IS IRELAND DYING?
Culture and the Church in
Modern Ireland

MICHAEL SHEEHY

Is Ireland Dying?

*Culture and the Church
in Modern Ireland*

HOLLIS & CARTER
LONDON SYDNEY
TORONTO

SBN 370 00466 3

© Michael Sheehy 1968
Printed and bound in Great Britain for
HOLLIS & CARTER LTD
9 Bow Street, London, WC2
by C. Tinling & Co. Ltd, Prescot
Set in Monotype Bembo
First published 1968

To those Irish writers
who have been driven into exile,
and to those who still fight
for cultural freedom
at home

CONTENTS

ACKNOWLEDGEMENTS

The author gratefully acknowledges permission given by authors and publishers to quote from the following publications:

From *The Playboy Of The Western World*, J. M. Synge, by courtesy of George Allen & Unwin Ltd; from an article, *America's Catholic Bishops*, Daniel Callahan (Copyright © 1967 by The Atlantic Monthly Company, Boston, Mass., 02116), by courtesy of the author and The Atlantic Monthly Company; from *George Bernard Shaw*, G. K. Chesterton, by courtesy of The Bodley Head Ltd; from *The Decline of English Murder*, George Orwell, by courtesy of Miss Sonia Brownell and Martin Secker & Warburg Ltd; from *The Informer* taken from *The Short Stories Of Liam O'Flaherty*, by courtesy of the author and Jonathan Cape Ltd; from *A Portrait Of The Artist As A Young Man* and *Dubliners*, James Joyce, by courtesy of the executors of the James Joyce Estate and Jonathan Cape Ltd; from *The Face And Mind Of Ireland*, Arland Ussher, and from *The Life Of George Moore*, J. Hone, by courtesy of Christy & Moore Ltd; from *The Irish*, and an article in '*The Bell*', Sean O'Faolain, by courtesy of the author and Curtis Brown Ltd; from *The Identity Of Yeats*, Richard Ellman, and from *West Briton*, Brian Inglis, by courtesy of Faber & Faber Ltd; from *Waiting For Godot*, Samuel Beckett, by courtesy of Faber & Faber Ltd., and The Grove Press Inc; from *The Collected Works Of George Moore*, by courtesy of J. C. Medley and R. G. Medley of Field Roscoe & Co; from *The Touch*, Liam O'Flaherty, by courtesy of Victor Gollancz Ltd; from *Vive Moi*, Sean O'Faolain, by courtesy of Rupert Hart-Davis Ltd. and Atlantic-Little Brown & Co. Inc., (Copyright © 1963, 1964 by Sean O'Faolain); from *That Lady* and *The Land Of Spices*, Kate O'Brien, by courtesy of the author and David Higham Associates Ltd; from *The Bootleggers*, Kenneth Allsop, from *Michael Collins*, Rex Taylor, and from *To Katanga and Back*, Conor Cruise O'Brien, by courtesy of Hutchinson Publishing Group Ltd; from an article by T. J. McElligott, by courtesy of *The Irish Times*; from *The Life And Times Of James Connolly*, C. Desmond Greaves, by courtesy of Lawrence & Wishart Ltd; from *Sean O'Casey: The Man And His Work*, David Krause, by courtesy of MacGibbon & Kee Ltd; from *James Stephens: A Selection* and from *The White Steed* P. V. Carroll, by courtesy of Macmillan & Co. Ltd; from *J. M. Synge*, D. H. Greene & E. N. Stephens, by courtesy of The Macmillan Company, New York; from *Anger And After*, J. Russell Taylor, by courtesy of Methuen & Company Ltd; from *The Victory Of Sinn Fein*, P. S. O'Hegarty, by courtesy of Mrs B. O'Hegarty; from *Ireland Since The Rising*, T. P. Coogan, by courtesy of The Pall Mall Press, London, 1966 and Frederick A. Praeger, New York, 1966; from *The Inquisition* and *The Martyr*, Liam O'Flaherty, by courtesy of A. D. Peters & Co; from an article by Rev. G. Perrott, S. J., by courtesy of the author and the *Sunday Independent*, Dublin; from *Lady Gregory's Journals*, 1916-1930, edited by Lennox Robinson, by courtesy of Putnam & Co. Ltd; from *Selected Poems of A.E.* by courtesy of Mr Diarmuid Russell; from *Death In Venice*, Thomas Mann, by courtesy of Martin Secker & Warburg Ltd; from *Ireland's Abbey Theatre*, Lennox Robinson, by courtesy of Sidgwick & Jackson Ltd; from *Man And Superman* and *John Bull's Other Island*, G. Bernard Shaw, by courtesy of the Public Trustee and The Society of Authors; from *Gas From a Burner*, James Joyce, by courtesy of The Society of Authors, as the literary representative of the Estate of the late James Joyce; from an article by Ciaran Carty, by courtesy of the *Sunday Independent*, Dublin; from a review by Harold Hobson, by courtesy of the *Sunday Times*; from *The Collected Works Of Padraig Pearse*, by courtesy of the Talbot Press Ltd, Dublin; from *Collected Poems Of W. B. Yeats*, by courtesy of Mr M. B. Yeats and Macmillan Company Ltd.

Introduction

PURITANISM HAS OFTEN been put forward as a cause of Irish ills. But what is meant by puritanism? It can mean a certain strictness in outlook and behaviour. In the present work it denotes a mentality which, seeing the human mind as essentially corrupt, obstructs its every vital expression. The evidence suggests that we are faced in Ireland with a cultural road-block which prevents any really vital advance in human growth. What then of religion? Can you have a religion without culture?

The Irish are pious in an ecclesiastical sense. They have the Faith; go to Mass; partake of the sacraments; pray; show a marked penitential spirit and go on pilgrimages to Lourdes and Lough Derg. If this constitutes religion, the Irish have it. But some contend this is not enough. Religion, they argue, should not be confined to church, convent or monastery, but should extend to daily life; should give a comprehensive character to thought, feeling and behaviour. So far from this being so – the complaint runs – the Irish Catholic clergy oppose vital human growth of every sort; discourage thought and art; stifle criticism; try to keep the public like an obedient flock of sheep. As a result, Irish Catholicism has no distinctive social, intellectual and artistic character; and it is this character which constitutes a culture.

Irish Catholicism became divorced from life because it instinctively distrusted it and feared the consequences of developing the human mind. The result was the adoption of a discipline of self-denial at the expense of self-expression. Positive human ideals, such as charity and justice, and vital human activities, such as philosophy and art, were shelved in the interests of self-discipline inspired by a real doubt as to the essential goodness of the human mind. For this reason the Catholic Church in Ireland was forced into a defensive position, mostly critical of intellectual and artistic life and depending mainly on censorship as a protection from them.

A

Christianity has always had a strong ascetic side which, apparently, many Christians have found to their taste. Artist as he was, Yeats was much impressed by this asceticism which he called the 'way of the saint who renounces experience' and is the 'bowman who aims his arrow at the centre of the sun'.[1] Christian asceticism, however, is a precarious means to holiness in a deeply puritan community, for such asceticism is apt to be conditioned by a distaste for the human mind. A vital love of man is a secondary but indispensable condition of Christian charity; and, without it, the life of the spirit must become arid and savourless, as it did for James Joyce. A cautious and bitter quality is to be found often enough in Irish spirituality, leaving the church-goer open to the charge of hypocrisy, turning him into an object of satire, a craw-thumper whose unkind treatment of others contrasts with his pious church exercises. This unsocial religion is sometimes unfavourably compared with the more considerate and scrupulous ethic of the agnostic or atheist. The agnostic has no god on whom to lavish his sense of duty and love; only man remains for him an object of concern.

However important self-denial may be, something more positive is needed for the majority who have to live in the world and create a Christian life. This means that thought and feeling must be used constructively in relation to man and nature, and find expression in social life, philosophy and art. To Christianise life means to seek a point of balance between grace and nature; between the importance of life and its transience; between the love of self and life; between sorrow and gladness; between the speculative and the practical; between the material techniques and spiritual fulfilment; between material security and insecurity . . . But many Christians today lack this complex Christian sense, and behave as if they had never heard of the Sermon on the Mount, extolling humility, sorrow, poverty, mercy and purity of heart. For the most part, modern Catholics find inspiration for their everyday life in some facet of Western humanism: this, taking man as the be-all and end-all of life, is now mainly concerned with making his brief journey to nothingness as easy, comfortable and pleasurable as possible.

The human mind is indivisible, and any doubt about its essential goodness must weaken vital human spirituality, whether it affects relations with God or man. The contrast found in Irish life between

[1] *Anima Hominis, Mythologies*, Macmillan, 1959, p. 332.

these two relations has no basis in orthodoxy or psychology. According to Catholic teaching, both are vital aspects of Christian charity, while, in psychological terms, the capacity to love man rests on the same basis as the love of God – a union of grace with the human heart. Either both are possible or neither is possible. In this, the Protestant reformers were quite logical, rejecting the possibility of any vital human spirituality because of the essential corruption of the human mind.

The social weakness of Irish Catholicism became more generally evident with self-government, when the Irish were able to devote more time to self-development. Those specially concerned with this – the writers in particular – found that whatever the struggle for freedom was for it was not for self-development; and it was during the opening decades of self-government that much was heard on the theme of Irish puritanism.

A quarter of a century of individual and social repression produced, in due course, its bitter fruits, culminating in a social breakdown in the fifties. By then Irish life had degenerated in practically every vital respect. The powerful flow of literary inspiration, expressed in the Irish Literary Renaissance (1880–1940), had diminished to a mere trickle. The popular mind had become soured, cynical, indifferent. Emigration doubled – from twenty to forty thousand per year – between the thirties and fifties, resulting in a population decline. Stung by the evidence of social disintegration, Irish officialdom adopted a more liberal social policy and took a closer look at the Irish reality. It found that Eire's vital statistics – marriage rate, alcoholism and insanity – were among the worst in the world.

Ireland's anti-social bias is a feature of the clergy rather than the people who, as is generally recognised, are kindly, easy-going and generous. The atmosphere of an Irish cottage or public house is far different from that repressive stringency which colours the outlook of Eire's ruling agencies, Church and State. This contrast in human acceptance found its most dramatic expression in the conflict between the clergy and writers who were the main target for clerical suspicion and animosity.

The new clerical liberalism is mainly the result of practical pressures, just as is the change from nationalism to internationalism under the administrations of Lemass and Lynch. There is as yet little awareness of the profound nature of such changes and of the quite different ethical principles which they evoke. A review of the history of modern Ireland is needed to clarify the forces and factors which have made for a denial to Irishmen of a full integrated life. Even now when the Irish are permitted to enjoy, in some part, the advantages of a positive social ethic, the Irish Catholic clergy do not yet, in fact, see man as a unity capable of a transcendent life whose virtue it is to transform the entire man and inspire all his activities. It will take some time before they come to see how a puritan sentiment has led them to make a purely pragmatic distinction between man's vital activities; between man as a sharer in the divine life, and man whose human and social nature lies largely outside Christian inspiration.

The actual outcome of the Irish clerical attitude is an artificial concept of man, involving an arbitrary division between man as a religious and as a social animal. From such a standpoint, the City of God is no concrete community, embracing the multifarious life of a real people who think and feel, work and play, drawing the inspiration of their complex activities from a single source. It is rather an invention of the mind, a figment of a schizophrenic mentality which artificially divides an intrinsic unity of force and activity. Such a religion rests on no sound basis, either human or social; and the priests who support it are advocates of no organic life, no vital order. Unless this organic unity is restored, a Catholic revival is impossible and a Catholic survival more than doubtful.

Evidence of an Irish decline, of an intellectual and spiritual stagnation over the last fifty-odd years since self-government, has become so clear as to shock even the complacent. Only a decade ago a study such as this would have been met with a disclaimer to the effect that there was nothing serious to worry about, plaintive outcries being characteristic of the Irish writers, and proof merely of a captious spirit. We can now expect a more responsible attitude.

The new Irish realism is due to the failure of traditional ideas. Hopes for an 'Irish Ireland', culturally and materially independent, are now seen to be unrealizable. Rising emigration and a falling population in the fifties compelled a revision of ultra-nationalist tendencies which became crystallised with the advent of the de Valera regime in 1932. The Irish emigrant to Britain proved a poor envoy, and his Catholic loyalty brittle; indeed, the Catholic allegiance of some who stayed at home was seen not to be above suspicion. The number of lapsed Catholics increased; and the measure of success won by the Jehovah Witnesses in the poorer urban districts was sufficient to provoke the clergy to sharp and sometimes brutal retaliation.

So pronounced was public apathy and cynicism that even the socially insensitive clergy began to feel the challenge to social stability and Catholic dominance. They were led to relax controls and to adopt a more liberal social policy. This trend was reinforced by public criticism. The impact of *The Vanishing Irish*,[1] edited by Fr. O'Brien, an American priest, was specially disturbing. This charged the clergy with a Jansenistic rigour of outlook which undermined the institution of matrimony. It was disquieting to be told by a conservative Catholic publicist, Alice Curtayne, that the 'results of Catholic family life in Ireland can occasionally be so bad that they become the subject of international concern . . .' Thus, by 1960, premonitions of danger, even of disaster, were upsetting the sentimental belief of the Irish Establishment that Eire could continue to drift securely in her chosen backwater, immune from the storms of modern life.

Waking up to a sense of reality can be a slow process, especially when the forces which obscure and distort reality – puritanism and ultra-nationalism – have had a century or so in which to condition the Irish mind. Eire now appears ready to take some criticism, though old prejudices are still sufficiently alive to resent a really frank critique. Thus, for example, a recent Irish critic refers to a 'hostile, denigrating depiction [of Ireland] from émigré writers and foreign observers.'[2] Whose judgment, one wonders, is to be trusted if not that of the Irish writers (émigré and otherwise) and foreign observers. It is therefore with some misgiving that I offer the public this study of Irish Catholicism, which charges it with the major responsibility for the Irish decline.

It is only fair to add that this interpretation of the part played by the Irish Catholic Church in modern Ireland is a very personal one, inspired by strong feelings. While my main theme does not lack support – some may even see it as hackneyed – it does involve a strong element of

[1] W. H. Allen, London, 1954.
[2] *Ireland Since the Rising*, T. P. Coogan, Pall Mall Press, 1966, p. xii.

personal judgment, especially in its interpretation of the detailed evolution of the many aspects of Irish life with which I deal. Often enough – partly for reasons I will give later – direct evidence to support my conclusions is lacking, and I have fallen back on the logic of intuition which some may consider inadequate. What is also disconcerting – some critics of this work have found it so – is that my deep sense of commitment has led me to deal harshly with some Irish leaders and personalities. I regret if an excess of feeling has led me to do less than justice to those I criticise. In a study such as this, detachment and objectivity are essential qualities; but these are apt to be elusive when one feels deeply involved. Even the gentle AE (George Russell) was once driven to declare 'one's country . . . is a brute to be kicked in the ribs.'

Another unfortunate aspect of this study is the need to concentrate on the defects in the Irish Catholic outlook, thereby tending to ignore its virtues. Limitations imposed by theme and logic may lead one to deal disproportionately with the seamy side, so suggesting an unduly depressing overall picture. Even Joyce felt that he was 'unnecessarily harsh' in dealing with his country. Irish Catholicism is at its best in its religious, as distinct from its social and cultural, life. Whatever coarseness or meanness of spirit may be found in the human or social field – in the factories, universities or in parliament – there does exist a genuine faith and refinement, the value of which it would be hard to overestimate in an age when mechanism and materialism restrict man's contact with the creative principles which give life wholeness and meaning.

'In the past,' Fr Fergal O'Connor stated at a 'Teach-in' at University College, Cork (December 3, 1967), 'Irish Catholics have not been renowned for . . . honesty. We have tended to speak our criticism in private, rarely in public . . . due to an excessive regard for authority. . . .' The regard of the Irish people for authority can hardly be seen as excessive in a situation where the clergy had an almost pathological dislike of criticism, and where public comment on their shortcomings was likely to have unhappy consequences for the critic. It was not until the late sixties that some honest public criticism of the Irish Catholic Church became a feature of the Irish scene, as at the above-mentioned 'Teach-In', an event which Lt.-Gen. Costello described on that occasion as the 'first time that a frank, fresh and comprehensive approach was taken to all the ills . . . of this country'.

It is not surprising that the volume of literature critical of the Irish Catholic Church is small enough. It grew rapidly during the fifties, however; and the best of it came from abroad. Apart from *The Vanishing Irish*, the best known of these critical studies are *Ireland and the Catholic Power* by Paul Blanshard, and *Mind You, I've Said Nothing* by Honor Tracy. The relative success enjoyed by *The Vanishing Irish* was due in part to its clerical authorship. This forbade the cavalier treatment which the clergy usually mete out to lay critics of the Church.

If a longer period is taken, it is interesting to note that the acutest critic of the Irish Catholic Church was another churchman, Dr Walter MacDonald, a life-long teacher in Ireland's leading Catholic seminary, Maynooth. This big-hearted priest had a bold, inquiring and original mind. He was almost alone among the clergy in seeing the need to revitalise the intellectual life of Catholic Ireland to meet the challenge of modern humanism. MacDonald died in 1920 of an incurable disease; and no doubt his death, like that of John Redmond two years before, was speeded by his realisation that he had no chance of averting the trend towards what seemed to him inevitable disaster. Now that the Catholic foundations of Ireland have begun to show serious cracks, there is reason to hope that his work, at present ignored and out of print, will receive more attention.

CHAPTER I

The Irish Dualism

THE BASIC PROBLEM posed by Catholic Ireland today is the need for a social synthesis. According to Sean O'Faolain the Irish never really succeeded in integrating religion and life. There was always a dualism, that is, the simultaneous use of a double set of values:

> One feels then from the beginning of the Christian period [he writes] in the presence of a delightful dualism – moderns call it split-mindedness – whenever one wanders into this early Irish world. There may be an overlay of stern Christian morality. At bottom there is a joyous pagan amorality. They believe in Hell. They also believe in the Happy Isles. They believe in the Christian doctrine of punishment and compensation in the after life. They believe, simultaneously, in the continuance of life's mortal joys for all beyond the setting sun and behind the dripping udders of the clouds . . .[1]

Yet, as Dr O'Faolain also suggests, the separation of religion from life in Ireland during those early centuries was not simple and clear cut. For while the early Irish showed evidence of a sound and fruitful humanism – as, for instance, in their knowledge of Greek and Roman culture – yet their Christianity had a profound penitential side; and their ascetical practices were taken to such extravagant lengths as to indicate the presence of a repulsively harsh view of the human mind. It is only natural that this caustic attitude should overflow into cultural life; and this may well explain that obscene and grotesque element in the Irish literary tradition, which some critics consider both constant and predominant, and whose most recent and best-known manifestation is to be found in Synge's *The Playboy of the Western World*.[2]

If one assumes a puritan element in the historic Irish Church, it is not

[1] *The Irish*, Pelican Books, 1947, p. 23.
[2] *The Irish Comic Tradition*, Vivian Mercier, Oxford University Press, 1962.

hard to explain the harshness of the modern Irish clerical outlook. For the traditional puritanism was reinforced towards the end of the eighteenth century with the introduction into Maynooth of teachers with Jansenistic leanings from Louvain. They imparted to the Irish clergy, as Dr O'Faolain points out, a repulsive and morbid view of human nature (p. 95 ff.).

Jansen saw the human mind as essentially corrupt. As a consequence he saw man's spiritual life not as a union of, but as a conflict between, redeeming grace and corrupting nature. He further identified the evil in man with concupiscence. This explains the typical features of the outlook of the modern Irish clergy. First, there is their exaggerated concern with lust, the 'sin of sins' in Ireland, as Christopher Hollis noted. Secondly, there is their repressive attitude to life. And, finally, there is their failure to give life a positive direction in the light of Catholic social ideas.

Indeed, the presence of an historic bias towards puritanism in the Irish outlook acquires further confirmation from the fact that not only did the Irish prove receptive to Jansenism, they also played an important part in creating it – through the teaching of the Franciscan, Florence Conry, Bishop of Tuam, and of two doctors of theology, Sinnich and Callaghan, both Cork men, the former a distinguished Louvain theologian. Conry's harsh interpretation of Augustine's views on grace and freedom, the *Peregrinus Jerichontinus*, was published in 1640, as an appendix to Jansen's *Augustinus*. Although, at its inception, Jansenism made little headway in Ireland, the fact that Irish ecclesiastics were among Jansen's most prominent collaborators suggests some kinship with the Jansenistic outlook.[1]

The fact that modern humanism has been a decisive influence in shaping the life of modern Ireland provides the strongest evidence of the Jansenistic bias of the Irish clergy. By humanism is here meant a view of life which, taking 'man as the measure of all things', has given a strongly secular and atheist direction to European culture. This European secularism has been super-imposed on Irish Catholicism, creating a hybrid life which partakes at once of Christian supernaturalism and atheist humanism. It shows itself in a narrow Catholic

[1] *Strangers and Sojourners at Port Royal*, Ruth Elvira Clark, Cambridge, 1932. See esp. Chaps. I, II and XIV.

life centred round the Church and in a quite other life in the market place and forum. Thus the Irish Catholic Church has shown an accommodating attitude to many forms of humanism, especially to those which place the creative emphasis not on man but on his environment. Thus it has, in fact, accepted ultra-nationalism which sees the Nation-State as the main creative force in life. It has accepted socialism which places its faith in the manipulation of the socio-economic environment. Also it is tolerant of materialist pragmatism, a view which sees the main purpose of life in the acquiring of money and material possessions. Unorthodox as these ideas are from a Roman Catholic point of view, they have been tolerated nevertheless by the notoriously stiff-necked Irish Catholic Church. True, they have been absorbed by osmosis rather than consciously adopted, taking in Ireland the form of social attitudes rather than ideas. The puritan clergy, shrinking from a positive Catholic social development, created a cultural vacuum which the alien ideas filled. Thus, it came about that Irish life is Catholic as it impinges on the man-God relationship, and mainly atheist-humanist in its social relations.

The Irish Catholic Church has, in fact, largely surrendered its control over life, in the sense of providing it with a positive social form. This does not mean that it does not interfere with life, but that its interference is negative rather than positive, destructive rather than constructive. The Irish Catholic clergy do not admit any such surrender, however; they do not admit that life is independent of Catholic moral direction. They preach and write as if they accepted the Catholic social ideal. That is why it is hard to prove, in explicit terms, that the Irish Catholic Church has opposed social and cultural growth. It is experience of their ambiguous attitude which shows that their instinctive fear of life is stronger than their orthodoxy. When it comes to the test, they come down on the side of reaction, of the *status quo*, against the vital and progressive. Indeed, during self-government, both social life and culture were largely strangled; and it is only in recent years that the binding cords have been loosened.

Moreover, it is hard to reconcile clerical hostility to the Irish writers with a positive cultural outlook. The real point here is not the cat-and-mouse relationship which exists between the clergy and the writers, but the rejection of the writers, individually and collectively, as a significant part of the social organism. This amounts to a complete rejection of human reason and intuition which are upheld by orthodox Catholic teaching.

The lack of rapport between Irish priest and writer touches the essence of the country's tragedy. When the writers have tried to give life a form, to make it vital, vivid, personal, intellectual and artistic, they have fallen foul of the Irish Catholic Church. Whatever their credentials – whether it has been a Newman, or a MacDonald, a Yeats or an AE – they got an equally unsympathetic hearing. Hence, the almost complete isolation of the Irish writers in a backward peasant community where they were popularly regarded as incomprehensible eccentrics, and whose most powerful agency, the Church, has been inimical to the exercise of their literary, artistic and social functions, even if the Church has stopped just short of open attack and condemnation. As summed up by Yeats Ireland is

> That country where a man can be so crossed;
> Can be so battered, badgered and destroyed
> That he's a loveless man.

In seeking to give life a form, the Irish writers have been, indeed, more truly Catholic than the clergy. But what ideas were the writers to use in shaping a social and cultural design? No vital Catholic social ideas existed in Eire. What there were of them had been dissolved in the puritan fermentation which the Irish Catholic Church had done so much to engender. Joyce alone really tried to use Catholic social concepts, but they were brittle and collapsed under his treatment. For the most part, the Irish writers have been forced to use humanist ideas, alone available to them, taking their stand on the side of natural evolution. The clergy took note of these anti-Christian literary demonstrations, apparently without surprise. After all it was, as they saw it, only life rearing its ugly literary head. The writers, they felt, were on the side of life; on the side of Satan who alone, it would appear, could have any interest in giving an intrinsically evil humanity a mature character and shape.

This, in effect at any rate, has been the tragic situation until recent years when the clergy began to discover that a devitalised community is a doubtful religious asset. They are now trying to create a more positive social outlook, fighting against their traditional fears and timidities. Meanwhile, the writers, who are an indispensable part of any real social revival, are by no means safe. Some are expatriates, like Paul Vincent Carroll, Samuel Beckett and Edna O'Brien; and some move uneasily in and out of Ireland like Sean O'Faolain and Kate O'Brien. By now the clergy should have some glimmer of the reason for Joyce's bitterness as expressed in *Gas from a Burner*:

> This lovely land that always sent
> Her writers and artists to banishment,
> And in a spirit of Irish fun
> Betrayed her own leaders one by one.
> 'Twas Irish humour, wet and dry
> Flung quicklime in Parnell's eye . . .

Irish Catholicism stands censured, or condemned, by the majority of intellectually distinguished Irishmen. Irish writers from George Moore to Patrick Boyle have been mainly critical of the Irish Catholic Church. If this critical attitude is less pronounced in the Anglo-Irish writers (excepting Sean O'Casey), that has been mostly due to their view – as of Yeats, Synge and Wilde – that Roman Catholicism represents a supernatural force in opposition to life; an ascetical, mystical power in a dualistic universe. Nor does the picture of Catholic Ireland seem more encouraging if one considers serious critics outside the country. Studies by such distinguished English Catholics as Christopher Hollis and Halliday Sutherland suggest that alarm as to the state of Irish Catholicism is by no means confined to Irish writers.

One is struck by the feeble impact Christian ideas made on the Irish writers. Oscar Wilde and George Moore did, it is true, much admire Christ as the supreme individualist, that is, as the highest expression of a purely human development, and, indeed, one of the most moving appreciations of Christian social ethics which has come out of modern Ireland is to be found in Wilde's *De Profundis*. Yeats allowed the ascetical Christian ideal a secondary place in his metaphysic. But, for the most part, Irish writers do not take Christian ideas seriously at all or, if they do, it is to treat them with the cold contempt of Joyce, the vituperative rhetoric of Sean O'Casey, the nose-thumbing blasphemies of Brendan Behan, or the wistful regret of James Plunkett.

It is a paradox that one of the most Catholic countries in Western

Europe has no major Catholic writer. Ireland has no Maritain; she even lacks a Belloc or a Chesterton. Our most Catholic novelist, Kate O'Brien, is Catholic only with regard to part of her work, and then with important qualifications. Our most Catholic intellectual, Sean O'Faolain, is hardly more than a liberal with a Catholic bias. Both these writers have shown an exceptional tendency to evolve from a liberal humanist to a Roman Catholic position. The work of James Plunkett shows, no doubt, some Catholic sense, but it evinces, no less, a conviction that Catholic social ideas are ineffectual.

The failure of the Irish writers to support Christianity is heightened by their contribution to humanism. This is most impressive – to name only Yeats, Joyce, Shaw, O'Casey and O'Flaherty. The irony of this situation seems to elude the Irish clergy. Out of Holy Ireland came no rude St John preparing the way for a Christian revival in Europe but, rather, a seductive Salome bearing his head on an exquisitely worked tray. The remarkable fact is that Joyce, Jesuit-trained and the most Catholic of them all, is an end-product of humanism; his work a *ne plus ultra* which captured the *avant-garde* of the Western world. Yet, Joyce's work struck no ominous note of warning for the Irish clergy, complacent in their belief that Ireland was safe from humanism.

What makes the Jansenist bias of the Irish clergy so hard to detect is that it is mainly subconscious, a sentiment never fully rationalised, of which the clergy themselves may be only imperfectly aware. It is in relation to marriage that, understandably, it comes closest to the conscious level. Here it constitutes a frank enough antimony between grace and nature; that is, between marriage, seen as a holy Christian sacrament on the one hand, and a natural union of corrupt natures on the other. It is with this anomaly that Fr O'Brien is principally concerned in *The Vanishing Irish*. The contradiction exists elsewhere, however, but it is for the most part implicit.

Confusion inevitably follows when one set of values is taught in theory and a quite other one put into practice. To the student learning his catechism by heart it seems that what the clergy most want to realise is the unity of all nations in charity and justice. But the mature student discovers that the Irish clergy are not really concerned with these aims, but with sexual purity. Irish youth is imbued by its teachers with a desire to bring back the old Gaelic culture, but, in practice, it finds no serious effort to do so. The old culture was aristocratic, pastoral and pagan-Catholic, while the official ideal today is democratic, industrial and puritan-Catholic. Fired at school with the dignified and generous spirit of Ireland's Golden Age, youth was confronted, until recently, by a national festival season, *An Tostal*, whose avowed purpose was to extend the period of tourist traffic, and so exploit still more visitors to provide foreign currency.

Sensitive to public opinion and nagged, one suspects, by a sense of unorthodoxy, the clergy try to camouflage their repressive social policy; to the point, indeed, of a certain dishonesty; of refusing to admit their real aims; of denying responsibility for what, in fact, they initiate or condition. The censorship of books, for instance, is a State matter. This the clergy will defensively point out when charged with responsibility for the narrow spirit in which censorship is exercised. Yet, one can be sure that it is the clergy who determine its precise character and function, all the more easily because of the presence of puritan minds in political and official circles.

Similarly cautious methods of control are used in the rural areas, where the clergy rebut criticism of rural backwardness by denying that the promotion of social and cultural activities comes within their province. The real point, however, is that they prefer a backward to an educated rural community – or did, at least, until recent years – and use their great influence to discourage progressive movements. This is not too difficult when dealing with a people whose cultural tradition is, at best, only a folk or undeveloped kind, and who are all too conscious of the importance of keeping on the right side of the clergy. Such cultural organisations as exist in the rural areas are usually well under clerical control, with a clerical chairman.

There is a liberal element in Irish Catholicism, though it was never strong enough to leaven the sour mass of clerical opinion. It was always to be found, in some real measure, among the younger clergy, but these have little say; and by the time they have evolved into parish priests and bishops, inertia has triumphed over inspiration. This liberal spirit was represented by Walter MacDonald, Canon Sheehan, the novelist, Canon Hayes, the rural organiser, and by the Rev J. C. O'Flynn who did so much for drama. In magazine form it was best represented by the

Jesuit-inspired *Studies*. Since the mid-fifties this liberal element has steadily grown. It is evident in a milder approach to the laity; in clerical addresses and sermons; in the Maynooth magazine, the *Furrow*; and in an increasing emphasis on the social and cultural side of Catholicism: this last is, indeed, the most striking feature of the new clerical outlook which has become preponderantly, almost obsessively, social.

This clerical liberalism inevitably overflowed into the social, political and commercial fields, and led to a more critical and realistic approach in press, radio and television. In fact, in the decade 1955–1965, there occurred a substantial revolution in the Irish clerical outlook which inevitably changed the entire Irish scene. This change came with no fanfare; without, indeed, any explanation or suggestion of a change in clerical policy. It just happened; and, indeed, one feels that the clergy would like to pretend that no change occurred at all, and that clerical social policy in the sixties was as it always had been.

To write appreciatively of this liberal clerical movement is to think rather of the point from which it started than of the point it has reached. Freedom is relative; and in the mid-sixties there was reason enough to be pleased with the progress made, and to know that it would continue. True, the growth of freedom was inevitably less than the Irish situation demanded, limiting the degree of honesty and objectivity needed to get to the root of the Irish problem as quickly as possible.

So far, clerical publicists have shown little awareness in public of the Church's responsibility for the Irish decline. The Rev J. Newman of Maynooth, dealing with the defects in the 'factual side of [Irish] sociology', blamed the Celtic disposition to 'react against the despotism of fact', and to lean 'towards the mystical and mythical'.[1] There may be something in this, but it ignores the realism in the Irish outlook which has triumphed over idealism in recent decades. Shaw warned in *John Bull's Other Island* against the facile assumption that the Irish do not know on which side their bread is buttered. Moreover, since 1922, there have been repeated efforts – for instance through such magazines as *Ireland Today*, *The Bell*, and the *National Observer* – to bring some rational order and sanity into Irish life; efforts defeated, at least in part, by clerical hostility and indifference.

[1] At Knockbeg College, Aug. 9, 1959.

The most prominent figure in the Irish Catholic revival is the Bishop of Cork, Dr Lucey, who foresees the end of present Irish trends in 'national bankruptcy, and depopulation, perhaps revolution, perhaps colonisation'.[1] Yet this forthright prelate is himself a symbol of the weakness at heart of the clerical reappraisal, refusing to see that rural reform depends on education, on a vital development of the rural mind and conscience. In making his main appeal to the State for a solution of the rural problem, he lays himself open to the charge that he fears what may result from educating the rural community. It is this unduly protective attitude which has gone far to create the problem.

By virtue of its negative social attitude, then, the Roman Catholic Church in Ireland has been disposed to acquiesce, by and large, in the humanist social design; condemnatory only when humanist ideology – as in the case of Marxism – was openly anti-religious. This attitude of dissociation reflects the posture of Roman Catholic puritanism which has had too little, as opposed to the liberal humanist posture which has had too much, faith in man.

What is needed is to revive Christian individualism which will make the social problem live again for the individual. This, however, demands confidence in the human mind; in its ability to identify itself with the needs of individuals, groups and society as a whole. The impetus for this has come from within the Church, but only recently. It was not until Pope John rallied Christendom that a Christian front began to emerge, instinct with a new liberal, critical and constructive spirit. Pope John's ideal was based on a positive intuition – a reversal of the traditional puritan spirit of the Roman Catholic Church – the effect of which was to introduce a more appreciative view of the human factor in religion and outside it. In this new vision, man gained a larger stature, a more responsible and coherent position. Dissident movements within the Church and humanist movements without it acquired an importance and integrity hitherto largely denied them. The world outside the Church ceased to be regarded too simply as 'evil', as Robert Kaiser suggests in *Inside the Council*, and the Church admitted not only concern but some responsibility for what happened in the world. Pope John's intuition of a Catholic humanism was an indispensable beginning for a

[1] At Skibbereen, May 9, 1960.

Catholic revival, but it was, of course, only a beginning. The real difficulty lay in the cultural weakness of the Church; its narrowly theological viewpoint as contrasted with the cultural viewpoint of those outside the Church. Pope John had granted, in effect at least, that the cultural standpoint – one depending entirely on the human mind – had a certain validity and coherence. But how were Catholics to communicate with humanists when they had largely ignored the cultural process, and when their theological ideas lacked vital expression in terms of thought, literature, art and sociology. Comments made by Catholic ecclesiastics on modern literature and art often indicate a lack of comprehension, dismissing them as pointless, chaotic, perverse, wicked.

The movement, however, is now towards a synthesis the absence of which, as this study seeks to show, has hampered the development of modern society – as is particularly evident in modern Ireland.

CHAPTER II

Inspiration from Two Wells

POST-REFORMATION attempts by humanists to create a better world were not without their price in human suffering and excess, as in the French Revolution. These had a sobering effect on the humanists themselves. Much more did they dismay the Catholic world whose deep sense of man's corruption was reinforced by the new evidence. More and more the Catholic mind shrank from human development, even from that modest development envisaged by Christian ideas. In this way did the humanists gain control of social and cultural life, and for this reason was the Catholic world forced to accept, however reluctantly, the social forms they created, for they had little of their own.

It was against this negative Catholic mentality that liberal Catholic thinkers had to struggle. So it was in England with Cardinal Newman and Lord Acton. Newman came to Ireland in 1852, at the invitation of Cardinal Cullen, to found a Catholic university, but he could not accept the restrictions which the Irish Catholic hierarchy sought to impose on lay freedom. In a letter to a friend, he wrote:

> On both sides of the Channel the deep difficulty is the jealousy and the fear entertained in high quarters of the laity. . . . Nothing great or living can be done except when men are self-governed and independent.

The Irish Catholic Church tried to combat new ideas by keeping the people ignorant; by restricting the circulation of books; by discouraging thought and art; and by a backward system of education. But experience has shown that though the Irish may not think, they are quick to absorb alien ideas and modes of thought. After all, a community cannot live in a social and cultural vacuum, without some ideals to give life a form and organisation; and, in spite of everything the clergy might do, external ideas or attitudes gained a footing – and, in some cases, a strong footing – in Ireland.

Of the modern ideals which helped to shape Irish life, the most congenial to the Irish Catholic clergy was ultra-nationalism which looked inward and backward to the Irish tradition, and which – during the period 1932–1959 – saw the perfection of the State as the main source of an Irish revival. From the clergy's standpoint, this view of Irish life had the advantage of shifting the emphasis from the individual to the State. And, indeed, when the clergy began recently to see the error of their ways, it was just this obsession with the State which some of the more liberal clergy attacked. Thus in a booklet, *Patriotism* (1958), Dr Philibin, the Bishop of Clonfert, criticised this element in Irish thought which is 'in the direction of a personified national entity', and 'away from the men, women and children who should be its beneficiaries'.

Closely linked with Irish nationalism was socialism of the moderate British brand which, by constitutional methods, gave the State a large place in the economic and social life of the community. This again delimited the scope of the individual in Irish life, and gave a strong impetus to State capital which has become a marked feature of the Irish economy. Because socialism was held in more doctrinaire distrust than ultra-nationalism, the Irish Catholic Church gave it less positive support. But it certainly tolerated it; and if the Irish Welfare State today is only a poor copy of Britain's, that is due more to lack of resources than to lack of will.

In spite of the opposition of the Irish Catholic Church to revolutionary socialism or Marxism (mainly because of its avowed atheism), it gained a secure bridgehead in Ireland after James Connolly founded the Irish Socialist Party in 1896. James Connolly – a revered Irish patriot – threw in his lot with the insurrectionists in the 1916 Rebellion, and thus helped to lay the foundation of national-socialism in Ireland.[1]

Marxism found its first advocates in the labour movement, and later – under self-government – in the extreme wing of the national movement. Though small in numbers, they have been the most consistently dedicated of Irish political groups and, in the late twenties and thirties, made an energetic effort to popularise Marxist ideas. They now work principally through the trade unions where they act as *agents provocateurs* promoting dissensions and strikes which have made Irish trade

[1] *The Life and Times of James Connolly*, C. Desmond Greaves, Lawrence and Wishart, 1961.

unionism one of the most disruptive organisations in the Western world.

In part at least, the growth of Marxism in Ireland may be seen as a result of the opposition of the Irish Catholic Church to any form of vital individualism – since the initiative must come either from the individual or his environment – and to be a consequence of the Church's toleration of socialist practice in Ireland. The most socially dedicated of Irish emigrants to Britain are Marxists. These, combined with the Irish writers, constitute a potent influence contributing to the growth of revolutionary ideas in the outside world.

The democratic ideal has also some influence on the Irish political system; though, as might be expected, only a very limited one in view of the Church's wish to keep popular life at a low ebb. True, under an ideal Catholic system, with pre-determined social and cultural values, democracy – which derives its guiding concepts from popular preferences expressed in the polling booths – can have only a limited application. But it is obvious that it has an important function in a Catholic system which sees moral growth in an extension of the sympathetic social vision, to which political (and economic) activity contributes. Sir Horace Plunkett tried to apply the democratic ideal to Irish rural life in the late nineteenth and twentieth centuries, but his co-operative movement failed to make headway against the anti-social policy of the Irish Catholic Church. In the early 1920's, Griffith and Collins appealed to the democratic ideal to save the Anglo-Irish Treaty, but this appeal – like many other such appeals in self-governing Ireland – made little impact on the hard shells of an autocratic Church and an autocratic State.

It was only during the period 1916 to 1922 that the Irish people played a significant part in the shaping of modern Ireland when, inspired by extreme nationalism, they destroyed the Irish Parliamentary Party and gave leadership to the extreme nationalists. Under self-government, they have had little or no say in the shaping of Irish policy. It was not only the people who suffered through this loss of creative influence. Neither the rank-and-file of their political representatives, nor the priests, had much of a part to play, both being strictly subordinated to their respective bosses, the party leaders and the bishops. Even under the more recent liberal regime, this situation has changed little; it has resulted, indeed, in a bitter struggle between the government and the people, as shown, for instance, in the conflict over the Gaelic revival and in a belligerent assertion on the part of the farming community for a share in the control of agricultural policy.

The Irish clergy took also a tolerant view of materialist pragmatism – that concession which the West has made to doctrinaire materialism, suggesting that if the social environment is not creative, it can at least be made comfortable. Hence Irish preoccupation with the pursuit of money, power and pleasure, which is so distinctive a feature of Western life increasingly sceptical of ideals. No doubt, such pursuits were seen by the clergy as a welcome diversion from the nobler but dangerous pursuits of ideas, literature and art. No great persuasion was needed to induce a people, long deprived of such congenial outlets, to take advantage of them; especially when they found themselves with little incentive or opportunity to make better use of their time.

The growing bourgeois outlook of the Irish people upset neither the clergy nor the politicians, whose self-interested behaviour was, indeed, one of the causes of popular cynicism. Centuries of insecurity resulted in an obsession with money, power and status. Only in the religious orders was there any real evidence of belief in 'Blessed are the poor'. The secular clergy – who are the real power in Ireland – made their preference for the society of the well-to-do quite evident. Their high standard of living was also an index of the extent to which they had forgotten the value of Holy Poverty. The snobbish attitude of the clergy and the nuns (especially in the teaching orders) reflects no less on their lack of Christian humility, and has left in the hearts of many of the Irish poor a deep sense of betrayal. It is in respects such as these that reform in Irish conventual life is needed, rather than in the 'modernisation' which increases contact between the nuns and life which, presumably, they wished to put behind them. This softening of conventual discipline seems a weak concession to a modern utilitarianism which sees a lifetime devoted to contemplation, prayer and penance as a sheer waste of time.

Most obnoxious, however, to the Irish Catholic Church was liberal humanism on account of its vivid faith in the human mind. Liberalism created an ideological split in Ireland, mainly expressed by the life-hating clergy and the life-loving writers. True, most of the best literature came from the Anglo-Irish writers who thought and wrote in the European tradition, though their links with the Irish tradition were profound. As far as vital vision went, the writers were the most valuable element in Ireland, whose influence on the world outlook was quite considerable but whose impact on Ireland itself was quite restricted. The Irish Catholic Church ignored them, just as Cardinal Logue prohibited the presentation of Yeats' *The Countess Kathleen* without even reading the play. In turning its back on the writers, the Church refused to face the basic problems raised by modern society which was departing more and more from Christian inspiration. Bound by a narrow ecclesiasticism, it withdrew into its ivory tower of piety and religious ritual, letting Irish life take what course it could in the light of modern influence and its own rigid prohibitions.

The Irish Catholic Church might argue that it could not be expected to sympathise with the deeply pagan and humanistic values of the Anglo-Irish writers. But its reception of the Irish Catholic writers was even more unwelcome. This was because these writers, with a surer Catholic instinct, bitterly attacked the Church's anti-social policy. It is only in recent years that the Irish Catholic Church has offered some nominal acknowledgment to such writers as Sean O'Faolain, Kate O'Brien, Brendan Behan and Edna O'Brien. A real concern for, or sympathy with, Irish Catholic problems was no guarantee of a clerical welcome, as witness the case of Paul Vincent Carroll, probably the most profoundly Catholic of the Irish writers, and who has remained a consistent and bitter exile.

The Irish Catholic writers – like the Anglo-Irish writers – found much inspiration either in the native pagan tradition or in humanism. So divorced was the Irish intellectual climate from Catholic inspiration that, apart from James Joyce, medieval Catholic thought made little or no impact. Modern Catholic writers – such as Maritain and Gilson – were scarcely read in Ireland. More striking, in an introverted community, was the failure of Ireland's greatest Catholic humanist, Fr Walter MacDonald, to give a direction of Irish thought. Ironically, MacDonald made his greatest impression on a writer with a Protestant background, Sean O'Casey, without whose constant reminders the name of this great priest would be practically unknown in Ireland today.

The failure of MacDonald to leave his mark on the Irish mind

31

indicates the divorce between Catholic ideals and life. This divorce is evident in one of the most earnest of Irish Catholic writers, Sean O'Faolain. For, on the one hand, he deplores the puritanism of the Church, and believes that 'priest and writer ought to be fighting side by side, if for nothing else but the rebuttal of the vulgarity that is daily pouring into the vacuum left by the dying out of the old traditional life.' (O'Faolain is here referring to the pagan tradition.) But what of Catholic social norms! Dr O'Faolain does not seem to have much sense of what M. Maritain calls the 'exigencies of the Gospel' where life is concerned. Attaching, as it does, certain values to grace, human freedom, ideas, sentiments, the State and the material environment, it is obvious that Catholicism – no less than Marxism – has a considerable stake in life. Thus, while admitting that the priest is 'indissolubly of heaven and earth', O'Faolain goes on to remark that it is this fact which makes him 'so slow to commit himself to any earthy fight . . . and it is this also that makes him come out of his cautious seclusion only when he finds the flood in full spate about him.'[1] The Irish Catholic priest did remain in 'cautious seclusion' to emerge only when the 'flood is in full spate about him'. The result is a complete anti-Catholic revolution in social outlook; and it is this which now confronts a worried clergy wondering how they can bring the largely autonomous social world under their control.

The welcome which Catholic Ireland gave to ultra-nationalism was partly due to the alliance which existed between Irish Catholicism and nationalism. The struggle against British rule was identified with a fight for both political and religious freedom. Faith and Fatherland were the twin inspiration. When, in Kate O'Brien's *The Land of Spices*, Miss Robertson asks the Bishop if the platform of nationalism does not cause him some uneasiness, the Bishop answers:

I personally feel none – but then, I believe it to be wrong that a nation fervently professing one Church should be subject to the rule of a nation professing an entirely other Church – so you see, for me, that platform is very closely allied to religion. And therefore I believe that, when such a state of things exists, education, for instance, should be very nationalistic indeed, even what is called

[1] *The Irish*, p. 122.

narrowly so, until such a political anomaly is renounced by the educational process. (p. 210)

The difficulty here is that the use of a narrow nationalism to counter British Protestant influence had consequences far worse than any possible effects of British Protestantism. It inspired the ideal of an autonomous Irish State, self-sufficient materially and culturally. It is hard to see how, politically speaking, the Irish Catholic Church could have made a greater surrender than when, in the interests of Irish independence, it turned its back on that universalist ideal embodied in the very name of the religion it professes.

Nothing so distresses the Irish clergy as a vital belief in man – unless it is a disbelief in God. It is their distaste for the human mind which explains their tolerance of those humanist forms – ultra-nationalism and socialism – which develop the extra-human elements in society. No wonder, Joyce noted that there is 'no heresy or no philosophy, which is so abhorrent to my Church as a human being'. The clergy were careful, however, to use these alien forms as surreptitiously as possible, keeping their ideal connotation to a minimum. Thus, though the Irish economy is socialist, the clergy resent such a description. This led Pendennis to remark in *the Observer* that in Ireland 'you can commit every sin in the book as long as you do not call it by its proper name'. The ambiguity of the Irish system which practises socialism but does not acknowledge it, induced Brian Inglis to join the Irish Labour Movement with the intention of giving expression to Connolly's 'explicit socialism'. He comments amusingly:

> To have to advocate nationalization would have damned us irrevocably, but there was little incentive to do so, as there was little left to nationalise.[1]

It reflects on the recent maturing of the Irish mind that Mr B. Corish, parliamentary leader of Irish Labour, openly advocated socialism at a Labour conference in October, 1967.

As was already mentioned, ultra-nationalism was the only social ideal for which the Irish clergy had a soft spot; and it was in the pursuit of this ideal that the Irish had most scope. It was only the intellectual with an ultra-nationalist bias who had any chance of remaining *persona*

[1] *West Briton*, Faber and Faber, 1962, p. 107.

grata with the clergy; and if he was a practising Catholic, he was a likely candidate for posts in the universities, schools and public administration. True, nationalism had to be handled with caution from an ideological point of view, so much so that Catholic Ireland never formulated a philosophy of ultra-nationalism. This, on broad humanistic lines, was provided by W. B. Yeats, and was one of the great contributions of the Anglo-Irish to the Irish national movement. So circumscribed, indeed, was Irish political life that the radical Irish Republican Army was the only vital political outlet for Irish youth.

Naturally, it was not so much with the bellicose I.R.A. that the Irish clergy felt most sympathy as with the more educated and refined language revivalists. Strongly conditioned by the schools, these were infected with both puritanism and ultra-nationalism, and are what Gabriel Fallon calls 'Calvinistic Gaels'. Ascetical and dedicated, their distinguishing marks are the Total Abstinence Pin, or pledge against intoxicating drink, and the *Fainne* or badge of the Gaelic speaker. This eunuch-like breed – a sort of Third Order of the Church – achieved considerable influence under Irish administration, and became a powerful adjunct to the clergy and the politicians, helping them to implement their reactionary social policies. In Ireland today, with its liberal trends, this influential body is more of an embarrassment to a Church and State seeking broader and more humanistic ideals.

Apart from the influence of Jansenism, historical conditions contributed to make the Irish Catholic Church the socially negative, timid and devious Church that it is today. Up to a century ago, the Irish Catholic Church was more concerned with survival than development. It had to steer a dexterous course between British imperialism and Irish nationalism, a nerve-wracking experience. There was need for tact and deviousness in dealing with successive British governments whose aim was the destruction of Irish Catholicism as well as Irish freedom. Even in the nineteenth century, with its great advance in civil and religious freedom, the position of the Irish Catholic Church remained difficult. Until the Church Disestablishment Act of 1869, it was dependent on the British government for the upkeep of Maynooth and had to submit to control and inspection. Small wonder if such a policy of appeasement left its mark in habits of evasiveness still observable in the clergy today; habits which suggest their origin when the clergy take a tougher line with the weak than with the strong, with the poor and ignorant than with the rich and educated.

The socially restrictive influence of the Irish priest was all the greater because of his unusually strong moral and intellectual position in Ireland. Until the onset of the present century, the Church – whatever its limitations – was the only educated body in Catholic Ireland. The education of the Catholic laity had been restricted by the Penal Laws and, during the nineteenth century, by harsh social and economic conditions. It was only in the present century that the Irish peasantry became proprietors, due to the Land Acts of Gladstone and others; and it was only then that a Catholic urban society began to emerge as a social force. An educated Catholic laity made its first real appearance under self-government; and its most vital expression was through the writers who, apart from those already mentioned, included Oliver Gogarty, Padraic Colum, Frank O'Connor, Conor Cruise O'Brien, John McGahern and Patrick Boyle.

The growth of the Irish Catholic writer was more hazardous than that of the Anglo-Irish writer who, belonging mostly to the ascendancy class, was more securely placed. The Irish Catholic writers lacked a cultural tradition; they had to start from scratch. This was quite a task since, for the most part, these writers came from simple homes whose only claim to education was that they tended to value it. Accounting for the slowness of his own development, Sean O'Faolain remarks that

> apart from my natural limitations, at least part of the explanation must be the fact that my father and mother, like the fathers and mothers of so many of my comrades at school and at the university, were not even townsfolk, let alone city folk. They were transferred peasants with small education and no worldly experience . . .[1]

The task of the Irish Catholic writer was not made easier by the fact that he found himself in an intellectual universe incomprehensible to his parents. Pitchforked from a naive world into one of great sophistication and cynicism, the intelligent Irish youth often found himself cut off tragically from his family, especially as he often enough lapsed from Catholicism. Joyce gives the classic description of this situation in *A*

[1] *Vive Moi*, Hart-Davis, 1965, pp. 132-3.

Portrait of the Artist as a Young Man. It was more typical of the early decades in the century before the collapse of Irish idealism.

But the most hampering of the limitations on the Irish Catholic writers was that they had to forge their way in a society officially inimical to their growth. Suspect by the Church, ignored by a philistine government and largely beyond the comprehension of the public, the tasks that faced them required heroic qualities. Few possessed these; and by the middle of the century – after a promising start – Irish Catholic literary inspiration was practically dead.

Understandably, the outlook of the Irish Catholic writers was marked by a certain bitterness and narrowness of vision as compared with the Anglo-Irish writers. Indeed, the contrast here is quite sharp. They also ran into trouble over the question of values. Joyce was the only major Irish Catholic writer; and his evolution illustrates the problem of values which faced his colleagues who, by the nature of their work, had to impose a vital form on life in an environment inimical to such a purpose. This led to a certain ineffectuality in Irish Catholic letters, which may help to explain Wilde's rather prophetic dictum that 'we are a nation of brilliant failures.' The mind of the writer was thrown in on itself, caught in a struggle with images or ideas which he could not marry with reality. Shaw well describes this frustrating condition in *John Bull's Other Island*, as when Larry Doyle exclaims:

> Oh, the dreaming! the dreaming! the torturing heart-scalding dreaming, never satisfying dreaming . . . an Irishman's imagination never lets him alone, never convinces him, never satisfies him but it makes him that he can't face reality nor deal with it nor handle it, nor conquer it.

The Irish Catholic clergy are bound, in principle, to accept a qualified individualism, that is, a belief in human development under certain safeguards. It is their practical refusal to accept this premise in their social philosophy which explains their negative social policy. One wonders, indeed, whether the Bishops were justified in discouraging the middle class from sending their children to the undenominational Queen's Colleges founded by Peel in 1848, seeing that they offered the only university education then available. If the defence of the hierarchy's action was based on the dangers of humanist influence, one must point out that these dangers are not much less in Irish universities today. Under a veneer of piety and orthodoxy, these largely remain, in fact, humanist. If, for instance, one examines one of the few remarkable works issuing from the National University and from a distinctively Catholic writer – *Money* by Dr Alfred O'Rahilly – one finds that, in tendency, it derives from the principles of national socialism rather than from those of Catholicism.

Irish clerical puritanism affected mainly that part of the community which was most in contact with the clergy – the educated who came under their influence in the schools, and the devout who were shaped by Sunday sermon, sodality meetings and retreats. It was the retreat – a week or weekend devoted intensively to pious exercises and lectures – which was specially responsible for creating this morbid fear of 'the world, the flesh and the devil'. James Joyce was the most distinguished victim of this morbid influence, and he gives a detailed sample of this kind of sermon in the *Portrait* . . . Another victim was President de Valera, who was a teacher in Blackrock College before he chose to man the barricades.

It was not, however, so much in politics – where qualifications appeared to depend more on the use of the gun than the pen – that puritanism was to be found, but rather in public administration, in the teaching profession and the public services, where a puritan attitude was a valuable, if unstated, qualification. Thus it is in official circles rather than in popular life that a sour suspicion of human vitality exists; and the visitor who mixes with the people in the street, shop or bus, may well fail to sense the presence of an administration which sets more value on the State than on the people who constitute it.

Jansenism contributed to cut the Irish clergy off from the vital scholastic tradition which was instinct with a spirit of intellectual inquiry. This had, indeed, produced one great Irishman, Duns Scotus (1265–1308) who was a rival of St Thomas in an era of intense disputation. Little of this spirit was to be found in the Irish seminaries, and the students who had it were regarded with suspicion, as Garry MacEoin – himself a seminarian – has pointed out.[1] One is reminded of Stendhal's Fabrizio del Dongo who, when about to enter a seminary, was advised 'Never raise any objection.' For over a century and a half, little of

[1] *Nothing is Quite Enough*, Hodder & Stoughton, 1954, p. 16.

37

intellectual value has come out of Irish clerical education, which was memorative, mechanical and arid. The only exception is Dr Walter MacDonald; and how unwelcome were his efforts to make contact with the Catholic intellectual tradition can be seen from his utter isolation.[1]

If the Church refused to encourage thought in the seminaries, it is unlikely that it would do so in the lay schools. These have been destructive of sensibility and creative idealism, as some of the more liberal clergy are now admitting. Behind a façade of progressiveness, they provide the surest means of undermining originality; and the graduates of these schools are mainly instinct with a self-centred and go-getting spirit which ensures that they are unlikely to be attracted by any form of idealism, unless it be a bitter nationalism. Under the recent liberal dispensation, improvements in education are slowest in coming. The system has been extended – as through the Post-Primary schools – but there is little reason to believe that education in the mid-sixties is more vital than it was in the mid-fifties.

The deterioration of the Irish popular mind is no less a tragedy than the decline in letters. For it is the strength and richness of the popular mind which conditions the production of writers, just as it provides them with material for creation. The Anglo-Irish writers were well aware of this; and, indeed, the vitality of their vision – as in the case of Yeats, Synge, O'Casey, AE and Lady Gregory – owes much especially to the rural mind with its pagan tradition.

The Irish public mind suffered through lack of use and through downright abuse. The Civil War destroyed its faith in ultra-nationalism, and no other ideal took its place. The people had no vital political function; and, indeed, their sense of social justice was outraged by a political system in which party loyalty was substituted for social justice. Political connections were far more important than personal talents, and 'influence' more important than inspiration. Indeed, integrity and intelligence were only an encumbrance when criticism was dis-couraged, and when discretion and hypocrisy were conditions of employment and promotion. Sean O'Faolain's parents may well have valued education for its own sake, but the parents of later generations

[1] *The Reminiscences of a Maynooth Professor*, edited by Denis Gwynn, Cape, 1925.

saw the schools merely as a means for getting jobs in a system in which jobs were scarce. It hardly surprises that the Irish have lost many of those simple qualities which are far more important than some of the sophisticated Irish now appear to think – kindliness, honesty, imaginative sympathy and a love of rhetoric if not of ideas.

Popular Irish cynicism showed itself in an indifference to the tragic drama of world events, as it did to the tragedy of life at home. The people had, in fact, no power to influence either. They found escape in drink, gambling, money-making and social climbing. They found inspiration in Hollywood and Radio Luxemburg. The unemployed and the disaffected (to the relief of the clergy) emigrated to Britain in vast numbers, as they did to America in the nineteenth century: but this time they could not blame an alien government for their misfortunes. Naturally, it was the poor, the helpless and the ignorant who mostly filled the emigrant ships. Sean O'Faolain summed up the position of the Irish peasant:

> . . . the poor fellow's defences are meanwhile being undermined by the vulgarities of the cinema, the radio, trashy books, cheap amusements, foreign fashions of every sort, and the chase of easy money, and by the effects of a hand-over-fist emigration to Britain under the worst possible conditions . . . He thinks he is safe behind formal religion, formal censorships, and an emotional nationalism which is, at least, a quarter of a century out of date.[1]

With the road to humanism (Catholic or otherwise) blocked, the Irish could find an outlet for religious idealism only in the service of the priesthood and the cloister; and this helps to explain the vigour of Irish Catholicism in this field – the many vocations for convent, seminary and monastery, the vitality of its missionary life. Here Ireland upholds a tradition which goes back to the Golden Age. And if there is any weakness in this cloistered life, it lies in the human taint which is a heritage of Irish Catholicism, shown in the neglect of human and social virtues, to which reference has already been made.

The decline in the quality of public life in Ireland was bound to reduce the number of religious vocations. Irish youth has not the same instinct for idealism, which distinguished it in the past. It has been infected with

[1] *The Irish*, p. 139.

the pragmatic spirit of the times, and looks rather to a secular career which emigration and the present Irish industrial revival make more available. Besides, increasing educational facilities – especially the provision of free secondary education for Irish children introduced in November 1966 – means that poorer boys will not have the same inducement to enter seminaries or join the religious orders. This fall in religious vocations – evident generally in the Western world – is likely to continue unless the Irish Catholic Church can restore the social idealism which it has itself done so much to undermine. This is one of its present urgent and difficult tasks.

A low estimate of human nature is bound to leave its mark not only on the social life of a people but also on its sacramental life, where a vital personal factor enters in as an indispensable condition of its efficacy. There is much that is mechanical – an effect of habit or custom – in Irish religious life. This is most evident in attendance at Sunday Mass, where a merely physical presence is deemed sufficient by no small numbers – especially in the rural areas – whose minds may well be preoccupied with matters far removed from religion, and who react to the ending of the short service with evident relief. It is often said that it is this semi-automatic attitude – partly conditioned by the poor quality of clerical preaching – which explains why so many Irish emigrants give up the practice of church-going even after a short stay in England. The recent movement to increase lay participation in the Mass was much needed in Ireland.

Much the same type of criticism can be made of Confession, though here the clergy insist more on the need for genuine contrition and a firm resolution in avoiding sin. Much of the criticism of Confession which comes from outside the Church stresses a type of absolution following a mere mechanical recital of sins, which the 'penitent' immediately proceeds to repeat thinking that his next visit to the confessional will automatically obliterate these in due course. One may presume some real basis for such a view but, in general, criticism of Confession which comes from unbelievers seems unfair and unsympathetic to genuine Catholics who find that Confession does help them in fighting temptation to sin. (What, in the penitent's view, constitutes sin is another question.) The church-goer who backbites his neighbour after leaving the church door is often guilty not so much of hypocrisy as of a distorted ethical sense which induces him (or her) to think that there is nothing seriously wrong about criticising one's neighbour. (Lack of charity ranks low in the Irish Catholic's category of sins: lapses from this primary ethic are often added as a conventional tail-piece in Irish confessions.)

Whatever about the Church or sacramental life, the Irish Catholic layman has little positive ethical guidance in his everyday life. He is largely in a moral no man's land, an amorphous world without Catholic definition, whose character remains undifferentiated from other social forms – liberal, democratic, socialist, fascist and materialist. No wonder, the Irish Catholic sees the everyday world as a hunting ground for material and social ambition; a pleasure ground for re-laxation, amusement and sport. George Moore saw this lopsidedness in the Irish Catholic ethic when he wrote in *Hail and Farewell*: 'Nothing thrives in Ireland like a convent, a public house or a race meeting.'

By the late sixties the Irish Catholic Church was fast acquiring a sense of the need for a vital individualism and internationalism – the primary features of the Catholic social ethic. At present the liberal Irish Catholic tends to be a liberal humanist, whose typical tenets are liberalism, nationalism and socialism. It is this triad of ideas which inspires the *Irish Times* and the Protestant university, Trinity College, Dublin. In April 1967, Mr O'Malley, Minister for Education, proposed integrating Trinity College and University College, Dublin, in a single multi-denominational University of Dublin, in spite of the fact that Trinity College lay under an ecclesiastical ban, rigorously enforced under pain of 'mortal sin' by Dr McQuaid, Archbishop of Dublin. This was the most striking evidence up to that time of the new liberal outlook of the Irish Establishment; and the difficulty of implementing Mr O'Malley's proposal is due not only to the problems raised by the academic integration of Ireland and Anglo-Ireland but also to the opposition of conservative Ireland, clerical and lay. If there is any danger to Catholicism in this enlarged concept of a University of Dublin, it is that the Catholic members of Trinity College (twenty per cent were Catholic in 1967) lack a vital Catholic social philosophy with which to defend their views. The advantage is with Trinity College which alone has a coherent cultural position. This is illustrated by the rapidly growing influence of the *Irish Times* among Irish Catholics.

CHAPTER III

Ultra-Nationalism in Practice

THE IRISH POLITICAL SYSTEM has a democratic façade, but its spirit is ultra-nationalist. There are elections every five years, but this does not mean that the people can influence government policy, or that they have much choice of representatives who are mostly the nominees of parties jealous of their political monopoly. This dual character of the Irish State arises from the separate ideals which shaped it – the humanitarianism of the eighteenth century and the nationalism of the nineteenth.

It was mainly on Northern Ireland that the ideals of Rousseau and Paine made an impact, inspiring the United Irishmen, when the non-conformists combined with the Catholic Irish to demand justice from England. This alliance broke down under sectarian bitterness, for humanitarian ideals found little sympathy in the narrow authoritarian outlook of Catholic Ireland, and were submerged by the national resurgence of the nineteenth and twentieth centuries.

Yet, in the literary field, this combination of nationalism and humanism resulted in one of the most humanly rich of contemporary literatures in the hands of the Anglo-Irish and Irish Catholic writers during the period 1880–1940, just when that part of Irish life under the control of the Irish Catholic Church became progressively more empty of human content – of imaginative vision, thought and sensibility. Nothing so much as this contrast illustrates the anti-human policy of the Irish Catholic Church. And, indeed, the rapid collapse of Irish humanism in the twentieth century was a consequence of political freedom when the Church found itself in a position to dampen its inspiration and to blight its growth.

No doubt, harsh material and social conditions during the nineteenth century did not make for orderly growth, turning the Irish mind towards revolutionary ideas and methods. Moderate leaders, such as O'Connell, Parnell and Redmond, were constantly imperilled by pressure from the left, especially after the foundation of the revolutionary Irish Republican Brotherhood in 1858, with its sister organisation in America, *Clann na Gael* (Family of Gaels). Towards the end of the century, their precarious rule was undermined as a result of the crisis which occurred with the discovery of Parnell's liaison with Kitty O'Shea. Offensive as this was to the Irish conscience, it may be doubted that the Irish clergy were wise in their unqualified public condemnation of Parnell – a clergy who, at the present time, observe without criticism Irish politicians lining their own pockets and those of their relations.

In helping towards Parnell's downfall, the Irish Catholic clergy showed little appreciation of its *political* outcome, that is, for political independence and the chance it would give of providing a native organisation, economic, social and cultural. It was not until the middle of the twentieth century that the clergy showed any concern for such needs, and then only when forced to do so by the breakdown of rural life. The rift between the people and the clergy really turned on that defect in the clerical outlook which exasperated a people only too aware of Parnell's importance to them. The people felt that if something had to be done they would have to do it themselves. Parnell was for them a symbol of such efforts and aspirations.

Nor did the Irish Catholic Church show much concern for the fact that the defeat of Parnell meant an encouragement of revolutionary ideas which found expression in the Rebellion of 1916 – an encouragement which was specially unfortunate at a time when Irish conditions were much improving due mainly to a settlement of the Land Question. But, indeed, by this time, the Church had begun to feel some sympathy with the national movement, from which it remained mostly aloof during the nineteenth century. It showed some tolerance of hate and violence when directed against the British occupation, and a tendency to think in the new nationalistic mode which accepted the autonomous nation as an ultimate premise in political and social thinking, a limitation observable in Dr Philibin's *Patriotism*, written half a century later. This isolationist trend in the political thinking of the Irish Catholic Church was an indispensable condition of the attempt to create an 'Irish Ireland' in the first half of the twentieth century.

The Anglo-Irish writers – especially Yeats and AE – contributed no little to Irish revolutionary tendencies, for it was their belief that human growth was a product of a creative combination of violence and spiritual energy. They had, however, a deep sense of the need for cultural vitality, especially in literature and art. This was lacking in the Irish Catholic clergy who, when confronted with what was for them a rather grim choice between violence and imaginative vision, between culture and conflict, preferred the crude methods of revolution. Thus, the shaping of the national movement fell more and more into the hands of intellectually unsophisticated revolutionaries.

The most intelligent of the men who moulded the Irish Republic was Arthur Griffith, who popularised his ideas through his liberal paper, *The United Irishman*, to which many Irish writers contributed. Griffith benefitted by a few years spent in the Transvaal where he worked as a type-setter and journalist, and gained some first-hand knowledge of the Boer Rising. Mostly self-educated, he was modest and sincere, deserving a better fate than to become the victim of a naive idealogue, Mr de Valera, into whose hands he unwittingly played. It was from Griffith that the hapless Republic got what few ideas it had to bless itself with.

Griffith admired the German economist, Friederich List. At a convention of *Sinn Fein* (Ourselves) in 1905, he introduced List's ultra-nationalist social philosophy, which, according to his biographer, Padraic Colum, was received with approval by his listeners.[1] According to List, a nation with its own distinctive life – its origins, history, language, literature, laws, institutions, customs and manners – forms 'one independent whole', and 'recognises the law of right for and within itself, and in its united character is still opposed to other societies of a similar kind in their national liberty . . .' In making the nation supreme within itself, and in setting it apart and in opposition to other nations, List's ideas contributed in Ireland, as in Germany, to an extreme nationalism which was to influence decisively the destinies of both countries. Why did the heresy-conscious Irish Catholic Church not condemn them? Had it some sympathy with the ideal itself; there is reason to believe that it had. It meant, of course, a self-contained Ireland in opposition to the 'godless, free-thinking' outside world: any political theory, apparently, was worth it, if it could keep that world at bay. Joyce was one of the few who saw the incongruity of fascism in

[1] *Arthur Griffith*, Dublin, 1959, p. 88.

Catholic Ireland, and gibed from the continent in a doggerel broadside, *Gas from a Burner*:

> O Ireland my first and only love
> Where Christ and Caesar are hand and glove.

Griffith himself did not take List's ideas too seriously, and was using them rather to increase Irish self-reliance, economic and cultural. A hero more to his taste was the Hungarian patriot, Francis Deak, humane and conservative, at any rate as drawn by Griffith in his pamphlet, *The Resurrection of Hungary* (1904). It was from Hungary Griffith got the idea of a Dual Monarchy, by which he meant that the King of England might have himself crowned King of a free Ireland. Griffith's democratic ideas, however, were little to the taste of the Irish Catholic Church; and these – the most important part of his social philosophy – lost ground in the ever-narrowing Irish humanistic vision. It was List rather than Deak who made the widest appeal in a situation of fast-growing national sentiment, and it was List's ideas – in that cloudy, sentimental form ideas take on in Ireland – which conditioned the Irish Republican Brotherhood and the leaders who were to emerge after the Rising.

Griffith misjudged the trend of his time which was not apt, as he hoped, to 'associate the idea of order and discipline with the idea of liberty.' A reactionary clergy and an ignorant people did not promise much in that way. Griffith ignored George Moore's warnings in *Hail and Farewell* regarding the clergy's opposition to culture; and declared in *The United Irishman* that 'neither of the two Georges had written anything by which we might profit considerably.'

Griffith's main mistake lay in disparaging the Irish Parliamentary Party, the most powerful symbol of political moderation in Ireland. Through its continued influence lay, in fact, whatever chance Griffith might have had of realising his policy of passive resistance, so that the people might not – as Deak admonished the Hungarians – 'be betrayed into acts of violence, nor abandon the ground of legality.' The choice between Redmond and the new insurrectionary leader, Mr de Valera, was a choice between reason and force; and in joining Mr de Valera, Griffith surrendered his main ideal, rational self-discipline. Griffith was critical of Redmond's modest Home Rule Bill, the implementation of which was interrupted by the First World War, and postponed with Redmond's consent until the war ended. He objected that the

Parliamentary Party was undermining Irish self-reliance by 'transferring the centre of the struggle from Ireland to Westminster'. The parliamentarians replied that the alternative to the Party was revolt; and this proved to be the case.

Griffith's own movement, *Sinn Fein*, grew rapidly after the Rising. But its character changed, became more militant. The I.R.B. infiltrated it; and it was shaped by new leaders of harder metal than Griffith; the fighting Michael Collins, out for a show-down with the British; the determined separatist Cathal Brugha; and the enigmatic Eamonn de Valera, the last commandant to surrender in the Rising: to his personality the vicissitudes of rebellion were to attach an aura of picturesqueness foreign to a mind more earnest than inspired.

De Valera dominated the new movement by identifying his powerful will with a separatist ideal of Ireland. Griffith made way for him, sharing the mystical belief of Yeats and AE in the emergence of a great leader or messiah. When asked, while a prisoner of war in 1918, what British terms he would accept, Griffith replied, 'I will agree to whatever de Valera agrees to.' Such a complete surrender of his own judgment – especially to one of whom he had little real knowledge – was unwise, as time was to prove. Griffith did what he could to moderate the insurrectionary movement, concerning himself mainly with the civil side, with the 'institutional rallying centre' which became known as *Dail Eireann* (Irish Parliament). This came to exercise no small measure of control over Irish civil administration, and gave a semblance of legality to what, in fact, was a rebellion.

But where was the movement going – in the direction of democracy or fascism? Wilson's principle of self-determination drew attention to the usefulness of the democratic ideal, and the new Irish leaders, seeking the support of the Paris Peace Conference, paid it some lip-service. A compromise declaration in the amended constitution of *Sinn Fein* in 1917 revealed how it wanted it both ways, asserting that

> *Sinn Fein* aims at securing international recognition of Ireland as an independent Irish Republic. Having achieved that status the Irish people may, by referendum, freely choose their own form of government.

It must have seemed odd to Wilson that the nationalist Irish, demanding the right to live outside the British Empire, denied that same right to the Northern Irish who wanted to live within it. Wilson naturally rejected an appeal by *Sinn Fein* which really meant that an Irish tyranny was to be substituted for an English tyranny.

Britain felt obliged to be more ruthless in putting down the Irish rebellion, sending over the undisciplined Black and Tans. Such measures recoiled on a Government assailed by liberal critics at home and abroad. In July 1921 a truce was called, for Ireland was feeling the strain of an unequal combat in which only half-a-dozen or so counties were engaged. Exchanges between de Valera and Lloyd George showed, however, that Britain would not grant Ireland full independence, and could not (the North dissenting) grant her unity. Nevertheless, in October, Griffith and Collins were sent to London to reach what de Valera called a 'compromise'. By December, the delegation had signed a treaty which granted dominion status to Ireland and provided that, if the North opted out of a Dublin government, it would have to submit to a Boundary Commission. Griffith and Collins too optimistically believed that such a commission would deprive the North of so much territory that it would cease to be a viable polity.

The treaty did not suit de Valera and his Cabinet followers, Brugha and Stack. They objected that it provided neither of the essential Irish aims – full independence and unity. It is hard to see how it could have been expected to provide both. The Northern enclave had made it clear that it wanted no part of a moderate Home Rule, much less in a fully independent Irish Republic. This it continued to assert with much vehemence and mustering of a defensive force, the Ulster Volunteers, that Britain had no choice but to pass the 'Better Government of Ireland Act' which came into force in December 1920, proposing separate governments for Northern and Southern Ireland. The North made use of this measure to set up its own Parliament.

In opposing the treaty, Mr de Valera showed no awareness of the material and cultural links binding Ireland (North and South) with Britain and the Commonwealth: links which time was to strengthen, bringing about, within four decades, a complete reversal of separatist aims. Nor did he sense the value of the Commonwealth itself in an era of expanding politico-economic organisation; and, indeed, he relished its dissolution, begun and inspired by the Irish breakaway.

By the early twenties, Irish political feeling had crystallised in an attitude which lent much support to the narrow political outlook of de Valera and his followers. The Irish Catholic Church was largely in line with this restricted vision of Ireland's destiny and responsibilities. Dr Walter MacDonald was one of the few clergy who asserted that this vision was unrealistic, retrogressive; he stressed the need for a principle of co-operation which he thought 'far more important than any principle of self-determination', and condemned those separatists who 'continue to struggle in isolation after a time when . . . they are no longer in a position to maintain themselves without combining with others'.[1]

The narrow regional outlook of the Irish clergy is best seen in their attitude to Partition. In 1917 a manifesto was issued by three Catholic Archbishops and thirteen Catholic Bishops deploring the fact of 'Ireland's dismemberment'. Their Lordships showed no concern for the fact that, as MacDonald pointed out, 'in race, religion and mentality, they [the Northern Protestants] and we are different' [p. 115]. Nor did they see that unity under an independent Irish republic would disrupt the organic connections between Northern Ireland and Great Britain. Even in 1921, when Irish nationalism had become extreme, the Catholic hierarchy described Partition as a 'sham settlement'. Nor did subsequent experience, which showed how impractical isolation was, lead to any clerical sympathy with the North's decision to remain part of the British polity. In 1956, Cardinal D'Alton described Partition as a 'glaring injustice'. Even as late as 1962, when it was widely understood in Eire that the unification of Ireland depended on strengthening the British and other external connections, the Bishop of Cork called for a patriot who 'would secure the unity of the country and break the link with any external State.'[2]

Yet, Mr de Valera denied holding extreme views. In a speech on the occasion of his election to the Second *Dail* on August 16, 1921, he claimed that '. . . we are not doctrinaire republicans'. Yet who but a doctrinaire republican would have rejected the treaty in favour of the doubtful prospect of achieving more in the face of civil strife? And

[1] *Some Ethical Questions of Peace and War*, London, 1920, p. 95.
[2] At Innishannon, May 7.

what did de Valera mean by 'republican'? Did he simply mean democratic, that is – to quote from the same speech of de Valera – 'a system which provides the Irish people with an opportunity for working out for themselves their national life in their own way.' But, obviously, there was more to 'republican' than that, since de Valera refused to accept the popular decision in favour of the treaty both in the *Dail* and in the polling booths.

For de Valera the term 'republican' also embodied the ideal of a united, Gaelic-speaking and independent Ireland. And, as such, it represented an ultra-nationalist ideal independent of public decisions. But how could such an ideal be described in any real sense as democratic? De Valera got round this difficulty by contending – as he did in his first public statement rejecting the treaty – that this ideal had the support of the 'majority of this nation as expressed freely in successive elections during the past three years.' Whatever the truth about such a claim, the people were entitled to change their minds, assuming the finality of popular preferences in a democratic society. But this de Valera would not grant. Thus he denied, in effect, that the Irish system was democratic.[1]

An adroit negotiator, Mr de Valera was confused with regard to political ideas and it would be a puzzle for future historians to see what really inspired him. Naive in vision and simple in his tastes, he was in sympathy with the traditional life; but more and more his mind unconsciously fastened on an ideal of the State, to which human and social needs were strictly subordinated. In regard to this ideal, Mr de Valera was, in practice, as consistent as he was capable of being, constantly stressing even to this day the three constituents of his ideal – a united, Gaelic-speaking and independent Ireland. Yeats had acutely noted that de Valera, Hitler and Mussolini had 'exactly the same aim', that is, they saw the State as a primary creative agent.[2] There were two important differences, however: first, that de Valera's ideal was inspired by a mood which never matured into an explicit idea or political theory, and, secondly, that de Valera's Catholicism (which places a unique value on the human soul) acted as a brake on his

[1] See P. S. O'Hegarty, *A History of Ireland Under the Union, 1801–1922*, Methuen, 1952, Chapter LXXVI.
[2] *The Letters of W. B. Yeats*, edited by Alan Wade, Hart Davis, 1954, p. 806.

state absolutism, moderating the inhumanity to which such an ideal logically leads. This logic was early evident in de Valera's treatment of Griffith and Collins, as it was in the Civil War (1922-3) which resulted from de Valera's refusal to accept the Anglo-Irish Treaty.

Lord Pakenham in *Peace by Ordeal* gives the classic account of the treaty negotiations in London. From this emerges the profound impression Griffith and Collins made on the British statesmen. But while the Irish delegates wrestled with as formidable an array of talent as ever assembled in council chamber – Lloyd George, Churchill, Birkenhead and Chamberlain – they were harried by their own colleagues in Dublin. One would not wish to see in the position of the Irish delegates what Collins called a 'trap', but one cannot but deplore the attitude of the influential section of the Irish Cabinet in Dublin which had an inhibiting effect on the delegation, as is suggested by the fears and anxieties which Collins confided in a friend:

> G. [Griffith] was particularly dour today. He said to me – 'you realise what we have on our hands?' I replied that I realised it long ago. He meant the Dublin reaction of whatever happens here . . . G. said 'What do we accept?' Indeed what do we accept? If we accept at all, it will be inferred as a gross act of treachery. What have we come for? I ask myself that question a dozen times a day . . . Rather the years that have gone before with all their attendant risks than the atmosphere which is part of this conference. Who should one trust – even on my own side of the fence, Griffith. Beyond Griffith, no one . . .[1]

The Irish people had little stomach for the Civil War which horrified by its brutality and dismayed by its apparent senselessness. When it ended, Collins had been shot, and Griffith was dead, succumbing like Parnell and Redmond to overwhelming and tragic pressures. The temper of the times showed in a moral decline consequent on the adoption of a narrow and bitter political ideal. The nature of this corruption is well described in a passage from a contemporary study by P. S. O'Hegarty, *The Victory of* Sinn Fein:

> We devised certain 'bloody instructions' to use against the British. We adopted political assassination as a principle: we devised the

[1] Quoted in *Michael Collins*, Rex Taylor, Hutchinson, 1958, pp. 165-7.

ambush; we encouraged women to forget their sex and play at gunmen; we turned the whole thoughts of a generation upon blood and revenge and death . . . We derided the moral law, and said that there was no law but the law of force. And the moral law answered us. Every devilish thing we did against the British went its full circle and then boomeranged and smote us tenfold; and the cumulative effect of the whole of it was a general moral degradation and a general cynicism and disbelief in either virtue or decency, in goodness, in uprightness or honesty. (p. 125)

Though much in sympathy with the separatist ideal, the Irish Catholic Church was disconcerted when the opponents of the treaty rejected the legally constituted Government of the Irish Free State. In 1922 the Church denounced the extremists. But this, like subsequent condemnations in 1931 and 1957, made little impact on the I.R.A. and had, indeed, only the partial backing of the clergy themselves; for, as T.P. Coogan noted, 'if the local priest refused the sacraments, there was always a 'patriot priest' . . . to minister to the devout militant.'[1]

In accepting – tacitly at least – the separatist ideal, it was inconsistent of the Church to condemn the use of force, since this normally impracticable ideal could be achieved only by force. For this reason the I.R.A. were in a logically strong position. And for this reason the policy of the Irish Catholic Church vis-à-vis the I.R.A. was ambiguous, resulting in a sharp contradiction, specially evident in education.

The Republicans, defeated in the Civil War, stood for elections but refused to take their seats in the *Dail* which they saw as a 'faked' parliament, an instrument of Britain. They did what they could to undermine it by violence and intimidation. The Government fought against anarchy with Public Safety Bills, and tried to force the Republicans to take their seats by passing a measure which required elected representatives to take their seats or forfeit them. Tired of the wilderness, Mr de Valera entered the *Dail* in 1927, taking as an 'empty political formula' the much-criticised oath to the British King. This move outraged his extreme followers. Nevertheless, de Valera's *Dail* group was, in the words of a party spokesman, Mr Sean Lemass, only a 'slightly constitutional party', whose real aim was to subvert the treaty-based

[1] *Ireland Since the Rising*, p. 229.

constitution of the Irish Free State. It was a kind of fifth column which, by virtue of its aims, remained in alliance – if an uneasy one – with the extreme or I.R.A. body.

De Valera's party, *Fianna Fail* (Soldiers of Destiny) held 57 out of a total of 153 seats in the *Dail*. Allied with Labour (13 seats) it was not without strength, which was used mainly to work towards a Republican status by breaking or weakening the links with Britain. Its efforts in this direction became more effective when, in the 1932 elections, *Fianna Fail* won 72 seats, and became the Government; this proportion it has largely succeeded in holding until the present day. Over the greater part of the next four decades, this party practically ruled Eire, interrupted only by two short intervals amounting to six years in all.

The success of de Valera's party may seem odd in light of the fact that popular interest in extreme nationalism had declined since the Civil War. The explanation lies in the fact that ultra-nationalist ideals were the only operative ones available, and that alternative concepts – such as the Commonwealth concept of *Fine Gael* (Tribe of Gaels) – could make no headway against the puritan-nationalist mentality engendered by the Church and the State. For both continued to assert the extreme ideals in the clerically dominated schools, especially those run by the Christian Brothers. These gave positive encouragement to the I.R.A., implanting a bitter and bigoted interpretation of Irish history, and firing the minds of the young with the do-or-die idealism of Padraig Pearse, a leader in the 1916 Rising. Besides, Mr de Valera had turned his back on force, and so met the needs of the moderately nationalist clergy. Thus, he was the best compromise the Church could find between the demands of unorthodox politics and Catholic ethics.

Mr de Valera did not declare a Republic, however, when he got into power, though he abolished the Oath and removed the British King from the Constitution. He retained the link with Britain and the Commonwealth through the External Relations Act of 1936, by which the King was empowered to act for the Irish State for certain purposes. The I.R.A. remained intransigent. De Valera tried with some success to win them over. They were pensioned like the regular army, compensated for wounds and property damage. They were recruited into a special Army Volunteer force, and into the police force where they formed an armed and trigger-happy detachment known as the Broy Harriers. Still, the hard core of the I.R.A. remained steadfast, and de Valera proclaimed the Organisation in 1936.

Like President de Gaulle, Mr de Valera might have declared that he was 'not of the left. Nor of the right. Nor of the centre. De Valera is above.' And, indeed, in his twistings and turnings, it would seem that he saw in his own mind a logic superior to the demands of his implicit state absolutism. Certainly he lived up to de Gaulle's egregious dictum by keeping in the armour of his ideas those which belonged to the right, left and centre. For de Valera's combined democratic and ultra-nationalist pretensions were not his only indulgence.

In his Constitution of 1937, Mr de Valera informed the country that his politics were Catholic, for their purpose was to promote the common good with due observance of justice and charity, so that the dignity and freedom of the individual might be achieved. Evidence to support such a claim would be hard to find. The Constitution also tells us that to the 'most Holy Trinity . . . our final end, all actions of both men and states must be referred.' Not quite all, however. Between man and the Holy Trinity there had been interposed a political trinity based on the absolutism of the State – a united, Gaelic-speaking and independent Ireland – and it was to this conception that the Irish people were sacrificed both politically and culturally.

The I.R.A. naturally tried to exploit the threat of Nazi Germany to Britain, and issued in 1939 a proclamation to the effect that the British Government should withdraw its troops from Northern Ireland. The bombing outrages in Britain were a reprisal for its refusal to do so. The Irish Government passed an Offences against the State Act, enabling suspects to be interned without trial, and a special criminal court was set up. There was, however, little suggestion of moral condemnation; and, indeed, the day of the execution of the two Irishmen connected with the bomb explosion in Coventry was treated almost as a day of national mourning in Ireland.

The I.R.A. were also active in Ireland where in December 1939 they successfully raided the army's ammunition dump in Phoenix Park, and later a British army camp in Ballykinlar, Co. Down. Yet, little came of the maximum effort they made during the first year of the war.

This was partly due to a division of aim between the Northern extremists, who wanted to unseat the British occupation forces, and the Southern, who wanted to overthrow the Dublin administration in the interests of a Republic. De Valera's tough policy also hampered the Organisation, whose more active members soon found themselves behind bars.

The success with which extreme nationalist ideas continued to penetrate the Irish mind was shown in the late forties when the *Irish Times* began to express some sympathy with them. More significant was the succumbing of the *Fine Gael* party to these same ideals. For this party – in a coalition Government led by Mr John Costello – did what de Valera himself refrained from doing and formally declared an Irish Republic on April 10, 1949. Even if one allows, as Lord Rugby suggests, that 'the government was up against political pressure from the extremist elements within it' – that is, from Sean MacBride's newly found *Clann na Poblachta* (the People's Party) – it was an extraordinary and unjustifiable move from a party which was the successor of the original pro-treaty group and pledged to uphold the Commonwealth connection.[1] Nothing better illustrates the effect of the continued propagation of the extreme ideals by the Church and the State, and the progressive stultification of the Irish mind at a time when it was becoming increasingly obvious that these ideals were having social and economic consequences which endangered the very survival of the nation. And, indeed, within ten years of *Fine Gael's* change of heart, *Fianna Fail*, under the leadership of Mr Lemass, rejected the extreme ideals and greatly extended *Fine Gael's* traditional policy of external co-operation.

In 1956 the I.R.A., realising that the opposition to unity came from the North and not from Britain, put special pressure on the North with hit-and-run attacks on its barracks and military installations. This led to a condemnation of the I.R.A. by the Irish Catholic Church in December, 1957. The clergy were of two minds, however. In January of the same year, no less than twenty priests attended the funeral of Sean South of Limerick, a member of the I.R.A. who had been killed in an attack on Northern Ireland. Even at the time of the hierarchy's

[1] *Irish Times*, July 4, 1962. Lord Rugby, as Sir John Maffey, was British Representative in Eire at the time.

condemnation, the I.R.A. were permitted to make collections at church gates after Sunday Masses in order to finance their terrorism. And, indeed, the schools continued with their bitter indoctrination; T. P. Coogan points out that 'the inflammatory teaching of Irish history has brought young men into the I.R.A. and to their deaths.'[1] Thus the clerically-run schools inspired the terrorists which the Church formally condemned. In 1958, the Christian Brothers published a pictorial history of Ireland which is a glorification of violence and revolution, a work described by Pamela Hinkson as an 'extreme example of Irish psychological blindness'.[2]

The teeth of the I.R.A. were drawn only when Irish officialdom was driven to accept a more moderate nationalism. This occurred under the realistic leadership of Mr Lemass, which began in 1959. Mr Lemass's moves to strengthen the ties with Britain were obstructed by the I.R.A., as when they murdered Constable Anderson in Northern Ireland in January 1961. At this time, Lemass was manipulating events so as to condition Irish opinion in the direction of membership of the Commonwealth. It is of interest to note that this change in external policy owes much more to economic realism than to Catholic idealism. The murder of Constable Anderson evoked only a perfunctory response from the Irish Catholic clergy, if one excepts the condemnation of Bishop Browne of Galway when he spoke of a 'crime crying to heaven for vengeance'.

The Government revived the Special Criminal Court in November 1961. Border controls were tightened; and at least ten of the attacking force – put by some critics as low as thirty operating at any one time – were captured and gaoled. With leaders and personnel well-known, the I.R.A. could not long withstand the opposition of a determined Government; and on February 22, 1962, they issued a public statement that the campaign against the North would cease.

Thus the back of the extreme movement was broken within three years of Mr de Valera's retirement from practical politics. De Valera's concept of unity was not vital; and during his long period of office he made no real effort to understand the Northern viewpoint. Under such circumstances, force alone remained as a means of bringing about

[1] *Ireland since the Rising*, p. 222.
[2] *Ireland, Old and New*, Dublin, 1958.

the mechanical political unity with which de Valera seemed content. When such a concept broke down, the I.R.A. lost its *raison d'être*, and isolationism was forced to give way to a more realistic ideal of Irish integration in a rapidly-growing West-European economic and political structure.

It was the end of an epoch (1919–1962) culminating in the defeat of Irish revolutionary nationalism, sustained, in good part, by the repressive social outlook and educational policy of the Irish Catholic Church, as well as by the personal power of de Valera. It is not simply, as P. S. O'Hegarty claimed, that Mr de Valera is an egoist. De Valera identified himself with Ireland; saw himself as its personification; saw his own predominance as indispensable, and so justified to himself whatever means were necessary to achieve it. These means are disconcerting to anybody sensitive to ideas. But de Valera is not sensitive to ideas. He is an idealist but not a man of ideas. He could reconcile the irreconcilable because he lacks the logic of intellectual coherence. He belongs, as somebody said of Joyce, to a 'secret nobility', whose essence lies in the intimate fusion of ego and idea, so that the self remains the unique manifestation and vehicle for the expression of the idea. It is characteristic of such people that they destroy others and survive themselves; survive, that is, with their own equivocal brand of nobility. Their followers, who lack their enormous moral power – combined with de Valera's talent for self-delusion or Joyce's lucidity – are broken under the strains of the contradictions on which their hero's life is built. Thus President de Valera is the noble father-figure of a community whose moral life has been reduced to chaos, and which now seems resolutely turned away from ideals and idealists, finding a refuge in the encompassing details of a mundane world and a mundane ambition.

CHAPTER IV

The Pursuit of a National Culture

NATIONALISM IN ITS DEEPEST SENSE is a philosophy of life. It presumes that each nation has its own distinctive genius which it is its duty to foster. If the mind of a people should be corrupted by alien influence, then its original character should be restored by making contact with the traditional culture of the race. Such represents roughly the ideas behind the national and, to an extent, the literary revival in modern Ireland, the popular assumption being that British influence introduced alien modes of thought and sensibility which gave a false orientation to Irish life. This is not, of course, the orthodox Catholic view, which holds no brief for basic racial differences, contending rather that the progress of a nation, like that of an individual, depends on the extent to which it realises a well-defined system of ideas, the most important of which is charity.

Irish cultural nationalism is basically realist, marked by a search for a spiritual reality which is presumed to have existed in the past, and which is still thought to exist in some embryonic and frustrated way. This idea was popularly put by Bishop O'Dwyer who told the citizens of Limerick that

> . . . there is deep down in the heart of Ireland the sacred fire of nationality, which such [British] influence can never reach, much less extinguish, and which will yet burn on the altar of freedom.

The Irish tendency, then, has been to interpret culture not in the Catholic sense of making life approximate to an abstract ideal but, rather, as a search for the indigenous character of a people, and in creating the conditions favourable for its evolution, one of the most important of which is isolation. Sean O'Faolain made this distinction quite clear when writing of the policy of *The Bell:*

This Ireland is young and earnest. She knows that somewhere among the briars and the brambles, there stands the reality which the generations have tried to reach – not, you notice, the Ideal . . . We are living experimentally. How can we have any policy other than to stir ourselves to a vivid awareness of what we are doing, what we are becoming, what we are. (Vol. I. October 1940).

Thus, as Dr O'Faolain saw it, we are not to impose a purpose on life, but to find one in it; not deliberately to create a social form but to expedite its spontaneous growth from its seeds in the national life. The ideal or abstraction he held to be the 'most egregious form of error', involving presumably the impertinence of imposing on life a shape which is artificial, untrue to life's inner nature and compulsion. Such ideas are a crystallisation of a mood which was dominant in Ireland in the first half of the twentieth century. It is found in O'Faolain's early work. He has sought – if with diminishing interest – an integration of life in

> that most powerful of all emotional pistons known to man, a blazing love of place and a fond memory for the lost generations of the tribe . . .[1]

What then is this national soul or genius? Is it embodied in the individual or in the community? Yeats thought that it embraced some form of collective unconsciousness:

> Is there a nation-wide multiform reverie, [he asks] every mind passing through a stream of suggestion, and all streams acting and reacting upon one another . . . ? Was not a nation, as distinguished from a crowd of chance comers, bound together by this interchange among streams or shadows . . . ?[2]

Yeats attached great importance to this *anima mundi*, this repository of collective experience which enormously enriches the life of the individual. The key to this collective life was to be found, he thought, in its associated images and, consequently, in the traditional literature. Thus, for him, the significant synthesis is inspired by the imagination (the image) and not, as in the Catholic view, by charity (love) and

[1] *King of the Beggars*, Nelson and Sons, 1938.
[2] *Autobiographies*, Macmillan, 1961, p. 263.

reason (the idea). Yeats adumbrated the solution of Ireland's cultural problem as follows:

> Have not all races had their first unity from a mythology that marries them to rock and hill? We had in Ireland imaginative stories which the uneducated classes knew and even sang, and might we not make these stories current among the educated classes . . . and so deepen the political passion of the nation that all, artist and poet, craftsman and day labourer, would accept a common design?
>
> (*Ibid*, p. 194)

Images were for Yeats what the Forms were for Plato, the source of integration, the creative factor making for new life. He continues:

> Perhaps even these images, once created and associated with river and mountain, might move of themselves and with some powerful, even turbulent, life like those painted horses which trampled the rice fields of Japan.

Yeats' view of the creative function of national art was bound up with his doctrine of the Mask. According to this doctrine, growth really depends on the individual or nation finding its antithetical self, that is, an ideal whose qualities are the opposite of those he actually possesses. It is in the struggle between the self and the anti-self that Yeats believed the dynamism of development lay. Yeats thought that the Mask of modern Ireland – a country shaped by cautious priest, merchant and politician – might be found in the bravery and nobility of Cuchulain's Ireland, 'terrible and gay'. Yeats' doctrine of the Mask is a modern variant of the Christian view which offsets the powerful egotistical tendencies in man's nature with the ideal of charity – the love of God and life.

In so far as they were aware of it, the Catholic Irish had little liking for Yeats' novel doctrine which reflected so unfavourably on their outlook and conditions. Nor did they really envisage any clear reforms to expedite a return to the old life. The pot of gold might well lie at the foot of a rainbow, but it was more likely to be found, they thought, under six feet of shop counter. They shied away from the explicit pagan character of Yeats' treatment, finding rather their exponent of nationalism in the Catholic Pearse. Yet Yeats' theory of a rejuvenation through national art inspired, in however sentimental a form, the national cultural movement as a whole. This it was which gave meaning to the nation-wide interest in the old legends, folk tales and literature.

The cultural idealism of the national movement found its strongest expression in the Abbey Theatre, whose initial aim was to show Ireland as the home of an 'ancient idealism'. Yeats, Synge and Lady Gregory gave their best work to this cause, providing the romances and fantasies, like Yeats' *Deirdre* and Synge's *The Playboy of the Western World*. Deriving from a cult of the ancient tradition was a cult of the peasant as its inheritor; it was peasants, tinkers and fisherman who inspired Synge's work. Romantic idealism could not last, however. Its short reign, between 1895 and 1910, was disrupted when reality began to assert itself. Lennox Robinson's *The Clancy Name* set the ball rolling in 1908. T. C. Murray and St John Ervine also took a realistic line. Lennox Robinson summed up the attitude of the realists:

> We young men, a generation later than Yeats . . . didn't see her [Ireland] as a queen, didn't see her in her purple and gold . . . we realists saw her faults too clearly . . . she was avaricious, she was mean, for family pride she would force her son into the Church against his will, she would commit arson, she would lie, she would murder and yet we would write all our terrible words about her out of our love.[1]

It is on this realistic note that the Abbey drama has continued until the present day, becoming slyly satirical in the work of Shiels and D'Alton; bitterly satirical in the work of O'Casey and Carroll; and finally degenerating to a level of almost complete mediocrity. The Irish Catholic Church liked neither the rich pagan idealism of the one, nor the critical realism of the other.

The national revival was not all of a piece. It had different elements which were hardly in harmony. Besides the literary, there was also a Gaelic and the political revival. These were closely linked with Catholic Ireland and were less free culturally. The Gaelic movement began with the founding of the Gaelic League in 1893, and saw a cultural restoration primarily in terms of a revival of Gaelic. Here there was a

[1] *Ireland's Abbey Theatre*, Sidgwick & Jackson, 1951, p. 84.

sharp difference in emphasis with the literary nationalists who held with Yeats that 'more important than questions of politics and language, it was to give a new artistic form to truth and beauty.'[1] The difference might be put by saying that whereas one group stressed the 'image', the other stressed the 'word'. The literary renaissance was consequently more profound, aiming directly at a vital cultural transformation. In a puritan Ireland it inevitably lost ground to the language movement which bogged down in an obscurantist cult of the language itself. It led in self-governing Ireland to a costly scheme of compulsory education in Gaelic. All the Irish youth got out of it was a language they did not really want and were unable to use. Today the Gaelic Revival is dying and discredited. It has little to show for itself except one poet, Sean O'Riordan, and one playwright, Mairead ni Grada.

The upsurge of political nationalism after the 1916 Rising gave a decisive cast to Irish revivalism. In the hands of de Valera, nationalism acquired a strong organisational character, concerned primarily with the State and its alleged needs – independence, unity and Gaelic in language. The central notion was the creative importance of the organised expression of the community; and thus was added a third key – the State – as an *open sesame* to the hidden Ireland.

It was the Irish Catholic Church which conditioned the form which Irish nationalism took under self-government. From the Church's point of view, the most important requirement was that it should be anti-individualist; hence the institutional rather than human character of de Valera's nationalism. This also had the effect of excluding men of honesty and ability from the Government – a fact which helps to explain the continued mediocrity, with some exceptions, of the members of both the *Dail* and the Senate. Thus, if the Irish State was an anti-cultural agent – supplementing the Church's anti-social policy – this was a condition of its existence. Apart from this limitation, however, the State enjoyed no little autonomy. This was due to the Church's implicit acceptance of the separation of religion and politics, as well as to the fact that the Church was, in some real measure, seduced by ultra-nationalism. The State was jealous of this autonomy and resented clerical 'interference' in politics, as shown, for example, by the summary rejection of Bishop Dignam's scheme for a comprehensive

[1] Speech on the *Reform of the Theatre*, March 14, 1903.

system of Social Insurance in 1945.[1] De Valera, in particular, was convinced of the autonomy of politics, a conviction which led him to take a strong line with the bishops – an attitude that has been much admired.

At the same time, relations between Church and State in Ireland were bound to be uneasy. Some doubts about national-socialism were inevitable, and the bias towards violence and revolution could not but be somewhat disquieting to a Church which had resolutely opposed these during the nineteenth century. Church-State relations improved with the adoption of a moderate nationalism by the Lemass administration, when political and clerical leadership found a common basis for national policy in an industrial expansion.

In order to understand the sad fate of Irish culture during 1932–1959, one must allow for the combined anti-cultural policies of the Church and of the State. Not that the State was anti-cultural so much as philistine, behaving as if culture did not exist. True there were some exceptions, like P. J. Little, a Minister in the *Fianna Fail* party, who tried to maintain some contact with Dublin intellectuals. To associate with intellectuals in those times, however, was only somewhat less indiscreet than associating with communists. For the most part, Irish politicians toed the clerical line. This meant no disturbing criticism, especially of the Church, education and censorship. And when the politicians stepped out of line – as in the case of Dr Browne – the Church rapped them smartly on the knuckles. So the situation remained, until recent times when a politician could make a critical remark without looking carefully over his shoulder – times, indeed, when a little honesty and intelligence might even help advance a political career.

Mr de Valera never gave his state absolutism a clear or explicit shape. It remained a mystique, never evolved into a philosophy. This did not diminish its potency, however, even if it obscured its real meaning. Thus Mr de Valera's politics were quite modern, up-to-date, and had departed almost altogether from the old tradition with which he was generally supposed to be in touch.

It is not easy to define what is meant by the old or Gaelic tradition.

[1] See O'Faolain, *The Irish*, p. 124 ff.

When in Kate O'Brien's *The Land of Spices*, the Bishop remarks to the Reverend Mother that Ireland's need was for a 'truly national' education, the nun replies, 'When Ireland decides what she means by that, my Lord, the *Compagnie de la Sainte Famille* will provide it.

There appear to be two answers as to what the Gaelic tradition really means. One is that the meaning cannot be precisely given because that tradition is evolutionary, unfolding itself with time, acquiring what Sean O'Faolain called a 'time-created character'. Paul Vincent Carroll gives us this interpretation in *The White Steed*:

> *Canon.* Now you are being silly and stupid Nora. You are not going back to England I hope.
> *Nora.* No, I will never leave Ireland again. There is something here that is nowhere else. It's away far back and away deep down. A man going down a moonlit road from a fair may know it, or a child reading on a broken window-sill of Niam or Aideen or Maeve, but they will tell you no name for it. They will look away from you and the tears will come with a sudden rush but the cry is within them forever, and neither money nor mating will make them happy.

One can see the difficulty of shaping a life for which no definition exists. The assumption of evolutionists is, presumably, that life itself will create, automatically meeting the challenge of needs as they arise. Was it not, indeed, our expectation that, as Sean O'Faolain expressed it,

> the sunburst of freedom . . . would solve all our problems with the descent of a heavenly human order which we would immediately recognise as the reality of our never-articulated dreams.[1]

The second definition of the Irish tradition is that it is pagan, relating to the native life which Christianity failed to assimilate. This is the life which Synge portrayed, and which Pearse tried to synthesise with Catholicism. The discerning Mr Carroll also provides this second definition in the same play:

> *Fr Shoughnessy.* The evil you assimilated in a pagan land is deep within you, woman.
> *Nora.* What I have in me that won't let me stoop I didn't get in England, for England hasn't got it to give. It was in Aideen when

[1] *Vive Moi*, p. 148.

63

she rode by Conor's side at the battle of the Grava. It was in Cuchulain when he tied himself to a pillar before he'd stoop to death; it was in Oisin when he rode back on Niam's white horse and found the land full of priests like you and little men like your poor schoolmaster here; and it's in me now, making me refuse to come to your council chamber and swallow the ancient draught of humility.

Mr Carroll seems aware of the pagan-Catholic dualism in Irish life, which he appears to accept as natural and normal. Professor Daniel Corkery – an outstanding Catholic apologist of the revival movement – gives the same impression. 'The companionship of the two cultures, Latin and Irish, in both native and Church schools [he wrote] was probably the greatest thing that ever happened in Irish history.'[1]

The old Irish cult of nature was pagan, treating nature as an absolute – as in Dagda, the Sun-God – or enjoying it merely as an end in itself. This paganism is typically Irish, and specially typical of rural Ireland. It is evident in the work of Liam O'Flaherty, and in later writers such as M. J. Molloy, Walter Macken and John B. Keane. Popularly, it is shown in the traditional interest in the ghost and fairy worlds; in stories of the 'little men' who enjoy sanctuary in rath or fairy fort; in the practice of witchcraft still to be found in the western parts of Ireland; and in tales of haunting along the lines of Eliott O'Donnell's ghostly melodramas. If the rural firesides today are less hushed in superstitious awe at the recital of those tales it is because of a general slackening of supernatural belief. In rural life, the local 'character' is often enough pagan with the lusty, imaginative quality one finds in Synge's *Playboy*.

Apologists of the national revival fight shy of using a racial basis for national distinctiveness, aware of the progressive dilution of the original stock by Dane, Norman and Anglo-Saxon; and aware of the shaky basis of the racialist theory, for, as Chesterton remarked, the notion of the Celt 'is dim to the anthropologist and utterly meaningless in anybody else'. Professor Corkery depends mainly on land and, like Yeats, sees its highest embodiment in literature:

. . . no landowners in any other country [he wrote] ever knew their territories as these Gaels knew their's since, in the literature, land and

[1] *The Fortunes of the Irish Language*, Dublin, 1954, p. 17.

64

literature were almost indivisible. Every bluff and brake they looked on they were aware was known at the other end of the country because it had at some time or other been enshrined in verse or a heroic tale. (*Ibid.*)

George Moore, on the other hand, preferred climate, contending in *Hail and Farewell* that 'ideas are climatic; the climate of Ireland had produced certain modes of thought, and these could only transpire in the language.' Yet, without the support of the racial idea, is there sufficient left on which to base Laurence Durrell's contention that 'any culture is after all the spirit of place'? Land and climate are hardly adequate. The blackbird sings as sweetly in Cornwall as in Cork, the purple of its heather is no less vivid.

A more sensible view of national differences is that they are secondary: a product of varying factors, partly human and partly environmental. Group sentiment has played a part by deliberately stressing and fostering differences, weakening our common humanity by creating regional rivalries. Ideological conflict has made for tangible and definable changes: as in the distinctive mentality and outlook of Marxist communities; or, even in a Christian context, as between British Protestantism and Irish Catholicism. A difference in the phase of social evolution is also relevant: perhaps the Elizabethan English more closely resembled the modern Irish than do their present successors. The nature of resources, whether agricultural or industrial, also affect views and ways of life. These and many others – geographical position, invasions, wars, famines, floods, earthquakes – are surely enough to explain why communities differ without having recourse to the radical assumptions of nationalism. Such is the conclusion of Boyd C. Shafer in his admirably lucid study of the misconceptions which underlie the pre-suppositions of nationalism.[1]

Padraig Pearse did most for the marriage of pagan and Catholic ideas in Ireland, greatly influencing the Irish administration in its aim to make Ireland at once Gaelic and Catholic. Pearse's syncretism inevitably meant a distortion of Christian values. In his work, pagan sentiments metamorphose Christian ideas. Humility is transformed into pride. Man himself is nothing, but with God's help he may become, not

[1] *Nationalism: Myth and Reality.* Gollancz, 1955.

C

gentle, but charged with a ruthless strength. This transmutation of values can be seen in Pearse's play, *The King*, as when the Abbot prays for the boy-king:

> O strong God, make strong the hand of this child. Make firm his foot. Make keen his sword. Let the purity of his heart and the humbleness of his spirit be unto him a magnifying of courage and an exaltation of mind. Ye angels that fought the ancient battles, ye veterans of God, make a battle-pen about him and fight before him with flaming swords.

Pearse glorifies war rather than peace; and this he does almost with a recognition of the conflict between Christian and pagan ideals. The Abbot's comment that the music of the fighters made drunk the hearts of young men inspires the following dialogue:

Second Monk. It is good for young men to be made drunk.
First Monk. Brother, you speak wickedness.
Abbot. There is a heady ale which all men should drink, for he who has not been made drunk with it has not lived. It is with this ale that God makes drunk the hearts of his saints.
First Monk. This is not plain, father.
Abbot. Do you think if that terrible, beautiful voice for which the young men strain their ears were to speak from yon place where the fighters are, and the horses and the music, that I would stay you, did ye rise to obey it? Do you think that I would grudge any of you . . . the dearest of these little boys to death calling with that terrible, beautiful voice. I would let you all go.

No wonder Yeats wrote of the birth of a 'terrible beauty' in connection with the 1916 Rising.

The Irish nation was treated as an absolute after the 1916 Rising, and the struggle to perfect it as a holy crusade. There came into being, as Sean O'Casey noted, a 'political catechism as well as one coined by the Council of Trent'. The apotheosis of the nation was marked by the use in connection with it of terms which belong strictly to religion. Those who died for Ireland were known as 'martyrs'. There was the 'gospel of 1916' which embodied the tenets of extreme nationalism. There were now, indeed, two faiths, the Christian and the Fenian, as Padraig Pearse called it. Thus Pearse could equate faith in God with faith in the Fatherland, declaiming by the graveside of O'Donovan-Rossa:

> . . . I may be taken as speaking on behalf of the new generation that
> has been baptised in the Fenian faith . . . I propose to you that here
> by the graveside of this unrepentant Fenian we renew our baptismal
> vows.

Here there is all the solemnity of a Christian baptism, a form of
initiation for the believers in the sacred character of the Irish nation.
The faithful must be prepared to give their lives for Ireland. MacDara
asserts in *The Singer*:

> One man can free a people as one man redeemed the world. I will
> take my pike. I will go into battle with bare hands. I will take my
> stand before the *Gall* [the English] as Christ hung naked before man
> upon a tree.

Pearse preached the need of a 'blood sacrifice', thus attaching a religious connotation to the I.R.B.'s traditional policy of force. Consequently, the 1916 Rising meant more than a military or propaganda
gesture; it was part of a quasi-religious ritual. It was a form of national
therapy, a Spenglerian catharsis which would renew the Irish soul.
This helps to explain why the Rising took place in spite of unfavourable
conditions; why, as D. J. Goodspeed shows, it was so haphazardly
planned and executed.[1] Even the rational Griffith was not unaffected
by the mystique of a blood sacrifice; and it coloured Connolly's Marxian
concept of revolution, helping to make him the most determined advocate of the Rising. Connolly noted that

> deep in the heart of Ireland has sunk the sense of degradation wrought
> upon its people – so deep and so humiliating that no agency less
> powerful than the red tide of war on Irish soil will ever enable the
> Irish race to recover its self-respect or establish its national dignity.[2]

He went on in the manner of Pearse to link the supreme sacrifice of
Irishmen with Christ's crucifixion, stating that 'for us, as for mankind
before Calvary, it may be truly said that without the shedding of blood
there can be no redemption.'

[1] *The Conspirators: A Study of the Coup d'Etat*, Macmillan, 1962.
[2] Editorial in *Worker's Republic*, February 1, 1916.

The nobility of the insurrectionists fired Ireland especially when their execution by the British completed their act of self-sacrifice. Even the clergy responded; and the Rev. P. Browne a Professor in Maynooth and later President of University College, Galway, identified the 'sacred fire' of religion and nationality:

> Our day has seen the sacred fire again
> Burst into flame and from the new-born glow
> We have relit the lamp within our souls
> Like the Church tapers lighted row on row
> On Easter Sunday from the Paschal coals . . .

The same priest, in a preface to Pearse's *Collected Works* published in 1917, described them as an *itinerarium mentis ad Deum* a journey of the mind to God. Fr Browne noted that the 'old divinities and figures of the sagas are there and the remnants of the old worship in the minds of the people are delineated, but everything is overshadowed by the Christian concept.' One wonders if this is not a modern sample of a type of rationalisation which enabled the original paganism to survive, and made possible that historic dualism to which Sean O'Faolain refers.

The revolutionary character of *Sinn Fein* ideals eluded no small numbers of the clergy who did not see that the social philosophy of *Sinn Fein* was anti-Catholic both as to ends and means. Christ died to assert the unity of man but the insurrectionists were at pains to assert Ireland's unique and separate nationhood. Christ upheld humility, conciliation and peace: the insurrectionists, pride, intransigence and war. There were not lacking bishops who supported the extremists like O'Dwyer of Limerick and Archbishop Mannix after he left Ireland for Australia. The younger clergy, in particular were infected, and some were to be found on *Sinn Fein* platforms seducing the people from the moderate Parliamentary Party. Of such was Fr Michael Flanagan, a Vice-President of *Sinn Fein*. The fever of Pearse's pseudo-sanctified fanaticism led Fr Dominick to describe Bloody Sunday – when a number of British agents were assassinated – as 'a glorious day for Ireland'.

The great nationalist writers had some faith in the Rising initially at any rate. They saw it as a crucial test of the hopes they placed in a creative combination of moral energy and violence. AE associated it with the familiar image of Christ's Resurrection, suggesting that 'it

has wrought that miracle among the ruins here . . .' But for Yeats and
AE, it lost its attraction when they saw that the outcome was the
destruction rather than the liberation of the national mind. AE complained in *The Freeman* in 1923 that the Revolution had 'triumphed
only in externals. Our spiritual, intellectual and cultural life . . . has
retrograded . . . The champions of physical force have . . . poisoned
the soul of Ireland.' Yeats warned prophetically:

> The mob reigned. If that reign is not broken our public life will
> move from violence to violence, or from violence to apathy, our
> parliament disgrace and debauch those who enter it; our men of
> letters live like outlaws in their own country.

AE tried to counter the trend towards force by urging the need for
'more intellect in Ireland', more sanity and honesty. Like Yeats, however, he found that he had little in common with the new politicians,
and could do little to influence them. The outcome of the Irish liberation
depressed him profoundly as it did Yeats, and he expressed his disillusion:

> The hills have vanished in dark air;
> The night without an eye is blind.
> I too am starless. Time has blurred
> The aeons of my life behind.
>
> Oh what in those dark aeons lay?
> What tumult, beauty and desire?
> I know not, all are lost beyond
> Sunsets of anguish and of fire.

The gap between the pagan and Christian elements in Irish nationalism
widened as a result of the Civil War and clerical censure of the extremists. The pagan forces found allies in the revolutionary ideas current
in Europe – nazism, communism, anarchism and nihilism – and were
transformed, in part, into modern humanism. Thus the old paganism
was shorn of some of its supernatural trappings; its marginal worlds
peopled by national divinities, fairies and ghosts. It was now adapted for
less esoteric, if for more urgent, needs.

Fiction rather than reality may give a better picture of the evolution
of extreme nationalism in Ireland. For Irish revolutionaries find it
discreet to hide their ideas, or lack the power to express them. In *The*

Martyr, Liam O'Flaherty's novel of the Civil War, Crosbie and Tyson, heirs to Pearse's syncretic ideal, defend their opposed interpretations. Crosbie, the Catholic nationalist, an officer in the anti-Treaty Irregulars, is torn between the claims of passive and terrorist resistance. He sees the Irish struggle as a 'fulfilment of our divine mission to Christianise Europe a second time'. Tyson, the humanist-nationalist, sees it as enabling Ireland to 'grow from tender infancy to something mighty'. He is an 'imperialist' who wants to make Ireland the 'birth-bed of an empire'. Tyson's view of God is anthropomorphic and nazi:

> God in relation to the State [he explained] is the poetic conception of the State; and religion which is a ritual for the worship of God, is the poetical expression of the people at large, their impulse towards immortality and the conquest of the universe.[1]

Tyson's position is more logical than Crosbie's, for in accepting the Nation – State as the supreme political principle, Crosbie is not justified in appealing to a Christian ethic. It is also the weakness in de Valera's position, as in that of the Irish Catholic Church in so far as it accepts the absolutism of the Nation but insists on the use of pacific means to realise it. Tyson attacks Crosbie savagely on this score, and thereby echoes the charges made against de Valera for his responsibility for the Civil War:

> A pacifist. By God! Yes. Are you still a pacifist? In war-time you're a pacifist. In peace-time you thirst for war. Spur on the fools . . . while you sit with the women . . .[2]

It is not hard to see why the radical brand of Irish nationalism is more alive than the moderate kind. The Catholic-nationalist is an ideological hybrid, whose ideas are in conflict, neutralising one another. He is an incompetent who is incapable of resolving the contradiction within him. The intelligent I.R.A. man either moves to the left, or leaves the Organisation, like Brendan Behan. The left-winger is consistent, adopting a coherent revolutionary idea, from which a sentimental Christianity has been ruthlessly pruned. The radical I.R.A. use the pietistic, Christ-invoking right wing as a respectable façade to

[1] Gollancz, 1933, p. 191.
[2] *Ibid.*, p. 189.

obscure their revolutionary aims. Tyson crucified Crosbie in a parody of Christ's death, and Crosbie was a willing martyr. But Tyson warned Crosbie prophetically that his inept brand of Catholic idealism would be destroyed, and that his hopes for a Christian revival were vain:

> You say that Ireland will rise again to spew me and my comrades from her bosom. My friend, she will rise too late for your ambitions. By then we shall have murdered martyrdom.[1]

In *The Hostage*, Behan attacked the 'earnest, religious-minded' revolutionary who prepares for a brutal murder in the afternoon with a fervent Holy Communion in the morning. Behan instinctively distrusted this bloody Catholic fanaticism, as well as criticising its narrow humanity which subjects social to political aims. It is in the first scene between Pat and the I.R.A. officer that this play takes on a real edge. Behan is here cold and deliberately insulting. Pat, a one-time member of the I.R.A., tells the officer that his main objection to going to prison for the national cause is his inability to stand the companionship of the other patriot-prisoners.

Irish revolutionary ideas, conditioned by the hate inherent in nationalism, savour more of the darker and destructive forces which go to make up modern political thought and sentiment; and there is a certain correspondence between the vital political and literary outlooks of modern Ireland, as expressed, for instance, by the later Joyce and Yeats. A vaguely defined nihilism underlies the more overt communist and anarchic conceptions of the extreme republican wing. This forbidding mentality is described in O'Flaherty's *The Informer* where Commandant Gallagher reponds to Mary's probe as to whether he has pity for the working class, or whether he believes in communism or in anything:

> No. I believe in nothing fundamentally. And I don't feel pity . . .
> Pity is a ridiculous sensation for a man of my nature. A revolutionary is incapable of feeling pity. Listen. The philosophy of a revolutionary is this. Civilisation is a process in the development of the human species. I am an atom in the human species, groping in advance, impelled by a force over which neither I nor the human species have

[1] *Ibid*, p. 197.

71

any control . . . to thrust forward the human species from one phase of development to another. I am at war with the remainder of the species. I am a Christ beating them with rods. I have no mercy. I have no pity. I have no beliefs. I am an automaton. I am a revolutionary. And there is no reward for me but the satisfaction of one lust, the lust for the achievement of my mission, for power maybe . . .

Modern Irish nationalism has little connection with the Gaelic tradition, especially 'orthodox' or de Valerite nationalism. The traditional culture was not nationalist. This can be seen in those Irish-speaking areas which it still informs; and where, as a critic of the Gaelic Revival noted, 'nationalism made but little impression . . . The political and cultural concepts of the doctrine were foreign to their spirit.'[1] The roots of the traditional culture, nourished on the Graeco-Christian ideas of the Golden Age, retained a vital sympathy with European culture, however drastically political conditions limited its exploitation. The old culture had a strong sense of individual and family loyalty – especially to its patrons among the old, Gaelic aristocracy – but of national sense it possessed little; too little, indeed, to enable it to overcome the organised Norman threat. Even when the traditional culture was mainly isolated from European culture – from the thirteenth century onwards – its historians supplied the nobility, Gaelic and Anglo-Irish, with ficticious genealogies extending back to the mythological deities of Rome and Greece until they reached biblical origins in Adam.

The intense hatred of England, so typical of modern Ireland, is a by-product of nationalism. It did not mark the Gaelic tradition which showed a more accommodating attitude to the invader, and adapted itself readily enough to the Anglo-Norman families which took the place of the dispossessed Irish. There may have been in this some element of opportunism, especially when, with the disruption of the old Gaelic society, the bards became desperate in their search for patrons. It was due mainly, however, to a broader human and more realistic approach to the vicissitudes of conquest. O'Brudair could write of a usurper, Warner of Castle:

It is God who created the world,
And given us one generous man for another who died

[1] *Studies, Revival and Survival*, R. A. Breatnach, Summer 1956.

> One who gives gifts to families, scholars and bards
> A champion not false but great of heart . . .

Sean O'Faolain describes this as a 'whine', but one wonders if we can do justice to O'Brudair's comment which was inspired by an outlook much less bound up than ours by a sense of ethnic and local differences. Perhaps a British patron of culture is better than none; and none the modern Irish writers have. The important thing for the bards was that the old life should continue, and, apparently, they believed that it could continue under any patronage, British or Irish. It was one of the great dreams of the last of the bards – O'Rahilly and O'Brudair – that the Stuarts would return, and with them the old secure patronage. The Irish nationalist culture of today has made a few converts, exciting only pity in Britain and fury in Northern Ireland. Perhaps there is more wisdom in the bardic approach which disarms an opponent by changing him into a contented member of an Irish society rather than by isolating him as a member of an alien class.

Neither had the traditional culture that democratic colouring which is part of the new synthetic Gaeldom. The notion of a popular sovereignty was utterly alien to the Gaelic tradition which was, on the contrary, aristocratic, even brutally so, concerned with the upper social strata – the nobles, the clergy, the learned and the bards. Its lack of interest in ordinary folk has led to some spirited criticism from some symphathisers with the Gaelic revival, as from Sean O'Faolain in *The King of the Beggars*. Not that the official Irish outlook today can be fairly described as democratic or aristocratic. It really appeals, in fact, neither to the values of a class nor to those of a collectivity, but rather to an inept and sentimental concept of culture, the product of a puritan nationalism. Because of its puritanism, however, its bias is democratic rather than aristocratic, that is, more in sympathy with the backward than with the progressive elements in the community.

Nor had the Gaelic tradition any sympathy with industrialism and urban life. Land and nature permeated the life and literature of historic Ireland. They entered strongly into modern Irish literature; into that of the Catholic Irish – as evident in the work of James Stephens, Padraic Colum, Liam O'Flaherty, Sean O'Faolain, M. J. Molloy, Walter Macken, and John B. Keane. It is in a feeling for nature and for

C*

the nation that the literatures of the Anglo-Irish and Catholic Irish come most closely together. So great was the exclusion of the influence of the writers that a sense of pastoral values has been markedly absent in the administration of self-governing Ireland. Under de Valera, Lemass and Lynch, policy has been primarily concerned with industry and the towns. The neglect of rural life and values led Dr Thomas Walsh, Director of the Agricultural Institute, to warn at a *Muintir na Tire* rural week that 'very shortly people born and reared in urban areas will be in such a majority that they will dismiss rural values as mere folk lore'.[1]

The Gaelic tradition had a strong pagan side to it, a lively and lusty love of life, which is acutely embarrassing to many of its protagonists today. This fresh and baudy quality can be seen in the English versions of *The Midnight Court* by Brian Merriman, a Gaelic poet, the translation of which by Frank O'Connor was banned. O'Brudair sang of marriage with a freedom which would make the Irish Censorship Board squirm with distaste:

> Here I put the gentle maiden
> gently up
> with her man in bed,
> no bed of straw,
> and loosen knees
> to furrow flesh
> and loose the austere belt
> until doors unlatch
> with kisses
> and there's blanket sport
> under the rose . . .

The introduction of Jansenism changed all that, substituting a frigid restraint for the free sensuousness of the older outlook. All Catholic Ireland could achieve, apparently, during her long history, was to leave the human imagination go its own way, as with the traditional culture, or, alternatively, to stifle it under the modern dispensation. Through Jansenism it was sought to resolve the dualism by an obliteration of the human element, as if – to quote the Rev Dr Alfred O'Rahilly

[1] Gormanstown College, Co. Meath, July 21, 1966.

74

– the 'supernatural replaced the natural instead of reinforcing it.' It is an irony indeed that a prudish government should commit itself to reviving a Gaelic literature about which the erudite Professor Atkinson of Trinity College, Dublin, said that

> it would be difficult to find a book in which there was not some passage so silly or so indecent as to give you a shock from which you would never recover during the rest of your life.[1]

The modern Irish view of the Gaelic tradition does it little justice, and what many revivalists want to revive has little existence outside their own distorted imaginations. They are guilty of the fallacy of reading the past in terms of the present, and seeing the Gaelic tradition through the prism of nineteenth-century ideas – nationalism, puritanism, democracy, and industrialism. The result is a synthetic ideal which the old bards would be the first to disown. For puritan Ireland, the old paganism was adapted to national socialism. For radical Ireland, it was transformed into an anti-Christian force, and became identified with the most extreme of modern revolutionary ideas. The outcome for both was the reverse of what was intended – a uniquely distinctive national culture – for Irish life today does little more than mirror West European political, social and cultural trends.

[1] Quote Mercier, *The Irish Comic Tradition*, p. 202.

CHAPTER V

George Moore

THE NATIVE IRISH MIND was unable to stand up to historical pressures. During the nineteenth century, it was afflicted with a morbid susceptibility to subversive ideas and sentiments – Jansenism and extreme nationalism. The last really great Irishman was Daniel O'Connell (1775–1847) whose broad and sympathetic vision was later a rarity among Catholic Irishmen.

The loss of this healthy instinct towards life was shown in the Catholic contributors to the Irish Literary Renaissance – in Joyce, Moore, Gogarty, and Edward Martyn of whom Yeats suggests that he compensated for a subconscious hatred of women by eating prodigiously.[1] What, for the most part, these writers could least stomach was contemporary Catholic Ireland; and their lives' work may be seen as a critique and rejection of Catholicism. They were representative of the immature and twisted Irish Catholic conscience which was to destroy the Irish mind when, under self-government, it was in a position to shape it.

Moore was the most humanistic of the above writers, but his outlook was marred not only by a profound hatred of Catholicism but also by a perverse and egoistic quality which made his relations with others brittle and variable. 'I am feminine, morbid, perverse. Above all, perverse', he wrote of himself. He was a stormy petrel whose support of any movement made him a doubtful asset; and his close friend, AE, advised against his association with the Irish literary movement. His strong aversion to Catholicism, however, as well as his snobbish attitude to the 'Catholic set', do not disqualify his criticisms of Catholic Ireland, though it limits his value as a reformer who might have helped to remedy the defects in its illogical anti-humanism. It must also be remembered that Moore spent the greater part of his life out of Ireland,

[1] *Dramatis Personae*, Cuala Press, Dublin, 1935, pp. 2–3.

so that his knowledge of Irish life was not as intimate as it might have been. He had a flair, however, for quickly appreciating the realities of any social situation, as he had for assimilating new ideas.

The works of Joyce and Moore provide the earliest and best assessments of modern Irish Catholicism. Two more dissimilar personalities it would be hard to find, for while Joyce was born with an almost ineradicable intellectual love of Catholicism, George Moore (1852–1933) had almost a life-long instinctive hatred of Catholicism. Joyce really belonged to the medieval Catholic tradition extending back to the humanism of Pelagius, and the Platonism of John Scotus Ereugina which the later Joyce totally inverted. Primarily concerned with ideas, Joyce clearly showed the essential contradiction which lies at the heart of Irish Catholicism – the anti-humanism of a religion whose main tenet is love of God and man. Mainly concerned with social realities, Moore described the human and social consequences of this anti-humanism.

Moore was born in Moore Hall near Lough Cara in a remote part of Co. Mayo. One may possibly see in his mixed Catholic-Protestant ancestry some part of an explanation of his love of 'dear sweet Protestant England', and why he became a convert to Protestantism. He was educated at Oscott, an expensive Catholic college on the outskirts of Birmingham. Here he quickly showed his anti-Catholic bias by refusing to go to confession; and here he also showed evidence of an incorrigible individualism by refusing to learn anything whatever, even to spell; his letters home were marked by an illiteracy worthy of a stable boy in his father's racing stable. Moore turned his back on a formal education, preferring, apparently, to educate himself. This may well have suited his curious personality – for Moore is one of the most complex and elusive of the Irish writers – but this method has obvious drawbacks, leaving him too exposed to contemporary influences, and giving to his outlook a certain dilettante and amateurish quality. Moore was a modern by the very nature of his type of education.

As Moore describes in the *Confessions of a Young Man* (1888) his first cultural inclination was towards art; and when he reached his majority in 1873, he went to Paris. Here he insinuated himself into the company of the Impressionist painters, whose attitudes and techniques left a marked impression on his mind; and here he had what he used to describe as a 'café education' which was his substitute for a university. Though he had a vivid appreciation of painting, he found that he had not the makings of a painter. Then he turned to literature. Zola was his first French mentor; and the ultra-realism of this writer influenced him profoundly, though it was later offset by Balzac whose more imaginative approach modified Moore's exaggerated preoccupation with the factual.

Moore's realism gave a salutary shock to English letters, as in such fine novels as *A Mummer's Wife* (1885) and *Esther Waters* (1894). Yet, oddly for a liberal, the overtones of these novels are moralistic in their reflections on theatrical life and horse racing; and no less oddly they have backgrounds in Protestant sectarianism – Wesleyism and the Plymouth Brethren. Though Moore had early declared his Christian agnosticism, Christianity remained with him a nagging obsession.

Moore's realism had less effect in Ireland where a literary consciousness of an idealistic kind was just developing. Susan Mitchell tells how W. B. Yeats had forbidden his sisters to read *A Mummer's Wife*, a prohibition which gives some indication of the profound change which took place in the outlook of Yeats, whose later work acquired a coarse, uninhibited quality.[1]

Moore's first novel dealing with the Irish scene was *A Drama in Muslin* (1886), which is concerned with the futility of the life of the landed gentry, mainly preoccupied with the problem of collecting their rents from a rebellious peasantry, and finding suitable husbands for their daughters in a travesty of social life centred on Dublin Castle. This is the best of Moore's novels dealing with Ireland, and contains only fleeting and disparaging references to the clergy, as in his portrait of Fr Shannon – 'large, pompous and arrogant'.

Moore's next Irish work, *Parnell and His Island* (1887) consists of a number of crude sketches in which Moore sees Ireland as a victim of the landlord, the terrorist and, to some extent, the priest. In the sketch dealing with *The Priest*, Fr Tom is shown as 'proud, overbearing and ostentatious', maddened by any opposition from his parishioners. There is 'much ostentation in his walk [and] there is treachery in the warm squeeze of his hand, and dissimulation in [his] unctuous words of

[1] *George Moore*, Talbot Press, Dublin, 1919, p. 43.

welcome . . .' His intelligence is of 'a limited and common kind', though he has some knowledge of politics and economics. He is a 'compromise between the priest of the last generation – the benign old man who loved his Horace . . . and the drunken demagogue of the present day who preaches assassination from the altar'. One of Moore's early tutors, the kindly Fr James Browne, belonged to the older generation of priests.

Of the clergy in general Moore noted that they are fond of the bottle but that they are chaste. This he rightly saw as a 'subject for physiological and psychological analysis' – how men who live so well and have so much leisure keep women at bay, especially as many of them live in such close proximity with their housekeepers. It is a phenomenon which has perplexed many another Irish critic, and seems to reflect on the general sexual devitalisation of Irishmen. For Moore rightly adds

that they sin and elude discovery, no one who knows the country, every eye fixed upon them, would believe for a moment.

In a later novel, *The Lake*, Moore hints that the Irish clergy's weakness for drink may be a means of assuaging the frustration of their empty lives. In that novel, Fr Moran says to Fr Gogarty:

We all suffer, you like another, and when the ache becomes too great to be borne we drink. Whiskey is the remedy; there's none better. We drink to forget and that is the great thing.

There is reason to believe that the Irish clergy's fondness for the bottle – a matter which is the subject of present investigation – finds part of its explanation in the repression of their idealism and social and cultural activities. This point is not so relevant in recent years when, as a result of the clerical revival, the activities of the clergy have been much extended.

Moore, as he often averred, was a creature of impulse, pursuing a zigzag course dictated by the inspiration of the moment. It is hardly surprising, then, that he joined Yeats, Lady Gregory and Edward Martyn in the beginnings of the Irish Literary Renaissance. He was genuinely attracted by the Gaelic revival; and for a while his attitude to

Ireland was concerned and sympathetic. Under this influence he wrote *Evelyn Innes* (1898) and its counterpart, *Sister Teresa* (1898), as well as a volume of short stories, *The Untilled Field*.

In these novels he made a genuine attempt to identify himself with Catholicism, describing the efforts of a celebrated opera singer to work out her salvation in a poor English convent. These works are not impressive; from a Catholic standpoint, though, it is of interest to note that Moore seems to favour the contemplative rather than the active religious life, and to recognise the importance of restoring traditional Church music, so dear to the heart of Edward Martyn. Moore's natural paganism and humanism continuously breaks through the religious pattern of convent life, and drives his Wagnerian opera singer to the edge of agnosticism and an early death.

In *Sister Teresa*, Evelyn reads an account of Sister Mary John's mystical experiences:

> One night . . . she had been awakened to see a soft light shining in the corner of the room which was quite dark. She lay with her feet and hands folded, watching the light until it grew wider until it descended upon her; and when she awoke again . . . an angel was beside her. She could just see him in the faint and tremulous light which his flesh emitted, and he folded her in his arms . . . and told her that he loved her, and watched for her, and he held her so closely that the two seemed to become one . . . she hoped that he would kiss her . . .

This religious sensualism is reminiscent of the later Yeats.

As Moore became more familiar with the Irish scene, his attitude to the Irish Catholic Church hardened; he began, as Joseph Hone stated, 'to side with the anti-clericals and Protestants who put the blame for . . . the melancholy waste in Irish life, emigration and so forth, on the puritan excesses of the Irish priest.'[1] So intense did his hatred of Catholicism become that it led to a complete estrangement with his brother, Colonel Maurice Moore, for whom over a long period he had the warmest regard – a difficult achievement for Moore's capricious nature.

Moore's criticisms of the Irish Catholic Church find expression in *The Untilled Field* (1903). In *Home Sickness*, for example, he describes how Bryden, a publican's assistant in New York's Bowery, returns to

[1] *The Life of George Moore*, Gollancz, 1936, p. 243.

Ireland to recover his health, but Irish conditions force him to go back to his former job. At Mass he listened

> in mixed anger and astonishment to the priest, who was scolding his parishioners . . . saying that he had heard that there was dancing going on in their homes. Worse than that [he complained] that he had seen boys and girls loitering about the road, and the talk that went on was of one kind, love.

The priest intrudes on one of these festive gatherings and Bryden observes that

> his eyes went towards the corner where the women were gathered and Bryden felt that the priest looked on the women as more dangerous than the porter.

Bryden falls in love with Margaret Dirken, but he cannot face the thought of marrying her and staying at home:

> His eyes fell on the bleak country, on the little fields divided by walls; he remembered the pathetic ignorance of the people, and it was these things that he could not endure. It was the priest who came to forbid the dancing. Yes, it was the priest.

In a story with a rather unconvincing background, *The Wild Goose*, Moore describes the return of another exile who marries the daughter of a rich farmer, and, with the aid of her money, devotes himself to politics, but he is thwarted by a reactionary clergy – especially the older clergy – who flourish while the people decline. He thinks that economic causes are not the real cause of emigration, but the kill-joy attitude of the clergy. In a public address he stated that

> the country was joyless . . . It will be said that the Irish are too poor to pay for pleasure, but they are not too poor to spend fifteen millions on religion . . . It was the duty of every Irishman to spend money on making Ireland a joyful country. He was speaking now in the interests of religion . . .

In spite of over-simplification, Moore put his finger on one of the vital causes of Irish emigration, which became even more significant under self-government. He complained of a 'mean intellectual atmosphere of nuns and rosaries'. He deplored the lack of 'any intellectual passion; there was not even religious passion, only religious formula'. He noted of an opponent, Fr Murphy, that

> He was clearly the well-fed, well-housed cleric who was making in this world an excellent living for his advocacy of the next, and Ned wondered how it was that the people did not see the a discrepancy between Fr Murphy's appearance and the theories he propounded.

Anticipating some modern innovators, Moore suggested – in a story, *A Letter to Rome* – that the secular priests should be allowed to marry in order to restrict emigration. He calculated that this would mean an increase of about four thousand children a year, and, indeed, children of the best stock, for

> The priests live in the best houses, eat the best food, wear the best clothes; they are indeed the flower of the nation, and would produce magnificent sons and daughters . . .

Undoubtedly Moore was naive to think that such views would meet any sympathetic response from the Irish clergy. He concluded of Ireland that

> This is no place for a man to live. This is no country for an educated man. It won't be fit for a man to live in for another hundred years.

Over half a century of experience has gone far to establish the truth of this grim forecast.

In spite of Moore's aversion to Christianity, he was (like Oscar Wilde, born two years before him) fascinated by the personality of Christ, and was an assiduous student of the Bible. In *Confessions of a Young Man* (1888) he wrote of Christ:

> Poor fallen God, I who hold naught else pitiful, pity Thee. Thy bleeding face and hands and feet. Thy hanging body; Thou at least art picturesque, and in a way beautiful in the midst of that sombre mediocrity towards which Thou has drifted for two thousand years.

His biblical studies led him to become a convert to Protestantism in 1903. In *Hail And Farewell* (written in three volumes between 1911 and 1914) Moore gives some reasons for this step. He criticises the anti-humanism of the Irish Catholic Church:

Ireland has lain too long under the spell of the magicians, without will, without intellect, useless and shameful . . . I have come into the most impersonal country in the world to preach personality – personal love, personal religion and personal art . . .[1]

This was cutting close to the bone for a religion whose asceticism left no room for self-expression, for philosophy, art and science. Moore saw that in Ireland 'men and women die without realising any of the qualities which they bring into the world . . .' He warned – a warning which holds an ominous ring even for the clergy – that '. . . if Catholicism degrades, corrodes, paralyses and stultifies the intelligence, it's day is over.'[2] Some years later, Joyce gave the same warning. In his lectures on Ireland in the Università del Popolo in Trieste, he said that in Ireland 'individual initiative is paralysed by the influence and admonitions of the Church'.

Moore also noted that Irish nationalism was marked by the anti-humanist attitude of the Church, sacrificing the individual to the national entity:

I have heard people speaking of working for Ireland [he wrote] but how can one work for Ireland without working for oneself? What do they mean? They do not know themselves, but go on vainly sacrificing all personal achievement, humiliating themselves before Ireland as if the country were a god.[3]

This sacrifice of individual talent became more marked after the Rising, when Yeats and AE deplored the evolution of a nationalism which became progressively more empty of a personal aesthetic and intellectual life.

Moore took the extreme view that Catholicism is opposed to culture, and demonstrated his contention by a detailed review of post-Reformation literature. Dogma and literature were incompatible, he thought, explaining that 'dogma draws a circle round the mind; within that circle you may think, but outside it your thoughts may not stray.'[4] In this Moore went too far. There are only two dogmas which make literature impossible; one which, like Marxism, denies the autonomy of the human mind; and the extreme puritan view which denies, in effect at any rate, its power of objectivity.

[1] *Collected Works*, Vol. 10, Heinemann, 1933, p. 209.
[2] *Ibid.*, Vol. 10, p. 236.   [3] *Ibid.*, Vol. 8, p. 221.   [4] *Ibid.*, Vol. 9, p. 198.

The Catholic cultural decline since the Reformation was due not to dogma but to puritan sentiment which undermined Catholic belief in human reason and intuition. True, all dogmas restrict, or rather, condition art; but so do all values. The humanist, no less than the Catholic, is bound by beliefs, whether the seeds of development are held to lie within life itself or to involve a transcendental relation. Humanism rather than Catholicism has culminated in a system of ideas – Marxism – which makes art impossible.[1]

Moore contrasted Catholic dogmatism with Protestant liberalism which 'leaves the mind free or very nearly'. He cited the strong literary development in post-Reformation England; omitting, however, to point out the manner in which Anglicanism rejected life at the front door to admit it at the back door. The Protestant rejection of the human mind as capable of a vital spirituality was to free it for a purely human culture. From Shakespeare onwards, English literature is inspired mainly by humanism, that is, by a belief in man himself. Moore rightly contended that we are indebted to agnostics for the greater part of modern literature. Naturally, since the belief of the agnostics in man gained, temporarily at any rate, from their disbelief in God, man became the centre of their hopes; and there can be no literature without a belief in man. Here they had the advantage of post-Reformation Catholics whose scepticism centred mainly on man himself, on his social, artistic and intellectual competence.[2] It is significant that possibly the two most distinguished Catholic writers during the last two centuries – Newman and Maritain – were converts from

[1] Wyndham Lewis noted that 'today it is far more from politics, usurping the place of religion . . . that the anti-artist currents come, than from the theologian proper.' *Man without Art*, Cassell, 1934, p. 279.

[2] Moore apparently failed to notice that the Anglicanism he embraced was having second thoughts about the freedom it permitted its adherents; and that throughout the nineteenth century it was trying to bring man under its control, as through the Oxford Movement which – as Geoffrey Faber noted in *Oxford Apostles* – 'was, in effect, a passionate assertion that the Church must rule society or cease to be Christian.' Like Catholicism, however, the Anglican revival broke on the familiar rock of human corruption, as can be seen from the moving writing of C. S. Lewis and Archbishop Temple's *Christianity and the Social Order* – the crowning achievement of the Anglican revival, and one of the finest attempts at a Christian social synthesis in modern times. The Archbishop failed to provide a basis for a Christian or individualist society, opting rather for a state solution for inequality. He was one of the founders of the British Welfare State.

Protestantism. George Scott points out that most of the modern British Catholic writers were also converts.[1] He also refers to the absence of 'any bulk of creative and clearly Catholic writing' from the descendants of the Irish emigrants in Britain, who are free to express themselves.

Moore's preference for Protestantism was due, in part, to its dogmatic vagueness; to the greater freedom it allowed the individual mind; as Joseph Hone put it: '... Protestantism with its "grace" and "election" is nearer to the artist than Catholicism which must always account the man of more intelligence, of more taste, of more imagination, as nothing compared with the veriest dullard who keeps the rules.'[2] Moore, indeed, saw Protestantism as merely a 'stage in human development, that is, a half-way house between Christian faith and agnosticism'. He hoped that 'when papists have been persuaded to bring up their children Protestants, the next generation may cross over to the agnostic side of the quadrille'.[3]

Whatever possible effects Moore's criticisms of Catholicism might have had on the Irish clergy were weakened by the evident agnostic and humanistic overtones of his work. His characters of spirit and intelligence tend to shed their Christian beliefs. So it is with Alice Barton in *Drama in Muslin*. Evelyn Innes' sustained loyalty to the Church is unconvincing. Likewise in *The Lake* (1905), where Fr Oliver Gogarty falls in love with the independent-minded music teacher, Nora Glynn, and denounces her from the pulpit when she is seduced. Her flight from the parish and her consequent loss of faith causes the priest remorse, and he tries vainly to induce her to return, though he realises that here he is likely to meet with opposition from his colleagues, noting that 'an independent mind is very objectionable to an ecclesiastic'. He also sees a difficulty in the fear that the nuns might not offer Nora enough to induce her to return, noting that 'nuns are always anxious to get things cheap.'[4]

[1] *The RCs: a Report on Roman Catholics in Britain Today*, Hutchinson, 1967, pp. 138–9.
[2] *Life of George Moore*, p. 250.
[3] *Collected Works*, Vol. 9, Heinemann, p. 145.
[4] They still are; and teachers who have worked in convents often complain about their dismissal after long service, when the convent acquires a nun qualified to teach their subject. No doubt, this is economical for the convent. But how can

Moore's interest in Christianity led him in 1914 to visit the Holy Land to collect material for *The Brook Kerith* (1916). This story has a curious dream-like quality suggestive more of poetic fiction than of history. Moore reconstructs the biblical story, denying the divine birth of Jesus and the validity of Christian revelation. The crucified Christ is secretly removed from the cross by Joseph of Arimathea, and He continues to live as a member of an Essene sect to which Moore claimed He belonged.

Moore had a strong faith in life but it was rather a confused one. As Yeats said of him: '. . . instincts incapable of clear expression deafened and blinded him'. Moore was typically modern in his distrust of ideas or dogma – a characteristic feature of the writers of the Irish Literary Renaissance. In the story, *Heloise and Abelard* (1921) – which Moore romanticises – the hermit D'Arembert tells Abelard, the philosopher, that dialectics are 'the web that the spider weaves to trap unwary flies'.

Moore had a strong bias towards paganism, expressed, for instance, in his joyful translation of the classic story, *The Pastoral Loves of Daphnis and Chloe* (1924). Heloise yearns for old pagan times; and thinks that, had it not been for Virgil

> I should only have known the story of the world as told in relation to martyrdom and miracles and have seen the world in the relics of the saints. But he [Virgil] unveiled my eyes, and by night and day the seas will be beautiful to me . . .

This is typical of the view of Roman Catholicism held by the Anglo-Irish writers, namely, that it is essentially and solely ascetic, lacking a positive humanism. Even Abelard feels the pull of paganism under the spell of Heloise. He reflects that he

> being a Christian, was perturbed by the paganism into which his life was falling, all things slipping away from him, even his Christianity, while he was with her . . .

Moore also had inclinations towards pantheism, due mainly, it seems, to the influence of AE. Heloise says to Abelard:

---

the nuns justify economy (unless they are very hard-up) when it is gained at the expense of lay people trying to make a living? This question ought to interest reformers of the conventual life.

But I am not talking, Abelard, I am thinking;
I am not thinking, Abelard, I am dreaming;
I am not dreaming, Abelard, I am feeling;
and at this moment I am consonant with the
trees above me, and the stars above me . . .
I am amid the roots of the hills.

The above passage is strongly reminiscent of AE.

Indeed, in *The Brook Kerith* there are hints that Moore had some sympathy with the quietism of Buddhism; a negation of all desire. For Jesus says to Paul:

. . . It has come to me to understand that all striving was vain, and worse than vain. The pursuit of an incorruptible crown leads us to sin as much as the pursuit of a corruptible crown. If we would reach the sinless state we must relinquish pursuit.

Moore's anti-clerical – if not anti-religious – attitude was typical of most of the Irish Catholic writers who followed him. There is an element of irrationality in his hatred of the Catholic Church, which aggravated his findings of the Church's stifling effect on human growth. Along with Joyce, however, he gave more consideration to criticism of the Catholic Church than did his successors; and one may regret his lack of real scholarship which would have made his criticisms more balanced and penetrating.

In his positive leanings, Moore was more in sympathy with the Anglo-Irish writers whose minds ranged over a wide historical and geographical field, seeking a synthesis which would elevate man from the prosaic and mundane life into which he was increasingly drifting. Moore's works are little read in Ireland today; and, indeed, most of them are unobtainable or out of print. He was an unfavourable witness, and consequently consigned to oblivion in a country which resents criticism, especially criticism of the clergy. Yet he ranks next to Kate O'Brien as Ireland's best novelist in the traditional manner; and his *Hail and Farewell* is – next to Joyce's *Portrait* – one of the best sources on the malaise of Irish Catholicism.

CHAPTER VI

James Joyce

THE MOST IMPORTANT of the Irish-Catholic writers is James Joyce (1882–1941). Joyce was the only major Catholic figure in the Irish Literary Renaissance. Second in greatness only to Yeats, his mind was spoiled by a defect in his sympathies, a deep distaste for human beings. This was a heritage of Irish Catholic puritanism which, in Joyce's case unfortunately, left an unusually profound mark.

Fr Noon, S. J., suggests that the reason why Joyce lost his faith must remain obscure.[1] But Joyce makes it clear enough that it was due to his inability to fulfil the social aspect of charity. This he states in *A Portrait of the Artist as a Young Man*, not only expressly, but with such an illuminating exposition of his own particular difficulties that this work is the most significant that exists on the state of Irish Catholicism today.

True, the *Portrait* is not simple autobiography, being rather a work of fiction inspired by Joyce's early experiences. Thus it cannot be taken too literally, and expresses rather an interpretation from a more mature standpoint in time and spirit. It seems reasonable, however, to accept its psychological essentials; to assume that the spiritual difficulties of Stephen Dedalus were Joyce's own, and that the reasons adduced for Stephen's rejection of Catholicism were those which led to Joyce's apostasy. This is more plausible when we consider that Stephen's spiritual crisis is so typical of Catholic Ireland, helping to explain not only the peculiar evolution of Joyce but also that of the community of which he was a part. Yet, Kevin Sullivan denies that Stephen's crisis is a 'psychological re-enactment of a similar crisis in Joyce's own adolescence'. He has not much to offer, however, in the way of an alternative explanation of Joyce's loss of Catholic faith.[2]

The importance of Joyce for Catholic Ireland need occasion no

[1] *The James Joyce Review*, Vol. I, No. 4, 1957.
[2] *Joyce Among the Jesuits*, Columbia University Press, 1958, p. 9.

surprise, in spite of his *succès de scandale*. It was what was Catholic in Joyce which gave impetus to his literary radicalism, like a diverted car which is carried to its destruction by the very power released to ensure its arrival at a determined destination. At no point in Joyce's career can his development be understood apart from Catholicism, or his view of it. Joyce was a Catholic philosopher *manqué*, a man of profoundly religious mind with a marked love of speculation and precise definition.

Joyce's unsettled family life did not help a youth over-sensitive yet deficient in sympathy. The father of the large Joyce family was not without a certain charm, but he was irresponsible and a drunkard; and Joyce's youth was marked by an enforced flight from lodging to lodging, leading to poverty and a hand-to-mouth existence. Apart from the hardship involved, this was a distressing experience for a youth in Ireland where Moore's sneer about Joyce's poverty is typical of the Irish view of 'God's poor'. A striking exception to this was the welcome Joyce got from the family of David Sheehy, M.P. This household must have been one of the very few in Dublin where the touchy and bitter Joyce could, as Patricia Hutchins remarks, 'become a normal young man . . . and freely enter into whatever amusement was going.'[1]

Joyce got his piety from his mother and his irreligion from his father; a common enough inheritance in Catholic countries where the culturally frustrated male has religious difficulties unknown to his matrimonially circumscribed spouse. Joyce inherited perhaps more from his amoral father than from his mother, drawing closer to him with the passage of time, and withdrawing from his mother whom he regarded as a personal symbol of Catholicism. This was one of the great tragedies caused by Joyce's defection from the Church – the conflict in a mother's loyalties, torn between the claims of a religion she would not relinquish and those of her most brilliant son who, after giving evidence of a high religious destiny, set his mind implacably against Catholicism. This tragedy was paralleled in the case of Joyce's wife, Nora Barnacle, who, on her death-bed, rejected with some hesitation the services of a priest so that (one suspects) she would not be disloyal to the memory of her husband.

Joyce was more fortunate in his schools than in his home. He had the best of Irish educators, the Jesuits; first at Clongowes Wood College,

[1] *James Joyce's World*, Methuen, 1957, p. 48.

and later at Belvedere. As usual in Ireland, however, it is wiser to look for the cause of educational growth in the pupil than in the teacher; and Joyce had a natural piety which enabled him to respond vitally to the religious environment of the Jesuit Colleges. An almost unique aspect of this response was its intellectual and artistic character, and Joyce made a real, if precarious, contact with the medieval scholastic outlook. In doing this, however, he had to depend too much on his own resources. In particular, his educators provided little of what he really needed – a warm humanism to strengthen his brittle affections and morbid nature. There is little evidence of such human wholesomeness in the *Portrait*. Nor does Kevin Sullivan's work, based on a sympathetic and factual study of Jesuit education in Ireland, suggest a much more favourable picture. In his recollections of his early education, Eugene Sheehy, a contemporary of Joyce's at Belvedere, comments on the oppressive dullness of the system, and suggests that the only way in which a schoolboy could preserve his intelligence was by adopting Shaw's policy of 'resolute idleness'.[1] As is usual in Irish schools, it was the intellectual and imaginative gifts of the pupil which enabled Joyce to transform the daily grind into a real mental exercise. Only genius can survive Irish education.

By an odd coincidence, one of the most pernicious influences on Joyce's life, Oliver St John Gogarty, was also a product of a Jesuit establishment, Stonyhurst in Lancashire. An intimate friend of Joyce during their university days, Gogarty was even more corrupt than Joyce, more derisive of religion, motivated, indeed, almost by a satanic wish to destroy. Gogarty's biographer, Ulick O'Connor, suggests a 'trace of Jansenism' in the Stonyhurst tradition, due to the fact that for a period during the penal days it had functioned in exile at St Omer.[2]

The social decline of the Joyce family had a disturbing influence on James, as circumstances matched less and less the well-to-do tradition of the family. The continuous harping of Mr Joyce on the status of gentleman must have stung James as he brazened it out, ill-dressed and even ill-washed, at University College, Dublin. Some critics, like Wyndham Lewis, make much of James' social consciousness in

[1] *May it Please the Court*, Fallon, 1951.
[2] *Oliver St John Gogarty*, Jonathan Cape, 1964, p. 14.

explaining his eccentric development, but this was only a secondary factor. Snobbery, a potent force in conservative Ireland, is of no great account in literary Ireland. There was some of it in George Moore though it hardly affected his writing. There was a good deal of it in Gogarty who was probably influenced by Mahaffy in Trinity College, Dublin.

Joyce was, to some degree, schizophrenic, as suggested by his extreme introversion, his touchy and withdrawn nature and, especially by that divorce between thought and feeling which, in his later life and work, amounted to a flat contradiction. The most conspicuous manifestation of this split-mindedness was his contrasted reactions to a single experience. In the *Portrait* he noted the way in which his corrupt feelings destroyed his image of a flower girl:

> The blue flowers which she lifted towards him, and her young blue eyes seemed to him at that instant images of guilelessness, and he halted till the image had vanished and he saw only her ragged dress and damp coarse hair and hoydenish face.[1]

Joyce had a profound fear of dogs and thunderstorms, and was certainly bitten on two occasions by the former, if he was not, as he suspected, victimised by the latter. By contrast, James' talented brother, Stanislaus, was morally robust, managing extraordinarily well to retain a goodwill and to resist the pernicious pressures to which his brother succumbed. Stanislaus was, in fact, a great stand-by to James, as well as being one of his most perceptive critics. Indeed, Stanislaus' selfless devotion to his brother is a bright spot in the grim story of James Joyce, recalling that classic example of kind brotherly relations, Theo and Vincent van Gogh.

In the light of all this, one might be disposed to question the value of Joyce's testimony, but Joyce had genius, and had much success in diagnosing his own malaise, like a doctor observing his own illness. The psychologist Jung noted that he was a controlled schizophrenic who deliberately exploited a mental disorder for a literary purpose. There was, in fact, only one weakness – if a serious one – in the logic of Joyce's repudiation of Catholicism, namely, his implicit assumption that his own emotional reaction was an adequate standard by which to

[1] Jonathan Cape, 1946, p. 192.

judge whether man was, in fact, lovable. Joyce was a puritan and, consequently, a biased subject for experiment in the field of social relations.

Joyce's morbidity showed in his view of man and, especially, women. In the *Portrait* he describes his reaction to a group of fellow students bathing:

> The mere sight of that medley of wet nakedness chilled him to the bone. Their bodies, corpsewhite or suffused with a pallid golden light or rawly tanned by the sun, gleamed with the wet of the sea . . . It was a pain to see them, and a swordlike pain to see the signs of adolescence which made repellent their pitiable nakedness. Perhaps they had taken refuge in number and noise from the secret dread of their own souls . . . (p. 192)

Joyce tried to create a more wholesome feminine ideal, such as the romantic image of Mercedes inspired by *The Count of Monte Cristo*, with the result that his mind was temporarily transformed by the prospect of a 'holy encounter' with Mercedes. His feelings were mellowed under the influence of the new romanticism; and as he sought in real life 'the unsubstantial image which his soul so constantly beheld . . . the peace of the gardens and the kindly light of the windows poured a tender influence into his restless heart.' (pp. 72–3) In this more exalted mood, it was the ideal of the Blessed Virgin which appealed most to him, however, so much so that 'if ever he was impelled to cast off sin and to repent, the impulse that moved him was his wish to be her knight.' (pp. 118–9) Joyce's cult of the Blessed Virgin shows his close identity with Catholicism; and, indeed, his praise of her reads like a paean from the *cantata* of the Church:

> And now thy very face and form, dear mother, speak to us of the eternal; not like earthly beauty, dangerous to look upon, but like the morning star which is thy emblem, bright and musical, breathing purity, telling of heaven and infusing peace. (p. 138)

Such attempts on Joyce's part to create in himself a mood more in line with Catholic or romantic orthodoxy have a pathos, doomed as they were to be overcome by what was corrupt in himself and in his surroundings.

Yet, one ought not to ignore some measure of organic soundness in the young Joyce, which disposed him for a while to adopt a somewhat moral role, a reformist aim. This side of Joyce is expressed in his early works, as in *Dubliners* and *Stephen Hero* – an early draft of the *Portrait*. *Dubliners* does not lack an idealism which lights up the sordid life it portrays. In these stories, one feels that Joyce has some faith in the human mind, but that some pernicious force in life defeats individual aspirations. Mr Duffy, a character in *A Painful Case* typifies that outlook:

. . . there was no harshness in his eyes which . . . gave the impression of a man alert to greet a redeeming feature in others but often disappointed.

Joyce defended the therapeutic realism of his stories to reluctant publishers. He explained to his friend, Constantine Curran, that he called the stories *Dubliners* to express 'the soul of that hemiplagia or paralysis which many consider a city'. He thought the people of Dublin would benefit by a study of their reflections in his 'polished mirror'. But that was not how priest and patriot saw it. They wanted to preserve a synthetic image of national innocence. Joyce believed that it was 'a mark of morality . . . to say what one thinks is true,' and he objected to those who judge 'an author immoral who refuses to be silent about what in any case exists'. But it was to take over half a century before Catholic Ireland showed any sympathy with Joycean realism. Joyce left Ireland in 1904 to work out his destiny in 'silence, exile and cunning'.

Joyce was well aware of his repulsive reaction to people, even to those of whom he thought highly as, for instance, the girl designated E–C–, identified by Stanislaus Joyce as Mary Sheehy. (p. 78) In the *Portrait* he makes his friend, Cranly, draw attention to this moral defect:

Do you love your mother?
Stephen shook his head slowly.
– I don't know what your words mean, he said slowly.
– Have you ever loved anyone, Cranly asked.
– Do you mean women?
– I am not speaking of that, Cranly said in a colder tone. I asked you if you ever felt love towards anyone or anything?
Stephen walked beside his friend, staring gloomily at the footpath.

– I tried to love God he said at length. It seems now that I failed. It is very difficult. I tried to unite my will with the will of God instant by instant. In that I did not always fail. I could perhaps do that still ... (pp. 273–4)

In the seventeenth year, Joyce had a phase of intense spirituality inspired by a 'fire and brimstone' preacher in a spiritual retreat. It was not fear that Joyce needed, however, but love, especially as it embraced man; and it was at this point that his heightened spirituality showed a radical weakness. He noted that

> to merge his life in the common tide of other lives was harder for him than any fasting or prayer, and it was his constant failure to do this to his own satisfaction which caused in his soul at last a sensation of spiritual dryness together with the growth of doubts and scruples. (p. 172)

When Joyce reflects on the reason why he turned his back on his vocation for the priesthood, he explains it obliquely, describing his reaction to a squad of Christian Brothers tramping along like a bunch of raw army recruits. He regrets that

> it was idle for him to move himself to be generous towards them ... idle and embittering, finally, to argue, against his own dispassionate certitude, that the commandment of love bade us not to love our neighbour as ourselves with the same amount and intensity of love but to love him as ourselves with the same kind of love. (pp. 188–9)

It is important to draw attention to the fact that, as Joyce describes it, his religious failure was due to a defect in his sentiments or moral nature. There is a tendency among American commentators on Joyce – evident in Fr Noon, for instance – to ascribe this failure to the impact of Parnell's downfall. There is no doubt that Parnell was a powerful symbol for Joyce. This is obvious in the searingly dramatic scene in the *Portrait* which deals with the clergy's treatment of Parnell; and one of Joyce's first works, *Et Tu, Healy*, was a condemnation of Tim Healy for disloyalty to his Chief. For Joyce, however, the clergy's rejection of Parnell was only a major expression of their rejection of life.

The Parnell crisis was, in no vital sense, pivotal or creative, either as it affected Irish puritanism or Irish nationalism. Rather did it quicken and heighten an existing division between the clergy and the people, between priest and writer: just as it conditioned the rapid growth of a revolutionary nationalism already in existence. The opening chapter of Herbert Howarth's fine study of the Irish writers is marred by such misconceptions, as when he writes that 'Parnell's fall involved sexual passions; prompted by that the Irish made sex one of their subjects'.[1]

Joyce's failure to be a Catholic priest led him to be one in what André Malraux called the 'religion of art'. At the end of the *Portrait* Joyce describes his setting out from Ireland on his secular mission which was inspired by a vision of life as seen through his corrupted feelings:

> The life of his body, ill-clad, ill-fed, louse eaten, made him close his eyes in a sudden spasm of despair and in the darkness he saw the brittle bright bodies of lice falling from the air and turning as they fell. Yes, and it was not darkness that fell from the air. It was bright-ness . . . His mind bred vermin. His thoughts were lice born of the sweat of sloth. (p. 266)

The elaboration of his literary view of life gave Joyce particular pleasure and amusement. It was bound up with the more animal side of man, which a puritan Catholicism tried to push under the carpet. Hence the importance Joyce attached to the human body in *Ulysses*, and his emphasis on its most intimate functions. The question inevitably arose as to whether Joyce's interpretation was more than a merely personal one. Did it also express the view current in his Irish Catholic environment, and, in particular, the view of the clergy?

L. Middleton Murray thought that Joyce's interpretation was that of a country which is 'at its least European, and is merely an immense reinforcement of puritanism'. Cecil Maitland, writing in the *Christian Witness* on August 4, 1922, went further and suggested that Joyce's view derived from Roman Catholic ideas. He thought that Aquinas would probably be more at home with Freud than, for instance, with G. K. Chesterton. This seems hard to sustain in the light of Aquinas' belief that 'reason is the first principle of all human work', an idea with which puritans have little sympathy; just as they would have little liking for Aquinas' view that the intellectual speculative virtues are

[1] *The Irish Writers, 1860–1940*, Rockliff, 1958, p. 20.

95

loftier (*nobilior*) than the moral virtues.[1] Nor does the interpretation of Aquinas' modern disciple, M. Maritain – as expressed in *Art and Scholasticism* – lend any support to the view that Aquinas had any sympathy with those who, like Freud, would diminish the place of rationality in art.

Cecil Maitland's contention might seem to find some support in Joyce's continued interest in scholastic speculation regarding aesthetics. But what really concerned Joyce in Aristotle and Aquinas was their philosophy of art. Joyce, following Aquinas, defined art as 'the human disposition of sensible and intelligible matter to an aesthetic end'. Within the framework of that definition, the scholastics regarded the artist as autonomous, independent of moralisers or interferers of any sort. It was *qua* man, or morally, that he was bound by the Christian interpretation. What Joyce did, however, was to divorce the scholastic concept of art from the Christian ethic and substitute an opposed interpretation.

Art is concerned with the expression of what is beautiful, but Joyce was no longer satisfied with the Christian interpretation of beauty. He shaped quite other pillars for his world of beauty than Christian love and human reason. With him, the Aquinian qualities of universal beauty – wholeness, harmony and radiance – were to find their rationale in an earthly vision, coarse and cynical. Stephen explains to Lynch in the *Portrait* this departure from the scholastic position:

> So far as this side of aesthetic philosophy extends, Aquinas will carry me all along the line. When we come to the phenomenon of artistic perception, artistic gestation and artistic reproduction I require a new terminology and a new experience. (p. 238)

Cecil Maitland is on firmer ground when he relates Joyce's vision to the modern Catholic outlook which has largely lost that faith in the human mind on which the Christian ethic of Aquinas depended:

> No one who is acquainted with Catholic education in Catholic countries [he wrote] could fail to recognise the source of Mr Joyce's *weltanschauung*. He sees the world as the theologians showed it to him. The humour is the cloacal humour of the refectory; his contempt is the priests' denigration of the human body, and his view of sex has

[1] *Sum. Theol.*, i–ii, Q. 58, a 2; and i–ii Q. 66, a 3, ad I.

the obscenity of the confessor's manual . . . If we consider Mr Joyce's work from this point of view, it becomes clear that while his study of humanity remains incomplete, the defect is not due to any inherent lack of imagination on his part. Rather that it arises from the fact that to a Catholic who no longer believes that he has an immortal soul, fashioned in the image of God, a human being becomes merely a specially corrupt animal . . .

So profound, indeed, is the modern Catholic sense of human corruption that, as Donat O'Donnell points out in his preface to *Maria Cross*, there exists a real doubt in the minds of many Catholic thinkers as to the very possibility of a Catholic literature and art.

Joyce's movement to the extreme literary left was modified somewhat by some success in human relationships. There was, of course, his early and Dantesque attachment to Mary Sheehy. But the main humanising influence on Joyce was Nora Barnacle, a Galway girl, with whom he left Ireland, and whom he married on July 4, 1931. She was his angel of mercy, in so far as he had one, just as Gogarty was his evil genius. She gave him some of that real companionship which his life so largely lacked. True, he was apt to see her with his characteristic split-mindedness. In a letter he tells her that 'one moment I see you like a virgin or madonna, the next moment I see you shameless, insolent, half-naked and obscene'. But he added, 'I have enormous belief in the power of the simple honourable soul.' Such a belief, however, was characteristically remote from the sceptical, misogynous outlook of Joyce.

The extent of Joyce's dependence on Nora is pathetic, as he appeals to her to 'save me from the badness of the world and of my own heart'. She would be a wife to him and a mother, so different from his mother-image of Ireland as 'an old sow who eats her farrow'. Joyce's bond with Nora disposed him to some humaneness in interpretation – as shown in a genial passivity in the character of Bloom – which relieves the sordidness of his work. Richard Ellman, in a magnificent biography, draws attention to her influence on the short story, *The Dead*, the most balanced and humane of Joyce's creations.[1]

Joyce's association with Nora had its disconcerting side, however, as

[1] *James Joyce*, Oxford University Press, 1959, p. 293.

D

Mr Ellman notes, creating an element of conflict in Joyce's mind. It clashed with his view that a genuine tie between people is impossible. This led him to doubt and question Nora's loyalty, to tease himself with the possibility of a betrayal by her. Joyce's obsession with the theme of woman's betrayal is shown in *Ulysses*, and in his play *Exiles* where Richard Rowan suffers a 'deep, deep wound of doubt' concerning Martha's loyalty, which leads him almost to connive at her betrayal of him.

As a test of Joyce's objectivity, it is instructive to ask if his picture of Dublin life is true. Shaw thought so, stating in his preface to *Immaturity* that 'James Joyce in his *Ulysses* has described, with a fidelity so ruthless that his book is hardly bearable, the life that Dublin offers to its young men . . .' Stanislaus, unsympathetic to his brother's later work, admitted that in it one finds 'Dublin stretched out before the reader, the minute living incidents start out from the pages . . .' But he thought that James had overdone the cynicism.

Though dealing with the life of Dublin's middle-class intellectuals, Joyce's view may be said to be generally true of Irish men but not of Irish women. These tend to place a higher value than men on sexual purity; and Irish women, possessing a more wholesome romanticism than their clerical mentors, take clerical recommendations to purity in the right spirit. The male view of sex, on the other hand, tends to depend on the quality of the cultural outlook, to be a by-product of a vision of life. But since a cultural outlook is denied to the Irish male, his attitude to women is typical of his generally cynical attitude.

Like most Irishmen, Joyce saw little in women to admire. A woman's love, he thought, is 'always material and egoistic'. Men, on the other hand, possess a 'fund of genuine affection for the beloved'.[1] This is not true of Ireland where the male has little affection, and less for women than for friends of his own sex. 'For the most part,' remarked Stanislaus Joyce more truly, 'women do not interest Irishmen except as street-walkers and housekeepers.'[2] Denying women affection, Joyce denied them the essential point of their existence, turning them into monstrosities. That, presumably, is what Nora Barnacle meant when she said of Joyce, 'he knows nothing at all about women'.

[1] Ellman, *ibid.*, p. 247.
[2] *My Brother's Keeper*, Faber & Faber, 1958, p. 164.

Irish women, it is true, have begun to kick against the goad. They no longer see their ideal in the Pietà but in the Mona Lisa, behind whose equivocal smile lies a threat to those who think that women can still be treated as slaves to husband and children. And in this development Joyce would see, no doubt, a corroboration of his view that his art provided a model for the future.

Joyce's revolt against the Catholic Church was a *cri de coeur* on the part of man, saddled, as Joyce saw it, with a corrupt and unredeemable nature. It was a cry inspired by hatred, indignation, derision and a sense of cosmic comedy, whose Faustian echoes are sent back by his Irish pupils, Samuel Beckett and Flann O'Brien.

Flann O'Brien contrasts modern and legendary Ireland in *At Swim-Two-Birds*. Finn McCool and mad King Sweeney are brought back to show how smug and hypocritical are the Irish today. What Flann O'Brien mainly glorifies in the past, however, is nature rather than man, as emerges from the fine nature poetry which his heroes copiously recite. The human quality in the ancients which he extolls is their asceticism, their power to endure. Flann O'Brien, like Joyce, scales the human mind down considerably, and his counterpart of Stephen Dedalus is stiff and lifeless, expressing little more than pride, boredom and crudity.

A denigration of life inevitably reduces the stature of the rebel and, as a consequence, the quality of rebellion. Nor, in an increasingly sceptical age, is it clear against what or whom man is rebelling. Joyce could rage against God because, in his reason at any rate, he believed in Him. But the concept of God has become progressively remote and shadowy. In such circumstances, there is little one can do except to kill time, as Samuel Beckett suggests in *Waiting for Godot*, waiting, that is, for the realisation of what is only a comforting fiction; and so, we fill up our days with activities which have some immediate point, and so help to obscure the fact that our lives have no ultimate point. Vladimir describes this technique of evading a paralysing sense of final meaninglessness:

> What's certain is that the hours are long, under these conditions, and constrain us to beguile them with proceedings which, how shall I say, which may at first sight seem reasonable until they become a habit. You may say it is to prevent our reason from foundering.

Waiting for Godot, the most popular of Beckett's plays, is a social satire which gains dramatically from the contrast between facetious human behaviour and an underlying despair. When Mr Beckett deals directly with his theme of utter hopelessness – as in *Endgame* and *Krapp's Last Tape* – the dramatic effect is weakened by the absence of human comedy and the grim monotony of his mood of pessimism. Drama presupposes some conflict and contrast, but these are possible only when faith of some sort exists. To the complete pessimist, social satire alone is available; and so, in the later work of Joyce's protégé, Samuel Beckett, we reach a literary impasse caused by a complete bankruptcy of faith or ideas.

Joyce appears as an ominous portent on the threshold of modern Ireland, and his apostasy may be seen as prefiguring the destruction of Irish Catholic values. For the Catholicity of Joyce's mind was really quite remarkable; almost unique, indeed, in a country which, in spite of its vehement protestations of Catholicism, has permitted the patterns of thought and sentiment to become quite alien to Catholic modes. When Mary Colum remarked, 'I have never known a mind so fundamentally Catholic in structure as Joyce's own,' she said something which, for Ireland, is literally true. Only from Joyce does one get a hint of the Catholic *weltanschauung*, that respect for traditional Catholic thought as in Aquinas, that taste for metaphysics which has become utterly dissipated in a country which has only contempt for ideas as such.

Herbert Gorman notes that some commentators on Joyce suggests that the young university men of Joyce's time 'lisped Latin in their cradles and devoured Aristotle as later generations of young men devoured Edgar Wallace'.[1] There is little evidence to support this view. In Joyce's time, University College, Dublin, provided some instruction in metaphysics and in mental and moral philosophy, but the impact of such courses was limited, as was that of the Academy of St Thomas Aquinas, with which Joyce had some contact.

Joyce's interest in scholasticism would seem to have been mainly the result of an accidental bias of mind. Some such interest, if to a lesser degree, was shown by Tom Kettle, a contemporary of Joyce's at U.C.D., and another product of Clongowes Wood College. Kettle was remarkable for his realistic assessment of Irish Catholicism which he

[1] *James Joyce*, The Bodley Head, 1949, p. 99.

saw as a 'contradiction in terms'. He was probably one of the few under-graduates with whose ideas Joyce had any sympathy, even if they stood on opposite sides of the Catholic fence. Nor, it may be added, did Aristotle and Aquinas get any more recognition in self-governing Ireland. Preaching on the Feast Day of Aquinas on March 7, 1960, the Rev Austin Flannery urged that 'Catholics who are unlikely to read a line of St Thomas should at least know that his system exists in the Church.' That is about the extent of their knowledge.

In a blasphemous prayer composed in a wood outside Trieste, Joyce called on the '. . . vague Something behind everything . . . Whoever the hell you are, I inform you that this [is] a poor comedy you expect me to play and I'm dammed to hell if I'll play it for you.' The Catholic Irish would be appalled by such sentiments (if they were sufficiently interested in Joyce to be aware of them) and with their touchy, immature piety, would not understand what had given rise to them, or see how they themselves were, in some degree, responsible for them. For while the Irish, especially the clergy, pay lip-service to man made in God's image, they lose no opportunity to show their contempt for him, especially for the articulate man, the writer. The Irish Catholic can stomach the degradation of Irishmen, the victims of cultural fears, social antagonism and political hates. But Joyce saw in them a travesty of the New Adam, a living refutation of Christian charity and justice.

It would perhaps gratify Joyce to know that the evolution of Irish Catholicism gives some support to his view of the futility of the human mind and of the Irish Catholic Church which he described as the 'scullery maid of Christendom'. For there have been few percipient heroes in Catholic Ireland since Joyce; few to challenge a Catholic ethic which has failed to realise its claims over men and society. On the contrary, Irish Catholicism has continued to disintegrate under the unseeing eyes of the clergy and the averted eyes of the laity. The claims of Catholicism to impose a form of life have been whittled away, and field after field – politics, economy, art, philosophy and science – have been progressively freed from its controls. Catholic values are being lost by default, by a pragmatic, piecemeal repudiation which must result in their insensible but complete defeat.

Joyce tried to bring life under the aegis of a Catholic ideal, to make our categories of thought and patterns of feeling conform to its requirements. In this he failed, but the fact that he tried establishes him as one of the few modern Irish Catholics who cared about Catholicism as a comprehensive ethic, whose claims to order the whole of life must be put to the test.

CHAPTER VII

Irish Catholic Writers after Joyce

THE IRISH CATHOLIC writers who followed Joyce had little of his keen Catholic sense. They felt the cultural vacuum in Ireland and tried to fill it, but with no clear understanding of the conflict between Catholic and humanist ideas. Those of them who tried to give it a Catholic shape faltered or blundered, and left untied the knots which bind religion and life. They achieved much more, however, than did the priests who feared these writers' experiments in integration, blindly content to accept and accentuate the Irish dichotomy.

The Irish cultural climate was as restrictive for Liam O'Flaherty (b. 1896) as it was for Joyce, but he took much less pains to understand what it is in this ancient religion which has made it so airless and reactionary. Like Joyce, he got what is called a good Catholic education, first at Blackrock College, and later at University College, Dublin. Far more than Joyce, however, he is typical of the Irish Catholic, intellectually incurious about his religion and unsubtle in his ideas. Nothing distinguishes him so much as his place of birth, the Aran Islands off the west coast of Ireland, whose untameable wildness is certainly in his blood, shaping his life and work with an elemental power beyond the control of ideas.

In a short story, *The Inquisition*, Liam O'Flaherty describes his own mind in that of Clery, a postulant in a religious order, who kicks against the settled life of the monastery and the limitations imposed on the mental freedom of its inmates. His decision to cut loose from this life creates in him an extraordinary sense of liberation, and he sets out to create a new world whose starting point is a rejection of everything and a hate of everything:

> . . . his mind exulted, ravenously devouring all sorts of new ideas, let loose into the whole cosmos of things without restraint. Free now and cunning . . . and securely hidden behind a thick wall of

deceit, through which nothing could pierce. Free and alone and hating everything. Free to found a new cosmos, to fashion a new order of thought and a new god. Through hatred to a new love. Through terrible suffering in loneliness to a new light. Through agony to a new peace.[1]

The similarity here with Joyce's revolt is striking, especially in the note of deceit and cunning which are only an instinctive assertion against the all-encompassing pressures of Irish Catholicism.

Mr O'Flaherty is, or was, more optimistic than Joyce, contemplating an ideal, if violent, evolution. Like the rebel teacher, Skerret, in a novel of the same name, he 'absorbed the doctrines of a philosophic anarchism . . . and mixed this philosophy with a mystical worship of the earth and the old pagan gods.' O'Flaherty puts the stress on nature, on a human passion which derives from a crude and violent concept of evolution, so that the characters in his novels are distended and distorted into symbols of a vast creative urge.

The characters in O'Flaherty's novels represent attempts to define the human in terms of the evolutionary, but so much of the force which inspires them lies outside the human mind that they seem hardly responsible. They are carried along on the flood of life, and shaped by the mysterious exigencies of evolution. They may be creatures of instinct like Gypo in *The Informer*, or tempered to a steel-like hardness and dynamism like Gallager in the same novel. They may be the expression of deep social conflict like Tyson and Crosbie in *The Martyr*, or exist in a cold remote world of ideas like Stapleton in *Insurrection*. But whoever or whatever they are, they tend to lack that autonomy needed for strict psychological development.

It is because of this insecure sense of human identity that O'Flaherty's short stories are finer than his novels, for the stories deal mainly with the influence of nature and environment on character. Besides, in them, Mr O'Flaherty is more content to recreate life as it is and not use it in the service of ideas. Some of his stories are, indeed, direct studies of nature – of bird, animal, fish and the elements in which they live. O'Flaherty, like Synge, shows a great sympathy with nature, especially in the storm-swept Western Ireland, and his description of it – or of

[1] *The Tent*, Cape, 1926, p. 156.

its impact on the human mind – can be very moving. This in the opening of *The Touch*:

> A white mare galloped west along the strand against a fierce drying wind. Her tail was stretched out straight and motionless. Her nostrils were blood red. Flecks of foam dropped from her jaws with each outrush of her breath. Hailstones, carried slantwise at great speed by the wind's power, struck with a loud noise against the canvas of her straddle. The two empty baskets, that hung on either side, shifted round the smooth pegs of the wooden yoke. A horsehair rope trailed from the holed bottom of each basket. The wind tore wisps from the loose straw that cushioned the mare's back against the rough canvas. They were maintained in the air by the fierce gale. They sailed away to the east, one after the other, gambolling like butter-flies at dance.
> Kate Hernon was riding on the mare's haunches . . .

The main driving force in O'Flaherty's work is a sentiment of hate, so powerful as to tell against ideological coherence; as illustrated by Crank Shannahan in *The Informer*, whose philosophy is a mixture of all sorts of political creeds, but its main basis is revolt against every existing institution, habit and belief. O'Flaherty's revolutionary energies petered out. His most recent novel, *Insurrection* (1950) shows the fires of revolt to have died to a pale ash.

Kate O'Brien (b. 1897) came close to working out a Catholic cultural synthesis, moving towards it from a liberal humanism which inspired her early novels, as *Without My Cloak* and *The Anteroom*. She was specially fortunate in her early education at a convent in Limerick under a French order of nuns, where the teaching seems to have been more intelligently Catholic than is usual in Irish convents. This was followed by a course at University College, Dublin. After graduation, Miss O'Brien spent some years as a governess in Spain, an experience which affected her profoundly.

The slowness with which Catholic ideas asserted themselves in Kate O'Brien's work shows how latent they are in the Irish mind. They made a tentative appearance in *Mary Lavelle* (1936) and became more marked in such novels as *The Land of Spices* (1941), *That Lady* (1946) and *The*

D*

Flower of May (1953). The finest of Kate O'Brien's work was done under Catholic inspiration; and it is her artistic tragedy that she never reached a point of full Catholic acceptance.

The best of Kate O'Brien's novels, *The Land of Spices*, deals with her early convent life, and it is the finest treatment of this theme in Irish literature. Its special virtue lies in its clarity of form, a firmness in outline, which the best of her other novels do not quite attain. Perhaps Miss O'Brien was here helped by her subject whose character and limits were defined by the nature of the life she interpreted. The charm of this novel lies partly in the contrast between the civilized and reflective content of the nuns' lives with the flurry and febrile excitement of the adolescent girls. *The Land of Spices* is the only really Catholic novel that has come out of modern Ireland. It was banned by the Irish Censorship Board, and later unbanned as a result of a storm of criticism to which the ban gave rise.

Kate O'Brien was not content to remain within the confines of the Catholic world where the human will is circumscribed by commandments and the monitory pleas of a traditional wisdom. For her, freedom has its spice, and the human intuition suggests delights which promise as much and more than those to be found in the safe haven of Catholicity. She has a marked fondness for physical beauty; and her attempt to synthesise physical and spiritual values suggests the renaissance spirit which tried to combine Christian and Greek artistic ideals. The result is – as in the case of much renaissance art – a distortion of both ideals, and also a certain sentimentality due to Miss O'Brien's extravagance of hope and a luxuriation in her own will.

In *That Lady*, Ana de Mendosa decides to continue her affaire with her married lover, Antonio Perez, and comments:

> My thinking tells me that I have a soul to save and that its salvation is paramount; my honour, which has nothing to do with my thinking, tells me that no retreat is possible now, and that everything, including my immortal soul, must wait on honour.

In *The Flower of May*, Fanny Morrow holds out against her religion with a personal, rational reservation. Her friend, Lucille, explains her own acceptance of religion as contrasted with Fanny's renunciation, by saying: 'I don't examine every idea in the light of my *own* comprehension.' When André de Mellin asks Fanny what she believes in, Fanny answers, 'the holiness of the heart's affections' and 'the truth of the imagination'.

Kate O'Brien, as a Catholic, places herself in a weak position in so far as she depends on a purely human or rational standard, since Christian values – or, indeed, any ultimate values – are only rational in part. They require for their acceptance that *sacrificium intellectus* which is implicit in the Christian concept of faith. A dependence on the human mind is more than ever dangerous at a time when the mirror of the human soul, as a measure of all things, is cracked beyond repair, and when rational standards are being superseded by the vital forces of evolution. No doubt, Kate O'Brien's movement towards Catholic values was conditioned by the decline of liberalism, and was an attempt to find a solution for the moral quandary in which the modern world finds itself. Her most recent novel, *As Music and Splendour* (1959) is inferior, and does not advance the solution of her liberal-Catholic problem.

It was also late in his career when Sean O'Faolain (b. 1900) came to some intellectual terms with Catholicism. For this he long had the Irish intellectual's distrust, if less intransigently than his one-time friend, Frank O'Connor. Much influenced by Irish nationalism, and taking an active part in the insurrection movement, he came, in due course, to doubt the adequacy of extreme nationalist ideas. In that stagnant period, 1940–1955, he was the main intellectual force in Ireland, a protagonist of cultural freedom, giving generous encouragement to young writers who found an outlet in *The Bell*. As mentor of the nation, he was succeeded by Frank O'Connor (d. 1966) who was, however, far less effective in this role.

Dr O'Faolain's first serious attempt to deal with the religious problem in Ireland was in *The Irish* (1947). Here he advanced the illuminating theory of an historic dualism, but when he reaches the modern period, he fails to work out the logic of his own ideas:

It is all very well [he wrote] for Lecky to say that the rise of liberalism has declared the union of politics and theology an anachronism by pronouncing their divorce. The priest does not recognise divorce. For him the two worlds are inseparable; the kingdom of earth is but the battle ground for the kingdom of heaven, and he will advance and retreat on that ground just like any soldier. (p. 118)

True, the Irish priest does not recognise, in theory, the separation of religion from politics. But he accepts it in practice. Indeed, he insists on it, in that he will use his whole strength and artifice to frustrate any attempt to introduce Catholic ideas into politics by making them responsibly individualist. From his practical standpoint, the kingdoms of heaven and earth are not so much inseparable as antithetical; and the battle for heaven is fought by rejecting life, by a progressive retreat from it.

It was not in Ireland but in Italy that Sean O'Faolain found his solution of the Catholic problem. There he noted that the Catholic had much more scope for cultural manœuvre; could, and did, adopt a variety of political and cultural positions.[1] Oppressed by the grim outlook of Irish Catholicism, he was charmed by the easy ambivalence of the Italian Catholic who, in combining the cults of Venus and the Virgin, manages to have the best of both worlds. What Italian Catholic life amounts to, however, is a pagan – or humanist – Catholic dualism whose edges are blurred by the overlapping of values. In Catholic Italy, as Morris West put it, the 'picture of the bambino is hung over the bed and the pagan horns over the barn door'.[2]

Sean O'Faolain is right, no doubt, to prefer the Italian dualism to the Irish – to prefer an ethic which allows you to be everything except possibly a communist to one which allows you to be nothing except possibly an ultra-nationalist – but neither ethic is really Catholic since neither allows Catholic ideas to inform life. One suspects that Dr O'Faolain's oversimple solution of the Catholic social problem would have led Joyce to reflect ironically on the cost of his own exacting orthodoxy. If, like so many modern Catholic writers, Joyce had been content to allow life its autonomy, he would not have had to renounce Catholicism in the interest of his art.

It is between the priest and teacher that the cultural fight in Ireland is carried on most closely and bitterly, even if the sounds of battle rarely

[1] *Summer in Italy*, Eyre & Spottiswoode, 1949. See especially pp. 20–4, and 156–87.
[2] *The Devil's Advocate*, Heinemann, 1959, p. 18.

reach the public; and it is in a play by an ex-teacher, Paul Vincent Carroll (b. 1900), that the Irish Catholic problem finds its most classic statement. *Shadow and Substance* is more successful as a play, however, than in its attempt to bring priest and writer together on a common social platform.

Mr Carroll is keenly aware that Irish Catholicism is anti-social, and he is surest of his ground when (like Fr O'Brien in *The Vanishing Irish*) he attacks the morbid clerical attitude to courtship and romantic feeling, as he does in *The White Steed*. But, apart from love between the sexes, he is not sure what social and cultural shapes Catholicism should take. This is the weakness in *Shadow and Substance*, where priest and writer, Canon Skeritt and O'Flingsley, never reach a common basis of intellectual agreement. The priest-reformer and the writer-reformer remain at sixes and sevens. It is the Canon's housekeeper, Brigid, the mystic, who affirms the basic alliance between them. She tells O'Flingsley: 'You have the same fine thing in you – the same thing that the Canon has.'

The Canon blames the humanists for the decline in classical standards. In the civilization they made, the 'passport to fame is financial scoundrelism, and the scholar of taste is ever the avowed enemy of the people'. Yet the Canon fails to point out that the Church is partly responsible for a cultural decline it never seriously opposed, and whose corrupting concepts – industrialism, nationalism and materialist pragmatism – it has largely absorbed in practice. Besides, the Catholic clergy have been far more opposed to the 'scholar of taste' than have the humanists. The Canon castigates the curates for introducing a gaudy oleograph of the Sacred Heart into the living room, and for dealing 'with a whitewash brush in terms of the divine'. Why has the Church failed to preserve standards of good taste within its own ranks? The humanists can hardly be blamed for that.

Both the Canon and O'Flingsley realise the cultural failure of Irish Catholicism, but neither can rise superior to its limitations. O'Flingsley remains a school teacher because he fears poverty, until he is fired by the Canon who wants the mediocre and tractable Francis for the job. The Canon dismisses O'Flingsley's requests for improvements in the school with the typical high-handedness of an Irish parish priest. He initiates the cynical match between Francis and Thomasina in order, as O'Flingsley put it, to have 'a rebel knocked out; a niece married off; and a school made safe for a stagnant tradition all in one move . . .' Neither the Canon nor O'Flingsley succeed in giving a tangible character to the 'fine thing' which, according to Brigid, they have in common. In particular, there is the Canon's preference for what Sean O'Faolain calls the 'lymph of authority' in dealing with O'Flingsley rather than an appeal to reason – to the criteria of that classical culture which the Canon claimed to possess and sought to realise.

Carroll's criticism of the Irish clergy – especially of their sordid view of love and marriage – was continued by subsequent critics. Dr Heenan, after a visit to Ireland, gave his impressions in an issue of *The Catholic Herald* on December 12, 1941. He warned of the intellectual sterility of Irish Catholicism, and referred to the current view of the educated in Ireland that it is 'tainted with Jansenism'. He concluded that 'in Ireland there is less loyalty to the clergy than in much-criticised England,' and suggested that this was due to sharp differences between the clergy and the people on social and political issues generally. Mervyn Wall took up the Jansenist theme which he dealt with obliquely but acutely in an amusing satirical extravaganza, *The Unfortunate Fursey* (1944). It was not until the mid-fifties, however, that the puritan question became a national one, with the publication of *The Vanishing Irish*. Meanwhile English Catholic opinion had become openly condemnatory of the social aspect of Irish Catholicism, as can be seen from Haliday Sutherland's *Irish Journey* (1956), and Christopher Hollis' *Along the Road to Frome* (1958).

The decline in creative power which marked the transition from the Anglo-Irish to the Irish Catholic writers born *circa* 1900, is continued as we move closer to the present day. The quality of the writer diminishes in the depth of perception, in imaginative and intellectual scope. The more recent development is closer perhaps to the work of Liam O'Flaherty than to any other member of the 1900 group. There is less concern with Catholicism and its problems, with the single exception of James Plunkett. The cultural mentality of the forties and fifties is best expressed by James Plunkett and Brendan Behan.

Most of the stories of James Plunkett (b. 1920) published in *The Trusting and the Maimed* (Devin-Adair, 1955) had appeared in *The Bell* and *Irish Writing*, and are some of the best Irish stories written between 1940 and 1955. James Plunkett is reminiscent of the young Joyce in his Catholic outlook which is marred by a cynical view of man. In the story whose title he has chosen for the published volume, Mr Plunkett shows how Casey's good intentions are frustrated by accident or providence. Distraught at getting a girl into trouble, Casey takes a walk in the Dublin mountains to decide whether to marry the girl or to procure an abortion. Deciding on marriage, he happens to break a leg in a fall, and his only means of getting help is a wounded carrier pigeon – a bird of destiny – to whose ring he attaches a message. The bird gets home but the message is lost, being displaced during flight; and so Casey remains to die and his girl is left to contemplate what seems to be his betrayal of her.

James Plunkett, like Joyce, is apt to recognise a Catholic social idea when he sees one – a rare achievement for a Catholic Irishman. And he is, like Joyce, critical of ultra-nationalist ideas. In *Weep for our Pride* he adroitly points the contrast between Catholic and extreme nationalist ideals. O'Ruarke, a school teacher, preaches, in an English poetry class, a bloodthirsty patriotism in which the main ingredient is hate of the British. O'Ruarke's teaching session is followed by Brother Quinlan on religious instruction. Here Christian charity is presented as paramount, and physical violence, vengeance and intolerance are condemned.

Yet, Mr Plunkett does not hold out much hope for the enlightened teacher in his struggle with puritan and patriot who insist that every plan must be 'set out on Irish-made paper which has been watermarked with the sixth commandment'. In *The Wearin' of the Green* Purcell tries to act on the belief that people 'must be allowed to develop themselves. They must learn, however dangerously, to run their own affairs.' But Purcell is finally driven from the school, and takes train, accompanied by a time-bomb intended for one of his opponents. Mr Plunkett suggests that even providence is on the side of reaction.

Mr Plunkett differs from Joyce in that he continues to accept Catholic social ideas though he has no faith in their efficacy, like the sun which cannot penetrate the fog and the grime of 'dear, dirty Dublin'. In *The Eagles and the Trumpets* – the finest of Plunkett's stories – Sweeney tells his girl that he will never forget her because he wants her too much. She warns that 'it's bad to want anything too much because you never get it'. So the girl waits in vain in the country town for Sweeney's return, and finally accepts the shy, unexciting commercial traveller, Cassidy, out of pity. Sweeney continues in his demoralising clerkship in Dublin with his demoralising companions, and holds on to the 'prescribed forms' of religion 'by which he might eventually drag himself out of the pit'. On the night Sweeney promises to meet the girl – an appointment which a malicious providence prevents him keeping – he goes on a spree, and observes a brilliant moon riding the August night. With what seems an invincible and impervious religious instinct, he comments *Corpus Domini Nostri*'. His friend, Ellis, with his eye on the moon comments more appositely, 'like an aspirin, like a bloody big aspirin'.

Mr Plunkett's acceptance of Catholic social ideas is not without sentimentality, for those ideas are supposed to be creative. In this Mr Plunkett is typical of the Irish today who continue to give loyalty to a Catholic social ethic in which they no longer believe. Such loyalty can only be temporary, of course, for the actual failure of a system of ideas (or a substantial part of them) results finally and inevitably in their explicit rejection. In the long run, Joyce's more logical repudiation of Catholicism will prove more significant. Evidence of this progressive rejection is not lacking in the work of Brendan Behan.

Brendan Behan (1923–1964) was not so much a writer as a personality whose writing has much in common with his conversation. Like Wilde, his personal appearances were as exciting as his plays; and this helps to account for the fact that he caught the popular Irish imagination to a greater extent than any other Irish writer. His liveliness and indiscretion were an antidote to the humbug and cautious timidity of official Ireland, though his quips and outrageous asides were sometimes either too bald or blasphemous for popular Irish taste.

Behan had a revolutionary background. Joining the I.R.A. in 1937, he was twice imprisoned for political offences, sentenced to three years in Borstal by a Liverpool court in 1939; and sentenced again by a military court in Dublin in 1942, serving nearly six of a sentence of fourteen years. He might appear as a jesting gunman, except for an acquired contempt for violence and revolution and, more important, a kind and simple nature. Behan's basic simplicity and sincerity are of fundamental importance to an understanding of his mind – qualities which emerge most clearly in *Borstal Boy* and help to explain his rather naive explosions and recklessness which brought him to an early grave.

In spirit, Behan is closer to Joyce perhaps than to any of the older writers. His mockery is of a very different kind, however, springing from faith, from a disappointment in the failure of life to live up to its possibilities. His malleable mind contrasts with the diamond-hard, deliberate quality of Joyce's. Behan was no Lucifer, but an avenging angel whose taunts challenged the sedate priest, the trench-coated revolutionary and the smug professional man. Indeed, it is in the absence of a cold, disciplined core of intelligence that one of Ireland's most recent literary spokesmen differs from his predecessors. The poet had turned into jester, the tragic muse into a Punchinello.

Behan's plays are therapeutic. They belong to that indispensable Irish institution, a night-out, when the hair is let down and frustrations dissipated in an alcoholic release. The atmosphere of *The Hostage* is not unlike that of an inspired pub. The conversation is uninhibited, and the humour is off the cuff. The ballads flow as readily as the beer. And when it is all over the pressures have been relaxed, and one can return to the business of living which partakes too much of business and too little of vital creative experience.

Behan's plays are in the urban tradition of O'Casey, though his characters do not belong to any clearly defined class. Those plays – especially *The Hostage* – suggest the revue or its archetype, the *Commedia dell' Arte*. In form, they resemble the work done in the Irish 'fit-ups' where actors and audience come together to share in the telling of a story and satirical comment on life. Behan did not make much of his characters which are thin and, sometimes, inconsistent, so that there is little psychological development in his work. He did not believe enough in his characters to draw them well, using them mainly for the purpose of social satire.

Behan had a collaborator in Joan Littlewood who directed the Theatre Royal at Stratford and used the 'fit-up' technique in the shaping and production of plays. She won much fame and many successes at this kind of work; and her first big success was Behan's *The Quare Fellow* which opened in May 1956.

The notion of collaboration in the making of a worthwhile play poses what seem insuperable difficulties but it appears that Joan Littlewood has this extraordinary talent. The manner of her working with Behan might be taken out of musical comedy. John Russell Taylor describes how

> Brendan Behan . . . was deposited in a pub opposite the theatre while his plays were being rehearsed, with the words pouring out of him and someone ready to note down everything good to cover that weak spot in the second act or replace the 'chunks of terrible sentimentality' which had to be cut from the original text right away.[1]

When one considers that the original Gaelic text of *The Hostage* was about one third of the length of the present English version, and consisted, according to Mr Taylor, 'of three long loosely connected scenes in Behan's most discursive style', one can appreciate the extent of the additions. More important than the additions, however, is the form of the play which would seem to demand a single personal vision. Who contributed this? A sense of form or organisation is something which, one suspects, Behan lacked.

Harold Hobson suggests that 'Behan is a dramatist in the line of O'Casey'. The resemblance in type of personality is perhaps more marked. Both had humanity, simplicity and a nostalgia for a more vital social existence. Both felt out of the present Ireland whose values take little cognisance of the human mind, and are consequently artificial and hypocritical. Twenty years before, Behan would probably have been a Marxist, and moved like O'Casey in the direction of *The Star Turns Red*. Now that time has shown that the stars have turned not so much red as bloody, this avenue is no longer so inviting. Yet Behan was not happy on the Western side of the Iron Curtain either. Despairing rather of the individual and ideas, he fell back on the concept of a vital democracy, in which the individual depends on a popular life and tradition. He was a revivalist in the vital Yeatsean sense; and so, combined with his Catholicism, his outlook suggests the old pagan-Catholic dualism. Like most Irishmen, Behan had little sense of Catholic social ideas.

That Behan's cynicism was not chronic is shown in the excesses of his

[1] *Anger and After: A Guide to the New British Drama*, Pelican Books, p. 102.

language and humour. The language foams like a too-fresh pint: 'Oh you lousy bastard. The curse of God meet and melt you and your rotten lousy leg.' The humour is often ingenuous and sometimes in bad taste: 'Gillchrist. In the name of Christ what kind of a name is Gillchrist.' Yet there is no real venom behind all this. It is a protest in the manner of the real robust Irish tradition, of which Behan was one of our best exponents as a singer of ballads. If the protests appear excessive, one must consider the provocation and the difficulty of formulating a more coherent objection. The only Irishmen in Ireland who behave with a sweet conformity are the fools and the rogues.

The breakdown of the Irish literary vision continued in the sixties as evidenced in the work of Edna O'Brien, John McGahern, Kevin Casey, and Patrick Boyle, whose fine short stories sustain a tradition which extends from Joyce to Plunkett. Here there is little sign of any unifying ideas, or of any vital social reality to provide unity. On the contrary, the tendency is towards the complete isolation of the writer and towards the isolation of individuals in society, doomed to decay in their corrupt separateness. This literary picture provides an ominous comment on the efforts of the Church and State to revive Irish life.

Of course, the decline in Irish writing had other causes than the opposition of the Irish Catholic Church. Catholic social ideas had dropped from practical currency. An idea ceases to exist in a vital sense when it ceases to work. When Brigid in *Shadow and Substance* asks O'Flingsley why he does not write a book which is 'full of love' rather than the bitter book he had written, he answers, 'I don't believe in love.' Why does O'Flingsley not believe in love? Is it because he finds so little of it in the life around him?

One must allow for the writer – whose material is life – when he finds that the professed values of a community have no place in its life; as when, in *A Moon for the Misbegotten* – Eugene O'Neill's study of Irish American puritanism – it turns out that Josie lacks the chastity which Tyrone seeks in her, while Tyrone lacks the wholesome humanity which Josie seeks in him. A writer's failure to find a reality embodying his ideal is very likely to undermine his faith in himself and in life, as it helped so much to cause the bitterly cynical outlook of Eugene O'Neill.

The position of the Irish writer today is aggravated by the failure of humanist ideas. To these he can no longer readily turn as did the writers of the Irish Literary Renaissance. The explosive optimism of O'Flaherty's Clery – 'free to found a new cosmos, to fashion a new order of thought and a new god' – is now largely outmoded; unless one hopes, like the French writer, M. Genet, to create a new spiritual reality through a reversal of Christian values – 'through hatred to a new love', as O'Flaherty put it. But there are no humanist gods left, except perhaps internationalism. Despair for the writer is Eugene O'Neill's conclusion in the modern situation. It is not without logic which springs from the writer's inability to find ideas with which to interpret and order life . . . Yeats expressed this profound disharmony between the individual mind and life:

> Turning and turning on the widening gyre
> The falcon cannot hear the falconer;
> Things fall apart; the centre cannot hold;
> Mere anarchy is loosed upon the world . . .

CHAPTER VIII

Puritanism
and the Anglo-Irish Writers

THE ANGLO-IRISH WRITERS saw Roman Catholicism as a lofty and transcendent principle but opposed to the vital needs of life itself. This view was expressed by Oscar Wilde (1854–1900) when he stated that

> the ideals we owe to Christ are the ideals of a man who abandons society entirely, or a man who resists society absolutely.[1]

Wilde was not without a sympathetic interest in the Roman Catholic Church and, indeed, was received into it shortly before his death. His tolerant view of Rome was, surprisingly enough, generally shared by the Anglo-Irish writers, in contrast with the hostile attitude of the bulk of the Anglo-Irish community. But, like Wilde, the Anglo-Irish writers saw little hope of any flowering of the human spirit under the aegis of Rome whose influence was, they thought, strongly directed towards a penitential repression of human impulse and aspiration. Referring to the revival of Greek and Roman culture in the post-medieval period, Wilde thought that

> Christ had no message for the Renaissance ... Medievalism with its saints and martyrs, its love of self-torture, its wild passion for wounding itself, its gnashing with knives, and its whipping with rods – Medievalism is the real Christianity, and the medieval Christ is the real Christ. When the Renaissance dawned upon the world and brought with it the new ideals of the beauty of life and the joy of living, men could not understand Christ. (pp. 934–5)

The puritan view of Christianity adopted for the most part by the Anglo-Irish writers was due not only to the influence of Catholic

[1] *The Works of Oscar Wilde: The Soul of Man under Socialism*, Spring Books, 1963, p. 934.

practice but also to their own Protestant tradition. One can readily see the impact of that tradition in the basic melancholy of Synge and in the sober habits of AE. But whether the effects were immediate or remote (as in the case of Shaw and Yeats) they cast a shadow over the human personality, resulting in distorted human ideals. Witness, for instance, Shaw's rejection of the material side of man and Yeats' progressive acceptance of it as a primary creative force.

Where puritanism is concerned, time had changed the roles of Irish Catholic and Protestant. The puritanism of Protestantism had gradually yielded to the optimism of humanism. Thus it is in an Irish Catholic writer, James Joyce, that one finds the deeper echoes of early Protestant puritanism as expressed, for instance, by Dean Swift (1667–1745); his *saeva indignatio*; his view of woman as an 'odious animal'; the grossness of his sexual imagery; his conclusion that 'life is not a farce; it is a ridiculous tragedy which is the worst kind of composition'. Joyce took his revenge by turning the tragedy into a farce; and this he did 'out of perfect rage and resentment', the motive which Swift said inspired his work for Ireland.

So widespread is the Irish allergy to matter that Arland Ussher writes in *The Face and Mind of Ireland* that

the Irishman is always at odds with Matter – with that lower and contingent creation . . . like Swift he feels vividly that Matter is dirt and that man is an unclean, irreclamable animal.

Ireland's two most original philosophers, the Platonists John Scotus and Bishop Berkeley, solved the problem by reducing matter to an illusion. George Bernard Shaw, the philosopher-artist (1856–1950) handled the problem differently. He did not belittle his adversary by the processes of logic. On the contrary, he frankly accepted matter, and set out in a businesslike way to get rid of it.

Chesterton saw Shaw's view of matter as characteristically Irish, remarking that

Bernard Shaw certainly has all the virtues and all the powers that go with this original quality in Ireland. One of them is a sort of awful elegance, a dangerous and somewhat inhuman daintiness of taste which seems to shrink from matter itself as though it were mud.[1]

[1] *George Bernard Shaw*, The Bodley Head, 1935, p. 13.

Shaw took Irish distaste for matter to an extreme. He was a complete puritan, anaesthetised against matter. To get rid of matter he first had to denigrate it. This he did by denying the sympathetic element in love, and so contributed to a typically modern situation in which, as J. B. Priestly noted, 'affection was banished from literature'.

All love, as Shaw saw it, was the outcome of an essentially selfish appetite. In *Man and Superman* he derides the idea that man is capable of a really generous impulse:

> *Octavius.* . . . It is out our deadliest struggles that we get our noblest characters.
> *Tanner.* Remember that the next time you meet a grizzly bear or a Bengal tiger, Tavy.
> *Octavius.* I meant where there is love, Jack.
> *Tanner.* Oh, the tiger will love you. There is no love sincerer than the love of food.

Here presumably Shaw is making an observation on the failure of love – whether Christian or humanist – to unify society. But he is also confusing two quite separate psychological trends, whose existence is a fact of every-day experience. Through sympathy man can offset the egotistical tendency in his nature. It is the moral point of his existence that he should do so.

Shaw's view of love destroys the basis of art which he regards as a useful guide to evolution. For creativeness presupposes just this contradiction, the tension set up by the opposed pulls towards self and life. The artist's moral problem is complicated, no doubt, by conflicting claims. For, morally speaking, he is obliged to treat people as ends in themselves; while, as an artist, he must, in some real measure, treat them as means to an end. But it is absurd to suggest, as does Shaw, that the artist is indifferent to the price others must pay in order that he may pursue his art, though temporarily he may not advert to it because of his singleness of purpose. This is to turn him into a villain, which Shaw hardly scruples to do.

> *Tanner.* But you, Tavy, are an artist: that is, you have a purpose as absorbing and as unscrupulous as a woman's purpose.
> *Octavius.* Not unscrupulous.
> *Tanner.* Quite unscrupulous. The true artist will let his wife starve, his

children go barefoot, his mother drudge for a living at seventy, sooner than work at anything but his art. To woman he is half-vivisector, half vampire. He gets into intimate relations with them to study them, to strip the mask of convention from them, to surprise their inmost secrets, knowing that they have the power to rouse his deepest creative energies, to rescue him from cold reason, to make him see visions and dream dreams, to inspire him, as he calls it.

Such scientific cold-bloodedness is self-defeating. The mind adopting it could never merge itself in an experience other than its own, and could never really find the material for creation. Here Shaw is perhaps rationalising his own limitations, as his vision was mainly scientific; a fact which helps to explain the poverty of his characterisation. Yet, his greatness emerges in the marked degree to which he identified himself with what he called 'life's instinctive purposes': though this he succeeded in doing more as a philosopher than as an artist.

Shaw did not see love or passion, in its complexity and subtlety, as enriching the human interpretation. Thus passion is to be scrapped in the evolutionary process, and with it will go the artistic faculty. The Ancients in *Back to Methuselah* are mostly creatures of pure intelligence, whose main problem is to reduce the dependence of mind on body. 'We have a direct sense of life', declares the She Ancient.

Shaw's human ideal is the most forbidding of Irish inventions. It simplifies life but it does not give it more point or interest. If man succeeded in evolving to the spiritual essence which Shaw desired, what then would he do? He would have no further aim, since there is nothing outside the human cosmos, as Shaw saw it: no transcendent life. Man in his final stage of evolution would have nothing to contemplate but himself. An eternity of self-contemplation is a prospect many would find unenticing.

More universal in his approach to the human problem was William Butler Yeats (1865–1939). He sought a synthesis which would reconcile the great historic systems, especially Christianity and paganism. He saw paganism as earthy, potent, creative, and Christianity as lofty, trans-cendental but humanly negative. These are the two main elements in his final metaphysic.

Of the great Anglo-Irish writers Yeats was perhaps the least affected by Protestant puritanism. He had a very liberal father between him and the Protestant tradition. Yeats' doubts about the human mind came mainly from a different quarter; from modern humanism which, distrusting reason, put an increasing emphasis on 'intuition' and 'instinct', which philosophers like Bergson and Whitehead were advocating. Yeats became increasingly suspicious of reason, whose abstractions were, he thought, an enemy of a vital and creative awareness:

> God guard me from the thoughts men think
> In the mind alone;
> He that sings a lasting song
> Thinks in the marrow bone.

There is, of course, no intrinsic division between thought and feeling. The division that arose in modern times was due to both Christian and humanist influence. The decline of liberal individualism involved a distrust of the human mind, and especially of human reason on which the highest hopes of the humanists were centred. The Age of Reason in the eighteenth century wilted under the influence of philosophical scepticism and the patent inequalities which resulted from the social application of individualism in the nineteenth century. Man fell, as the Christian God had fallen. The humanists were divided into those who placed their creative hopes in man's environment and those who thought that really vital inspiration lay in the human subconscious. From the vantage point of the latter, thought and will were seen as dry, inhibiting or distorting forces, cutting across vital human instinct and intuition which were the surer guide to human and social growth. In the melodramatic dictum of James Stephens: 'Reason sits howling over an intellectual chaos.'

The growing preoccupation with feeling did not mean any regard for the highest of the human sentiments – sympathy – which was sacrificed to the raw forces of the unconscious mind – ego and sex. Consequently, Yeats was prevented from achieving his dearly sought synthesis of man, nature and supernature; for reason and sympathy are the only integrating forces. The only way out for Yeats was to conceive life as an evolutionary conflict of spiritual and material principles, which, altering in a set way, determined the nature of life at any given period.

Such was the view he put forward in *A Vision* first published in 1925.

Nor was 'frigid Rome' any help to Yeats in remedying the defects in the contemporary outlook, since the Roman Church was even more sceptical of the value of the higher human faculties than were the disillusioned humanists, so much so that Catholic thought and art were pushed into the background of modern life.[1] Thus Yeats could not use – as did Aquinas in the Middle Ages – an intellectual basis to unify the Christian world with what preceded it.

Early in life Yeats assumed that the Christian ethos was opposed to life and art. Richard Ellman points out how the hero in Yeats' unpublished novel, *The Speckled Bird*, hoped to humanise the Christian ethic; thinking to find

> somewhere in the east a doctrine that would reconcile religion with the natural emotions, and at the same time explain these emotions. All the arts sprang from sexual love and there they could only come again, in the garb of religion, when that reconciliation had taken place.[2]

In his first long poem, *The Wanderings of Usheen*, Yeats opposes St Patrick (the Church) and Usheen (the artist), making St Patrick admonish Usheen for 'dalliance with a demon thing', namely, life:

> You who are bent and bald and blind,
> With a heavy heart and a wandering mind,
> Have known three centuries, poets sing,
> Of dalliance with a demon thing.

Later in *The King's Threshold* (1904) Yeats deals specifically with this theme. In this play, Seanchan, the chief poet of Ireland, is asked to leave the Council of State. Among the reasons for this are those advanced by the Monk who charges the poet with being a man who 'hates obedience/Discipline and orderliness of life . . .' This is the most valid of the charges which can be made by the churchman against the artist.

The moral dangers to which the artist is exposed are vividly portrayed in *Death in Venice* by Thomas Mann. In this story, a staid, highly respected writer falls madly in love with a beautiful boy; and this perver-

[1] Well may Hans Küng be concerned with the problem of an 'isolationist Church' in *The Council and Reunion*, (Sheed & Ward, 1961).

[2] *The Identity of Yeats*, Faber & Faber, 1964, p. 52.

ted love leads to the writer's complete dissolution and death. In the spirit of Plato in the *Phaedrus* Mann reflects on the manner in which an artist's preoccupation with feeling leaves him open to the domination of sexual passion:

> For mark you, Phaedrus, beauty alone is both divine and visible; and so it is the sense way, the artist's way, little Phaedrus, to the spirit . . . it is a path of perilous sweetness, a way of transgression, and must surely lead him who walks in it astray. For you know that we poets cannot walk the way of beauty without Eros as our companion and our guide. We may be heroic after our fashion, disciplined warriors of our craft, yet we are all like women, for we exult in passion, and love is still our desire, our craving and our shame.[1]

There is some truth in this, and the artist who explores and develops feeling is open to temptations to which the ascetic (who constrains feeling) is less subject. To the artist, *qua* artist, the discipline of ethics is not as relevant as that imposed by his art: his special job is to make a beautiful work. Whether a man can be an artist and live a good life according to the strict requirements of the Catholic ethic is open to some doubt; for whereas art requires a wide experience, ethics – especially as it affects marital loyalty and sexual continence – demands a highly controlled and limited one. The artist, *qua* artist, and the artist, *qua* man, may well be somewhat at loggerheads.[2]

Mann, however, would seem to do less than justice to the therapeutic value of art which, by a repeated action of the sympathies, ennobles both feeling and thought. Eros is not normally the guide of the artist but of the libertine. When Eros is the artist's guide – as he is today – that is because the rational and sympathetic foundations of art have broken down, and the artist has little choice but to use what inspirational forces remain. In such circumstances, the consequences for the artist are closer to what Mann envisaged – as can be seen from the coarsening of Yeats, so evident in his verse; but, even so, the artist tends to achieve a dignity and speculative purity – no less evident in Yeats which are a justification of the artistic approach and method.

Yeats' spiritual and material principles became more sharply con-

---

[1] Martin Secker, London, 1928, pp. 113–14.

[2] See *Art and Scholasticism*, Jacques Maritain, Sheed & Ward, London, 1950.

trasted as modern values centred more and more on the sexual and egoistic drives of the unconscious mind, which came, in time, to be vulgarly, if graphically, associated with the 'kitchen sink'. In the cyclic explanation of history towards which Yeats was working, the gross principle took on an increasingly sinister aspect and was seen as a 'rough beast, its hour come round at last/Slouches towards Bethlehem to be born.' Yeats first suggested the supercession of the Christian era in a poem, *The Magi* (1915) when the elements of disorder and bestiality would take over:

> Now at all times I can see in the mind's eye
> In the stiff, painted clothes, the pale unsatisfied ones
> Appear and disappear in the blue depth of the sky
> With all their ancient faces like rain-beaten stones,
> And all their helms of silver hovering side by side,
> And all their eyes still fixed, hoping to find once more
> Being by Calvary's turbulence unsatisfied,
> The uncontrollable mystery of the bestial floor.

In *The Player Queen* (1922) the bestial element is combined with its antithesis, a principle of purity and nobility. In this play, Septimus announces the end of the Christian era and the advent of a new dispensation. This centres on the unicorn which is represented as coupling with a dedicated and mystical queen. 'Man is nothing,' says Septimus, 'till he is united with an image. But the unicorn is both image and beast; that is why he alone can be the new Adam.' Likewise in *The Resurrection* (1931), Yeats portrays the risen Christ showing Himself above a street in which a crowd of Asiatics – the 'dregs of the population' – mutilate themselves and copulate in abandonment in order to bring back the old gods.

As the material element in Yeats' metaphysic became more gross, the spiritual element became more rarified, identified with a mystical power which does not seem to have any definable content at all. Yeats was apt to equate this spiritual power with Christian sanctity whose essence lies in charity or love. But Yeats had serious doubts about love; even if, on rare occasions, he felt a sense of beatitude 'the moment I cease to hate'.[1] For Yeats, love became that 'crooked thing', and hate a

[1] *Anima Hominis, Mythologies*, Macmillan, 1959, p. 315.

more potent force than love: there is 'more substance in our enmities/ Than in our love.' The barrenness of this moral factor, love, Yeats expressed in a dialogue between Heart (Artist) and Soul (Saint):

The Soul. Seek out reality; leave things that seem.
The Heart. What, be a singer born and lack a theme?
The Soul. Isaiah's coal, what more can man desire?
The Heart. The heart struck dumb by the simplicity of fire.
The Soul. Look on that fire, salvation walks within.
The Heart. What theme had Homer but original sin?

Evidently, for Yeats, the Christian heaven left much to be desired, consisting in some indefinable bliss in which art and thought had little place. Yet, Yeats could never quite lose faith in the power of this mystical element, clinging with his extraordinary intuition to a belief in its efficacy. Writing to Mrs Shakespeare in 1932 about his *Collected Poems*, he remarked that

The swordsman [the artist] throughout repudiates the saint, but not without vacillation. Is this perhaps the sole theme – Usheen and Patrick – 'So get you gone, von Hügel, though with blessings on your head' (?)[1]

Where the Catholic Church was concerned – and heaven to which it was the gateway – Yeats was in a quandary. He knew that the Church must have some virtue to produce such saints as Teresa of Avila; and for this reason he did not wish to turn his back on it:

Must we part Von Hügel, though much alike for we
Accept the miracles of the saints and honour sanctity?
The body of St Teresa lies undecayed in tomb,
Bathed in miraculous oil . . .[2]

The question was what sort of virtue had the Church. If Yeats' concept of the ideal Catholic life is lacking in depth and richness, so it must be admitted was the contemporary Catholic reality. For that was marked by neither thought nor sensibility.[3] Had it charity? Hardly in a human

[1] See Richard Ellman, *The Identity of Yeats*, p. 268 ff.
[2] Von Hügel was a Roman Catholic mystic.
[3] Evidence of the anti-rational bias of Roman Catholicism today may be seen in the attack on the Scholastic tradition by G. F. Pollard in *Objections to Roman Catholicism* (ed. Michael de la Bedoyere, Constable, 1964).

or social sense. Irish life, for instance, was instinct with much hate, political and otherwise, as Yeats well knew:

> Out of Ireland have we come
> Great hatred, little room,
> Maimed from the start.
> I carry from my mother's womb
> A fanatic heart.

So Yeats can hardly be blamed for turning away from an arid-seeming Roman Catholic ideal to a pagan world rich in human experience:

> Homer is my example and his unchristened heart.
> The lion and the honeycomb, what has Scripture said?
> So get you gone, Von Hügel, though with blessings
> on your head.

Yeats thought that Christian art depended on pre-Christian life for its inspiration. Even the art of Dante Alighieri, the 'chief imagination of Christendom', Yeats saw as inspired by Dante's lecherous life and his appeal to a pagan image 'that might have been a stony face/Staring from a Bedouin's horse-hair roof/From doored and windowed cliff . . .' Hence Yeats' return to a pagan world to find an aesthetic to supplement Christian self-denial, and so to provide a comprehensive ethic which would cater for both ascetic and humanist, for monk and layman.

The importance of Ireland for the Anglo-Irish writers was due not only to the fact that they were part of it, but because they saw Ireland as their own special field of experimentation, a relatively isolated region, largely free from the evils of industrialism and commercialism. Thus Yeats, with some justice, regarded Irish nationalism as 'my' nationalism. Besides, it was of special interest to writers who wanted to create a universal synthesis, for it contained both Christian and pagan elements. The popular pagan tradition was pregnant with sensousness and sensuality, with violence and potent superstition. This pagan world became more completely Yeatsean with the more recent addiction of spiritualist and occult practices, to which Yeats himself was much given. It was a great disappointment to the Anglo-Irish writers when self-governing

Ireland proved inimical to culture. Yeats complained bitterly: 'for all that was sung/All that was said in Ireland was a lie . . .'

Yeats' religious syncretism is of exceeding interest; inspired by an attitude which was relatively conservative and traditional. Its constituent elements, artistic and moral, characterise the distinctive Western viewpoints of the churchman on the one hand and the writer and artist on the other. The Church's practical policy is practically empty of any real human content. Even charity is doubtfully present, as Catholics, in their everyday lives, view one another with much the same competitive hostility which marks their humanist brethren in what has come to be called a 'rat race'. Humanism has degenerated from its original lofty conception of man until today when he is seen as driven by powerful sub-conscious forces which are destructive and divisive, even if not downright evil as expressed by Francis Bacon in his *Three Studies for a Crucifixion*. In such circumstances, reform – involving essentially a restoration of belief in the integrated human mind – seems problematical indeed.

The Yeats' Summer School in Sligo, set up in 1958, suggests that the Irish Catholic Church has come to take some interest in Yeats' work, the evolution of whose values provides a parallel to changes in the Irish scene. For while Yeats' individualism weakened, so did that of Catholic Ireland; with this difference, however, that while Yeats was forced to give ground in his claims for human imagination and reason, the Irish Catholic Church deliberately made war on thought and the sensibilities. What colossal ineptitude for a Church to wreck deliberately one of the two pillars on which its foundation depends. If, as Nietzsche claimed, we have 'killed' God, then it is not only humanists who are responsible for this but those Christians – and, especially, the clergy – who have derided and repressed the human mind which remains the best evidence we have of the existence of a divine mind. The anti-human policy of the Irish Catholic Church specially contributed to Yeats' failure to achieve a unified system, since it was on Ireland his hopes were specially centred, and he was specially influenced by the outcome of his Irish experiment.

Yeats' synthesis is the best of the vital interpretations which has come out of modern Ireland. Synge had expressed to Yeats the essence of the spiritual problem when he noted that 'we must unite asceticism, stoicism and ecstasy; two of these have often come together, but not all three'.[1] This was a shrewd assessment. Ireland may be said to have all three, but not together. The Church has provided asceticism and stoicism; but ecstasy, when it is to be found, usually belongs to an older, pagan tradition. Yeats tried to create a unity by a synthesis of paganism and ascetical Christianity. What could be more natural, traditional and inevitable?

More modest than Yeats in his expectations of life was John Millington Synge (1871–1910). He was satisfied with the contemporary Gaelic reality which he found in tinkers, fishermen and farmers who were the inheritors of the traditional culture. Synge's relish of this popular life was all the keener because, in his dour Protestant home, he was taught to expect little from life. His evangelical mother, in particular, filled him with a deep pessimism, based on her belief that 'man was essentially wicked and, by justice at least, entitled to nothing but damnation'.[2] Synge never quite rid himself of this sense of doom. His later delight in life was ever mixed with a vivid sense of corruption and mortality.

The native life Synge found was not all of a piece. At one extreme, the tinkers lived almost exclusively by a pagan tradition, looking on priest and parson with the tolerance of those who believe they possess a richer inheritance. Next came the fishermen whose life contained Christian and pagan elements. Finally, there were the farmers and, especially, the villagers and townsfolk, whose puritan-Catholic and bourgeois prejudices prevented them from living vitally at all. The tinkers and fishermen lived as fully as circumstances permitted, and Synge dramatised their lives in such plays as *The Tinker's Wedding* and *Riders to the Sea*. But the villagers could savour life only through the imagination, through dreams and fancies. It is about these who are closest to the middle-class urban Irish that Synge wrote his finest play, *The Playboy of the Western World* (1907).

In spite of their puritanism, the human ideal of the villagers is pagan. When Sean Keogh, engaged to Pegeen Mike, remarks that their marriage can take place when they get a dispensation from Rome, Pegeen answers:

[1] Preface to the First Edition of *The Well of the Saints*.
[2] *J. M. Synge*, D. H. Greene and E. N. Stephens, Macmillan, New York, 1959.

It's a wonder, Shaneen, the Holy Father'd be taking notice of the likes of you; for if I was him I wouldn't bother with this place where you'll meet none but Red Linehan, has a squint in his eye, and Patcheen is lame in his heel . . .

She goes on to note the decline in local vitality, the loss of courage and dare-devil brutality:

Where now will you meet the like of Daneen Sullivan who knocked the eye from a peeler; or Marcus Quinn, God rest him, got six months for maiming ewes, and he a great warrant to tell stories of holy Ireland till he'd have the old women shedding down tears about their feet . . .

The villagers delight in the entry of Christy Mahon who claims he has killed his own father. 'I just ris the loy,' explained Christy Mahon coolly, 'and let fall the edge of it on the ridge of his skull, and he went down at my feet like an empty sack, and never a grunt or groan out of him at all.' In Christy, the villagers see the hero of their dreams, the man who realised their own longed-for experiences. On him they lavish their delight in the imaginative personality and in rhetoric – the two great human preferences of the traditional culture.

It was this frustrated mentality which produced the stage Irishman who, though dismissed by many Irish critics as a malicious invention, was a logical product of the Irish environment. He is aptly named, a self-dramatiser, who compensates in the creation of fantasies for his inability to come to grips with life. Dion Baucicault made much use of this rogue-hero in his melodramas which delighted Irish audiences. After seeing one of them in 1904, *The Shaughrawn*, Synge noted favourably its 'good acting comedy – its broad farcical humour – and its naive . . . personal humour' which contrasted with the 'impersonal wit' of playwrights such as Wilde.[1] What Synge did – and O'Casey later – was to turn Baucicault's popular hero into a tragic hero, presenting him in the inhibiting context of the life which produced him.

The pietists and the nationalists had little liking for the low comedy of Baucicault or for the satirical comedy of Synge. Both groups – in reality they had largely coalesced into a single puritan-nationalist body – sought a synthetic national ideal which was chaste in sentiment,

[1] *The Academy and Literature*, June 11, 1904.

vacuous in thought and belligerent in will; and whose highest dramatic expression was Yeats' *Cathleen Ni Houlihan* (1902). No drama with any claim to humanity could pass so exhausting a test; and not even the innocuous comedies of Lady Gregory really did so.

It was not so much Synge's satire which distressed the nationalists – that largely eluded them – but his outspokenness and realism. Thus, they objected to the use of the term 'shift', and the theme of a young wife leaving her aged and crusty husband. Their censorious and humourless mentality is well expressed in the *Playboy* by Shawn who, when asked to stay the night in order to protect Pegeen from the disorderly tinkers, cries out in terror for his modesty:

> Let me out . . . Oh, Father Reilly, and the saints of God, where will I hide myself today . . . ? Leave me go, Michael James, leave me go, you old pagan . . . or I'll get the curse of the priests on you, and of the scarlet-coated bishops of the Courts of Rome.

Synge's *In the Shadow of the Glen* (1903) and the *Playboy* caused riots in the Abbey Theatre. Even the Abbey managers, the Fays, were uneasy, as were, indeed, the actors, some of whom left the cast of *In the Shadow of the Glen* as a protest. The extent of public indignation is suggested by the fact that one of the objectors was Arthur Griffith, who attacked Yeats and Synge in *The United Irishman*. This was the first real clash between the vital writers and the sentimental Irish public whose leaders in the Gaelic League began to take fright at what a real cultural revival might involve.

It was a drawback for Synge – as, indeed, for every serious modern Irish writer – that his critical and literary canons were not generally understood in Ireland. For while the Irish are pre-eminently a people of feeling, they know little of organised emotion or art. To look at life as it is; to interpret it out of direct emotional and imaginative response, is now how the Irish see the writer's job. They would have him boost Irish life and pretensions; propagate the notion that the Irish are a pure, upright and noble people, courageous victims of a harsh destiny. It is this immature attitude which has alienated every serious Irish writer from George Moore to Edna O'Brien, and has caused their works to be seen (and often banned) as deliberate travesties of the Irish reality.

How true was Synge's vision of the contemporary Gaelic reality?

If the testimony of anyone could be trusted, it was that of Synge. He loved the Gaelic reality, and distrusted ideas and preconceptions; writing the *Playboy* 'directly as a piece of life, without thinking . . . whether it was comedy, tragedy . . .'[1] Besides, Synge had a well-trained mind; learned in Celtic studies which he pursued in Trinity College, Dublin, and at the Sorbonne, Paris; well-versed in literature, especially French. He had, as his friend, Stephen MacKenna claimed, a 'passionate' concern for truth. Yeats thought very highly of him and urged him to go to the Aran Islands. True, Synge's view of the Gaelic reality was an interpretation, involving a selectivity both as to human types and language; a pointing of the significance, as he understood it, of what he looked at. But there is no other kind of 'realism' in art.

The Catholic revivalists were in the ascendant, however; and their image of life – in fact, an image of death – prevailed over that of the writers. The result was war on the human personality; on integrity of purpose, honesty of thought and richness of imagination, while language degenerated to officialese and journalese, whose main purpose was to obscure thought. Yeats, when replying to Griffith's attack in *The United Irishman*, pinpointed these groups who falsified the Irish reality:

> There is the hatred of ideas of the more ignorant sort of Gaelic propagandist who would have nothing said or thought that is not in country Gaelic . . . There is the obscurantism of the more ignorant sort of priest who, forgetful of the great traditions of his Church, would deny all ideas which might perplex a parish of farmers or artisans or half-educated shopkeepers. Third, there is the obscurantism of the politician and not always of the more ignorant sort, who would reject every idea which is not of immediate service to his cause. (October 24, 1903)

Like most of the Anglo-Irish writers, Synge underestimated the Irish clergy as an agent of destructiveness, even though he was well aware of their humanly negative attitude; for his Saint in *The Well of the Saints* is solely – like Yeats' St Patrick – a symbol of asceticism. Indeed, the mildly critical attitude of the Anglo-Irish writers to the Irish

---

[1] *A Letter to a Young Man*, in *The Works of J. M. Synge, Vol. I, Plays*, Allen & Unwin, Revised Collected Edition, 1932, p. vii.

Catholic Church seems due to their view that the Christian ethic has no constructive human reference; and that, consequently, the clergy are quite logical in their opposition to thought and art: though, as in the above passage, Yeats suggests that the role of the Church had once been more humanly positive. It is the Irish Catholic writers who have been the bitterest critics of the clergy.

In modern Ireland it was mainly the Anglo-Irish writers who were critical of material growth; they were in sympathy with the medieval attitude expressed by Henry of Ghent's stricture: *summa periculosa est venditionis et emptionis negotiatio.* That trade should be avoided because of its moral perils would seem a novel heresy to modern Catholic Ireland. The Anglo-Irish distrust of commerce derived partly from the traditional Gaelic culture, and partly from the Christian-Platonic tradition which found expression in England, as in the work of Samuel Butler, D. H. Lawrence and Dylan Thomas. This same ideal inspires Arland Ussher, the most distinguished contemporary spokesman of the Anglo-Irish. Mr Ussher shows his liking in *Spanish Mercy* for the relics of the old order in Spain. He values the aristocratic character of its life, even if its ecclesiastical and social basis is rather narrow. He admires the Spanish contempt for modern 'progress', and sees that to democratise and industrialise Spain would spoil its traditional life, rich in character and colour, and happy even in its material exigency. He warns that 'those who love Spain desire humane reforms most deeply; but those reforms would do away with the Spain they love'.[1]

The threat to the Gaelic reality which Synge feared most was commercialism, whose destructive advance he observed in the Aran Islands where the traditional life was at its best. Synge, as Alan Price emphasises in a perceptive study, was profoundly aware of the conflict between security and imaginative richness; of the indispensable link between a vital popular culture and a hazardous life lived close to land and sea.[2] In this, Synge was at one with Yeats and AE; and, indeed their preference for a rural environment and material simplicity, was perhaps the most valuable of the lessons they vainly tried to teach the new Irish State. But the growth of commercialism in Ireland – now proceeding by leaps and bounds – was expedited by the official cold

[1] Gollancz, 1959, p. 215.
[2] *Synge and Anglo-Irish Drama*, Methuen, 1961.

war on the human personality which took to the contemporary pursuit of wealth when it was frustrated in its traditional pursuit of beauty.

From the official and bourgeois viewpoint of the new Irish State, there seemed little to be said for the tinkers; and, indeed, in the middle sixties, there was a movement to 'civilise' them; to incorporate them as permanent members of the urban community. The protagonists of this movement showed little awareness of the virtues – moral or otherwise – of the tinker class, which James Stephens elaborates in his story *The Demi-Gods*. Of the tinkers, John and Mary MacCann, Stephens wrote that

> they had no property, and so they had no prejudice, for a person who •
> has nothing may look upon the world as his inheritance, while
> the person who has something has seldom anything but that.[1]

It is odd that the townsman can condemn the petty thefts of the tinkers with little sense that his own business world exploits far more consistently and ruthlessly.

Synge's work has come to be largely accepted in Ireland because in a country with an intense consciousness of drama, it is hard to avoid presenting some of its classics. Yet, Synge's plays still cause some unease among the clergy and the nationalists. It is no accident that the Abbey Theatre has never presented *The Tinker's Wedding* which brings together two of the most sharply contrasted of Irish attitudes, that of priest and tinker.

Of the Anglo-Irish writers, it was Sean O'Casey (1884–1964) who was most conscious of Irish puritanism – Catholic and Protestant – and of its inhibiting effects; for he was in closer contact with his Catholic compatriots. Both types of puritanism find clear expression in his work. Susie in *The Silver Tassie* illustrates the Protestant type, ranting from the Old Testament and calling down fire and brimstone on the unrighteous. Fooran in *The Bishop's Bonfire* is an example of the more subtle kind of Irish Catholic puritanism which makes chastity rather than charity the central ethic.

The Irish public which responded indignantly to Synge's work reacted even more caustically to the work of Sean O'Casey. O'Casey

[1] *James Stephens: A Selection.* Introduced by Lloyd Frankenberg and with a preface by Padraic Colum, Macmillan 1962, pp. 165–6.

did for the proletariat of Dublin what Synge did for rural society. In the Dublin slums life was rich and vital, if rather chaotic, lacking the discipline or form to be found in the life of fisherman or even the tinker. Both these urban and rural worlds were concerned with human realities – with food, drink, life and death – and in both there was human warmth and imagination. O'Casey, like Synge, was on the side of life; and, in his opening trilogy of plays, created a wonderful picture of a people trying to cling to human realities during a period of national insurrection.

The slum dwellers in Eire's cities were among the most culturally independent in urban Ireland. Their lack of education saved them largely from the influence of the old puritanism and the new nationalism. Thus, during the period 1918–1923, with which O'Casey's first plays deal, the people of the Dublin tenements were rather remote in spirit from the extreme regional sentiment which inspired the independence movement, even if they were some of its victims. O'Casey's sympathies were strongly on the side of the slum dwellers, and opposed to the idealists who would cut Irishmen off from the human family and from a rich human tradition.

If the slum dwellers benefited in some ways by being left to themselves, they suffered in others. They were the forgotten ones, the outcasts. They lived under appalling conditions which O'Casey's biographer, David Krause, briefly describes.[1] The Irish Catholic clergy looked on passively at what they regarded as the inevitable plight of the Dublin poor, and supported, for the most part, their employers whose ruthlessness goaded Jim Larkin to exclaim, 'You'll crucify Christ no longer in this town.' It was the beginning of serious labour agitation in Ireland – in which O'Casey played a part – and whose first major achievement was the General Strike and Lock-Out of 1913.

The Dublin poor met the challenge of life with courage and good humour, but hopeless conditions drove them – especially the men – to fantasy. They were not afraid of life in the sense in which Synge's puritan villagers were afraid of it, but they could not solve its problems; and the result was comparable in that they were driven to dramatisation. O'Casey's plays abound with stage Irishmen, such as Captain Jack Boyle and Fluther Good.

[1] *Sean O'Casey: The Man and his Work*, MacGibbon & Kee, 1960, pp. 4–8.

David Krause rightly points out that O'Casey's characters do not understand their malady (pp. 75–6) – that excess of imagination which Larry Doyle deplores in *John Bull's Other Island*. But one may ask how well did Shaw himself understand it. Larry Doyle contends that the Irishman 'can't be religious' because the 'inspired churchman that teaches him the sanctity of life . . . is sent away empty . . .' Such inspired churchmen are rare indeed; for it is the sanctity of God not the sanctity of man which Irish churchmen are apt to extoll. Man is not seen as vitally responsible, and is cut off from the humanly moral, intellectual and artistic development. David Krause rightly notes that '[Irish] men are dreamers by default', that is to say, when deprived of a vital process of growth.

It is only the women in O'Casey's plays who are heroic – Minnie Powell, Bessie Burgess, and Ginnie Gogan. Mr Krause suggests that they are 'realists by necessity'. It would be more pointed perhaps to say heroines by limitation. For it is the personal outlook of their sex – their concern with husband, children and home – which makes it possible for them to try and meet their obligations in a community which has a very strong family sense. It is when one goes outside this personal world in Ireland and enters the impersonal that one feels the cold wind of official discouragement and the poverty of ideas. Indeed, one may see in this an explanation of why, in other Catholic countries such as Spain and Italy, the female retains her religious faith longer than the male.

O'Casey left Ireland before any radical change in his plays became manifest. The reception of his trilogy in Ireland disgusted him – *The Shadow of a Gunman* (1923), *Juno and the Paycock* (1924), and *The Plough and the Stars* (1926). The *Plough . . .*, in particular, offended the pietists and the chauvinists, causing riots in the Abbey. O'Casey concluded that Ireland 'galled the hearts of her children who dared to rise above the ordinary'; but while there is envy, and to spare, in Ireland, it was fear and anger rather than envy which inspired the attack on O'Casey. O'Casey emigrated to England, to a more congenial environment where his *Juno . . .* won the Hawthornden Prize. He was thus removed from the Dublin poor he loved, and exchanged the confined hot-house atmosphere of a narcissistic Ireland for the free play life and ideas in London. Dramatically speaking, however, it was an exchange of doubtful value.

O'Casey was one of the most politically conscious of the Anglo-Irish writers; and, indeed, his interest in reform contributed to undo him as a dramatist. His anti-heroic view of man induced him to switch his interest to ideas and social systems; and his next play, *The Silver Tassie* (1928), deals with the Great War. Mr Krause defensively urges that ideas can 'usually be found in the best literature of all ages'. But they should be implicit: inferences from character and the play of character rather than directly motivating. The loss of richness in the characterisation in *The Silver Tassie* dismayed many of O'Casey's admirers, including W. B. Yeats; and it was this play which brought about the break between O'Casey and the Abbey Theatre.

The loss of individuality is more evident in *Within the Gates* (1933), where the characters are symbols of social and ideological groups – the Bishop, the Atheist, the Dreamer – who struggle for control of society symbolised by the Young Whore, Janice. This is the best of O'Casey's later plays, more consistent in style than *The Silver Tassie* which departs from naturalism in the first act to expressionism in the second. The theme is also more interesting, dealing with the problem Yeats faced, that of a social synthesis.

O'Casey's solution of the modern problem is to combine the best of Christianity and liberal humanism. Following Yeats and Synge, he is apt to see Christianity as a purely ascetical religion, though, in his later plays, he is not quite consistent in this. David Krause remarks of the religious characters in *Within the Gates* that the 'God-fearers turn out to be life haters'. Janice, the illegitimate daughter of the Bishop, has been brought up in a convent where she becomes obsessed with the idea of sin and the 'fire that cannot be quenched'. This dark religious sense draws her to the Bishop. Her strong sense of life, on the other hand, draws her to the Dreamer or Artist. She finds her salvation by taking what she needs from both; and, in the final scene, she dances the joyful dance of death with the Dreamer and then receives absolution from the Bishop. Thus, O'Casey finds the human and cultural qualities which Christianity lacks today, not in the Christian system itself, but in modern humanism.

In his final phase, O'Casey returned to his most valuable theme – an affirmation of faith in man against the Irish clergy; and this brought him into the news again, into the Irish news at any rate. In *Cock-adoodle*

Dandy (1949) – a lively fantasy – an apocalyptic cock, a symbol of life, tries to introduce a spirit of love and laughter into an Irish village. The presentation of *The Bishop's Bonfire* in Dublin in 1955 caused the usual Irish rumpus, the Catholic *Standard* making itself ridiculous by charging O'Casey with 'bitter venom' against the Church. *The Drums of Father Ned* had to be dropped from the Dublin Tostal Festival of 1958; but this last snub to O'Casey was more apparent than real, for, at that time, Fr Ned's drums were rallying support in the ranks of the clergy themselves; and the roll of these drums was soon to be reinforced by the clarion call of Pope John for a fresh spirit of Christian realism and co-operation.

O'Casey suggests three kinds of individualism – pagan, Christian and modern humanist. The joyous people in *The Drums of Father Ned* appeal not only to Aengus, the Celtic god of love, but also to Christ who 'must have listened to the people singin' and been caught up in the rhythm of the gentle harp and psalter . . .' In O'Casey's later plays the effect of the puritan priest is modified by the presence of a humane priest, such as the Brown Priest in *The Star Turns Red*, Fr Boheroe in *The Bishop's Bonfire*, and Fr Ned himself. The contrast between the harsh and mild priests is extreme, 'black and white types, with no subtle shades of grey', as David Krause puts it. It is evident that O'Casey had no clear idea about the Catholic social ethic – by contrast with his knowledge of Marxist ideology – and the most he could manage was to give it a positive but naive form.

O'Casey died just when official Ireland had begun to soften its harsh attitude to the Irish writer. A few more years would probably have lessened that bitterness in O'Casey's heart, a bitterness so deep as to move him to forbid the production of his plays by the Abbey Theatre and Radio Eireann, and, what is even more telling, to forbid the return of his remains to Ireland. Of all that betrays the unsympathetic treatment of the Irish writer in his own country, nothing is more eloquent than this decision, on the part of one of the kindest of Irish writers, to remain an expatriate even in death.

CHAPTER IX

Cold War on Culture

ONLY A HANDFUL of writers have survived in self-governing Ireland. But whatever the writers might achieve personally, with the aid of British publishers, there was little they could do in a co-operative or social sense. Vital theatre and magazines need some official support, morally if not materially. But this they did not get in Ireland. On the contrary, the Church and the State saw to it that such cultural growths were unobtrusively strangled.

The Abbey Theatre was the most valuable cultural institution the Irish State inherited. But it was rather because of its world repute that the Irish Government thought it discreet to keep it in existence. The history of the Abbey Theatre may be divided into three periods; from 1904 to 1924 when it was free; from 1924 to 1940 when it was semi-free; and from 1940 onwards when it was, in fact, well under State control.

The Abbey Theatre reached the apogee of its powers when it staged *The Plough and the Stars*, the last of O'Casey's fine opening trilogy. Up to that time, the Abbey's career had been astonishing. Without a dramatic tradition, it had, in a quarter of a century, found a producer, Frank Fay, and two playwrights, Synge and O'Casey, who brought it to the forefront of world drama, sharing the laurels with the Moscow Art Theatre.

Oddly, it was Yeats who suggested putting the Abbey Theatre under the National Government. He did not appear to see the danger in this, as did Lady Gregory, who expressed in her *Journals* the doubt that 'they [the Government] would leave it in any way under our control, or subsidise it unless it was strictly theirs . . .' Originally £850, the Abbey subsidy is now about £14,000 yearly. In return, the Abbey Theatre agreed to put on a number of productions in Gaelic each year; to subject the actors to a proficiency test in Gaelic; to submit its directors to the approval of the Government; and to allow Government representation on the Board of the Theatre.

Government influence on the Abbey soon made itself felt in the treatment of the work of Sean O'Casey. The first Government appointee on the Board – Dr George O'Brien, Professor of Economics at University College, Dublin – strongly objected to *The Plough and the Stars*, but was outvoted by the Board. This should have been a warning to Yeats and Lady Gregory of the dangers of Government interference; and David Krause rightly concludes that if they had reacted 'by actually choosing their freedom and promptly handing Dr O'Brien and the subsidy back to the Government, the recent history of the Abbey might have been a brighter picture'.[1]

If O'Casey's first plays were distasteful to officialdom, so much more were those that immediately followed – *The Silver Tassie* and *Within the Gates*. True, both Lady Gregory and, especially, Yeats had grave doubts about *The Silver Tassie* (1928), though the Abbey did later see fit to stage it in 1935. The early rejection was, as Lennox Robinson admitted, an 'error in judgment'. Shaw objected to Lady Gregory:

> Why do you and W.B.Y. treat O'Casey like a baby . . . you should have done the play anyhow . . . Yeats should have submitted to it as a calamity imposed by an act of God, if he could not welcome it as another *Juno* . . .'[2]

Within the Gates and *The Star Turns Red* were never presented by the Abbey. True, these plays are dramatically inferior to O'Casey's early work, and their themes are radical. But should not a theatre present the work of its major dramatists no matter what its conclusions? Is not a failure to do so a shirking of responsibility, a refusal to face up to contemporary realities?

The growth of Government influence at the Abbey was expedited by the decline of the old guard. Lady Gregory died in 1932 at the age of eighty. Yeats' continued interest in the Abbey was limited by his failing health and by his appreciable absences from Ireland since he ceased to be a senator in 1928. Lennox Robinson was fast learning the value of

[1] *Sean O'Casey: The Man and his Work*, MacGibbon & Kee, 1960, p. 128.
[2] *Lady Gregory's Journals, 1916–1930*, edited by Lennox Robinson, Putnam 1946, p. 110.

discretion in self-governing Ireland. It was his influence which tipped the scales against *The Silver Tassie*.

The Abbey Theatre's treatment of Paul Vincent Carroll was hardly less discouraging than that of Sean O'Casey, in spite of the fact that Carroll's *Shadow and Substance* was the only major Irish play to follow Synge and O'Casey and to compare with the best work of these writers. Furthermore, it was the only significant Catholic play to come out of modern Ireland. And yet, Frank O'Connor stated that 'I had to fight hard to get . . . Mr Carroll's *Shadow and Substance* produced at all.'[1] Carroll's *The White Steed* was never presented by the Abbey. Dramatically inferior to *Shadow and Substance*, it is, however, a much better play than many which the Abbey has seen fit to stage; but it is pungently critical of clerical Jansenism and so, presumably, unpalatable to official taste.

There was little native work of value to follow O'Casey's plays in the Abbey Theatre. T. C. Murray's best work, *Autumn Fire*, was staged in 1924. Robinson, in his dull and politic history of the Abbey Theatre, states that the 'best plays were piling up almost to an embarrassing degree'.[2] They were embarrassing, however, only in their mediocrity, for the new plays, coming from the pens of George Shiels, Brinsley MacNamara and Lennox Robinson, lacked distinction; they were, as Tyrone Guthrie noted, 'commercialised stereotypes of Irish life, bearing little relation to any realities in Ireland, or indeed, to any realities at all'.[3]

The last evidence of any real vitality in the Abbey Theatre was during the late thirties when the excellent Hugh Hunt was producer. Frank O'Connor became a member of the Abbey Board in 1935. But even during those years the Abbey directors were at loggerheads, as O'Connor explained to the International Summer School in Sligo on August 22, 1963. The principal cause of the quarrelling (according to O'Connor) was Lennox Robinson, who was a 'deadweight on the theatre . . . and only approved of dreary farces'. F. R. Higgins made trouble between Yeats and O'Connor. Even Yeats and O'Connor had their quarrels, 'bitter and regular, like man and wife'. By 1940, however,

[1] *Sunday Independent*, September, 8, 1963.
[2] *Ireland's Abbey Theatre*, Sidgwick & Jackson, 1951, p. 153.
[3] *A Life in the Theatre*, Hamish Hamilton, 1960, p. 261.

Yeats and Higgins were dead, and O'Connor had left the Abbey, being 'ousted by political manoeuvres'.[1]

A few years before Yeats died, he co-opted Ernest Blythe, an ex-Minister of Finance, onto the Abbey Board to help with the business side of the theatre. This dour Presbyterian from Co. Antrim had become infected with the mystique of Irish nationalism. He had that puritan-Gaelic outlook so congenial to the Irish authorities. According to Seamus Kelly of the *Irish Times*, the 'new boy was planning his own palace revolution' in the Abbey. But he was, indeed, only a front man for the authorities. He became the Theatre's Managing Director in 1941, and exercised almost autocratic control of the Abbey for more than two and a half decades.

Under Mr Blythe's direction, plays in Gaelic began to filter into the Abbey programmes, usually in the form of one-acts supplementing plays in English. In 1945, Gaelic pantomimes made their appearance and were a sentimental hotch-potch of the legendary and the modern. Under Mr Blythe, 'it has been,' he informs us, 'the policy of the theatre not to take on any new players who are not able to perform in both English and Irish'.[2] The narrowing effect which this policy had on the Theatre is obvious and led, for instance, to the automatic rejection of Peter O'Toole. It is noteworthy that the Abbey was not able to hold Siobhan MacKenna, who can act superlatively well in both English and Irish.

In spite of its reactionary policy, the Abbey Theatre has managed to retain a competent company and some very able players such as Maire ni Domnall, Philip O'Flynn and Geoffrey Golden, because it was the only Irish theatre which provided its players with financial security. Yet, a loss of its best actors was always a real threat to the Abbey even in its early and vital days. The greater dramatic and financial opportunities offered by London and Hollywood were hard to resist. Thus between 1914 and 1918 practically every Abbey actor of talent took wing – the Algood sisters (Sarah Algood and Maire O'Neill), Arthur Sinclair, Fred O'Donovan and J. M. Kerrigan. Later the drain continued with the departure of Barry Fitzgerald in 1934; Liam Redmond in 1944; Cyril

[1] *The Genius of the Irish Theatre*, edited by Sylvan Barnet, Norton Herman and William Burte, Mentor Book, 1960, p. 10.
[2] Robinson, *Ireland's Abbey Theatre*, p. 151.

Cusack in 1945; Siobhan MacKenna in 1946; Joe Lynch in 1954; T. P. MacKenna and Ray MacAnally in 1962. From the forties onwards the pull of security was not enough to prevent Abbey actors of courage and inspiration from preferring the risks involved in joining Dublin's independent theatres which more and more staged whatever vital theatre the city could boast of.

The Abbey Theatre, under Mr Blythe, seemed hardly to value its best actors. How else account for the fact that Mr Blythe gratuitously dispensed with the services of Jack MacGowan, the best character actor the Abbey had since F. J. McCormick, who died in 1947? Another example of its lack of enterprise was its refusal to provide the stage designer, Sean Kenny, with some modest employment at the outset of his career.

Of the later Abbey productions, only M. J. Molloy's *The King of Friday's Men* (1948) can be said to have done any real justice to the Synge tradition, written in the 'beautiful and vivid language' which the young Yeats valued. After 1940, the general trend of the new dramatic writing was satirical; and the more biting the satire the more it pleased Irish audiences. Some of the best Abbey productions were of this kind, as evidenced by such plays as G. B. McCarthy's *The Whip Hand* (1942). This satire became more violent and derisive in the fifties, as in such plays as Louis D'Alton's *This Other Eden*, and Richard Johnson's *The Evidence I shall Give* which the Abbey reluctantly presented after blunting the edge of its bitter criticism of life in a Catholic orphanage.

The Blythe-administered Abbey Theatre soon came under criticism, which steadily mounted until Mr Blythe became one of the most discredited of Irish public figures. On July 29, 1944, the *Irish Times* commented on the 'Abbey's Decline', and suggested that the £1000 subsidy 'looms too largely over the directors' choice of plays'. On August 11, O'Casey suggested in the same paper that the cause of the decline was that the playwright 'must write nothing to displease the powers or the nominees who place the power there'. Going deeper, P. V. Carroll noted in the same issue that

Dublin's censorious, provincial and pietistic attitude is chiefly responsible for the Abbey débâcle. The introduction of foreign puritanism has proved inimical to native art. Ireland has shed immortality and clothed herself in the rags of a bogus, bombastic freedom. Here lies the ruins of the glorious Anglo-Irish European tradition.

In 1947 the policy of the Abbey was attacked from the auditorium of the theatre by Valentin Iremonger and Roger MacHugh, who complained that the Abbey had lost the 'fine glory' of the Yeats' tradition. And, indeed, it became more and more obvious that the new directors could neither live up to the Theatre's past nor adapt themselves to the present. Hence, they fought shy of the work of Brendan Behan, the best native dramatist to follow P. V. Carroll. The Abbey never presented *The Hostage*, and only got round to the production of *The Quare Fellow* when the Pike and Joan Littlewood's Stratford company had made it famous.

Critics of the Abbey Theatre sometimes put the blame for the decline in Irish dramatic writing on the Abbey directors, but it would be more to the point to see the decline of the Abbey and of drama as the twin consequences of a national anti-cultural policy. Because Mr Blythe was doing the reactionary job expected of him, he could afford to ignore his liberal critics, and declare, as in a radio commentary on the Third Programme, that 'I'm a politician and I have a thick skin, so I don't give a damn what they say about me – not a damn.'

With the advent of more liberal times, a politician with a thick skin was not quite what the Government wanted in control of the Abbey Theatre. Even in the late fifties, the Abbey was reluctant to move out of its comfortable rut, and made no worthwhile contribution to the Dublin Festival which – according to Harold Hobson, writing late in 1963 – had moved 'into first place in the theatrical festivals of these islands'. Of course, a liberal change was not to be effected without a struggle; and, indeed, the Festival set off to a bad start in 1958 when the Dublin Tostal Council had to abandon the presentation of works by O'Casey, Samuel Beckett, and a dramatisation of Joyce's *Ulysses*, titled *Bloomsday*. This ban owed much to the influence of Dr McQuaid, the Archbishop of Dublin. Mr Blythe was not without powerful allies, but nevertheless the trend of the times was towards realism and freedom.

The intrinsic poverty of the Abbey Theatre was high-lighted by a decision of the Government to provide the Abbey with a splendid new building – the original Abbey building was destroyed by fire in 1951 –

estimated to cost £250,000. 'Time only can tell,' commented the *Irish Times*, 'whether this stone was also a foundation kind for Irish drama, or, as some have been averring of late, a tombstone.' The Blythe administration got its hardest blow in 1964 when its offerings for the quater-centenary of Shakespeare – O'Casey's *Plough* and *Juno* – got a poor reception from the British critics.

The Irish Government's first serious attempt to reorganise the Abbey Theatre occurred on February 16, 1965, when it appointed a second Government representative on the Abbey Board, and extended the number of shareholders by twenty-five members. Among the new shareholders were Micheal MacLiammoir, Cyril Cusack, Lady Longford, Arland Ussher, Shelah Richards, Mairead ni Grada and Mrs Mary O'Malley.

The part which the Abbey Theatre plays in the life of contemporary Ireland will be seen in better perspective when the other main theatrical movements have been considered. The most important of these was the Gate, which developed much of the international side of the Abbey Theatre's work.

By the year 1918, Yeats had come to realise that the Abbey Theatre was too narrowly concerned with the peasant type of play which was, in any case, becoming too prosy and realistic for his taste. The Dublin Drama League was founded, with Yeats as President; and on Sunday and Monday nights, the Abbey was given over to a wide variety of continental works. Modern drama, however, did not find a congenial place in the Abbey tradition which was being progressively narrowed by official regionalism; and it is not surprising to find that this experiment fell into other hands, those of Micheal MacLiammoir and Hilton Edwards, who took over the Drama League in 1938, and who were to achieve some real distinction in this field.

The Gate Theatre grew from its beginnings in the Peacock, an off-shoot of the Abbey, which Edwards and MacLiammoir rented for two seasons. They then moved to the Rotunda, and their aim was 'to establish in Dublin an international theatre for the production of plays of unusual interest.' The Gate Theatre is the greatest cultural achievement in self-governing Ireland. It came ironically to a close in 1956 when Eire was just beginning to recognise the existence of the outside world. The extent of the Gate's debt to the State was a generous gift of £4000 on an occasion of bankruptcy.

MacLiammoir had come under the influence of Yeats and a Gaelic writer, Padraig O'Conaire. He had sympathy with the ideals of the Abbey Theatre. But like a sceptical Sir Galahad, he had begun to share the growing suspicion that the jewels in the hilt of Excalibur were paste. 'Was this national-aesthetic movement,' he asked, 'all a dream . . . in the mind of a besotted individual, a species of dangerous and seductive opium . . .'[1] The Gaelic side of the Gate enterprise was expressed mainly through the Gaelic Theatre in Galway, which opened in 1928 with an original play by MacLiammoir, *Diarmuid agus Grainne*, one of the best works that came out of the Gaelic revival. Apart from his work at the Gate, MacLiammoir directed the Galway Theatre until 1931 when he took on the Gaelic Drama League in Dublin instead.

Hilton Edwards believes that drama is the domain of the poet, and that its function is 'revelation'. It is no accident then, as he suggests, that the 'Gate approached nearer to the vision of Yeats than did his own theatre'.[2] The absence of a vital national outlook affected the Gate which, as Mr Edwards pointed out, was not a national theatre but simply a theatre. Any theatre worthy of the name, however, cannot help being a national theatre, that is, it will express the vision of the community of which it is a part. Unfortunately, the period of the Gate's life was one in which the Irish were progressively losing faith, especially in nationalism.

Indeed, the Gate scored one of its great successes with the presentation of a satire on nationalism, Denis Johnston's *The Old Lady Says 'No!'* which the Abbey rejected. Apparently, Lady Gregory could not stomach so harsh a critique of her ideals. Yeats was more in sympathy with what the Gate was doing, with its critical vitality and its willingness to deal with the 'ugly things' which dismayed Lady Gregory. When the Gate played a London session in 1935, it presented Johnston's work and Lord Longford's *Yahoo*–a study of Dean Swift–as the best of the most recent Irish plays.

A more positive experiment of the Gate's was Maura Laverty's *Liffey Lane* whose human freshness and free form offered scope to a

[1] *All for Hecuba*, Methuen, 1948, p. 31
[2] *The Battle of Harlequin*, Dublin, 1958, p. 4.

producer eager to dispense with conventional sets and scenes. Sensitivity and imagination were qualities, however, which became rare in self-governing Ireland; and it is ironic to reflect that it was a Protestant Englishman, Hilton Edwards, who upheld Catholic and romantic values against the Abbey which coarsened the human imagination with its conventional peasant comedies.

The Gate managed far better than the Abbey to keep its best actors, who included Meriel Moore, Betty Chancellor and Coralie Carmichael. The scope and virtuosity of its players were greater than those of the Abbey actor, for whom the naturalistic method tended to degenerate from an art to a bad habit. Gate performances ranged from those required by the Noh drama in Japan to experimental work along Brechtean lines. Some of the best Irish actors played at the Gate one time or another – Eithne Dunne, Geoffrey Quigley and Siobhan MacKenna who made a wide reputation in Shaw's *St Joan*. To the Gate came young actors, some of whom were to achieve distinction; Geraldine Fitzgerald, Peggy Cummins, James Mason and Orson Welles. The only guest celebrity to play at the Gate was Dame Sybil Thorndyke as Mrs Alving in Ibsen's *Ghosts*, a role which Mrs Campbell played in the Abbey Theatre.

The Gate would probably have had a shorter life without the financial help given it by Lord Longford in the early days when he was on the Board of the Gate. Playwrights and translators, Edward and Christine Longford added some plays to the Gate's repertoire. Their attitude to the theatre, however, was marred by a certain sentimentality which cut across intrinsic theatrical needs, and a break finally occurred after the Gate's season in Cairo. The outcome was the formation of the Longford Productions which shared the Gate premises with Edwards and MacLiammoir. The Longford productions were mainly of eighteenth and nineteenth century plays. These lacked able direction; and the fact that they outlived those of Edwards and MacLiammoir was due mainly to strong financial backing. The death of Lord Longford early in 1961 brought his company to an end.

The passing of the Gate brought no tear to the Irish eye, and its founders were left to fend for themselves. It is quite possible that they would have done better for themselves abroad. The spectacular success Micheal MacLiammoir subsequently won suggests as much, with his reading of a pastiche based on the work of Oscar Wilde, and his commentary on Ireland: *I Must be talking to my Friends*.

With the collapse of the Gate, the Irish theatre fell on hard times, and had to depend on short-lived ventures housed in make-shift theatres, as in the Gas Company in Dun Laoghaire, or the Eblana in the basement of the central bus depot. The most important of the first experiments was the Globe (1954) which was well served with Jim Fitzgerald as producer, and with actors such as Norman Rodway who was to achieve distinction, and Geoffrey Quigley and Denis Brennan, who had already proved themselves, Brennan at the Gate and Quigley at the Longford Productions. Mr Quigley, who left Ireland after the failure of the theatre, later angrily defended his exile, pointing out that an actor in Dublin could not be expected to live on five pounds a week.

Other ventures which broke on the rock of finance were Barry Cassin's 37 Theatre Club, and Alan Simson's Pike which presented Behan's work, and showed a preference for the daring and sensational type of play, such as Beckett's *Waiting for Godot* and Tennessee Williams' *The Rose Tatoo*. Here he got into trouble, however, being prosecuted in 1957 by the State for indecency for showing *The Rose Tatoo*. Though acquitted of the charge, he was obliged to pay the costs of the action; and this brought his theatrical venture to a close.

Trouble with the Church and the State did not help the new groups, for, simultaneous with Simson's trial, there was the rumpus about the plays scheduled for the 1958 Dublin Festival. These inhibiting pressures, initiated by Dr McQuaid, Archbishop of Dublin, led the normally discreet Hilton Edwards to comment:

> What this really means is that there is, as there always has been, a rigid censorship of plays and everything else. It is working in different ways, and putting pressure on things. All right – I am no rebel. If the people of this city think the play [*Bloomsday*] is not for them, I'm not upset . . . I think it is a very exciting work for the theatre . . . the Festival will end up like the kind of silly joke for the rest of the world that most things that have happened here (*sic*). Everyone will feel very smug and very pure here, and they will be wrong as usual.[1]

[1] Quoted David Krause, *Sean O'Casey*, p. 217.

The most important of the new theatrical groups active in the early sixties were the Gemini, Orion and Vulcan companies, founded by Phyllis Ryan, a former Abbey actress. Co-directors were Norman Rodway who, in 1962, scored his best success in *Stephen D.*, and Hugh Leonard who made this fine adaptation of Joyce's *Portrait*. Mr Leonard was the most prolific of the new dramatists, providing the Dublin Festival in 1963 with two plays, *The Poker Session* and *Dublin One* – another fine adaptation of Joyce's *Dubliners*. Joyce's work did much to inspire Miss Ryan's companies which presented two other adaptations from the novels of Joyce, *The Voice of Shem* and *Bloomsday*. Other productions by Miss Ryan's companies were works by Tennessee Williams; plays by Irish writers and expatriates, Thomas Murphy and Patrick Galvin; and Eugene McCabe's *The King of the Castle*, which appeared in the Dublin Festival of 1964, as did Brian Friel's *Philadelphia Here I Come*. The 1964 Festival also presented a fine play in Gaelic, *The Trial* by Mairead ni Grada.

From this sketch of theatrical life in Dublin, it is evident that it is a long time since the Abbey Theatre can be said to have fulfilled a vital national function. More and more have Irish dramatists had to depend on other theatres for a presentation of their work. The best Irish producers – Hilton Edwards and Jim Fitzgerald – are not in the Abbey: and most of the best Irish actors have either left the Abbey, or owe little or nothing to the Abbey at all – Rodway, Quigley, Edward Mulhare, Richard Harris. Many of these actors are expatriates, or have only a precarious contact with Ireland. All this is widely known, and has been the subject of much comment. Frank O'Connor thought that Phyllis Ryan's groups should be recognised as the national theatre; so does Gerald Colgan in a review of the post-Gate theatre, *Threadbare Harlequin*.[1]

There is little doubt but that some substantial change in the Abbey Theatre's administration is likely; and that the Irish Government is well enough aware that the Abbey, as it stands, is a costly piece of hypocrisy, no longer tolerable to a Government with any liberal or realist pretensions: better to increase the old-age pension than waste money on a sham culture. There have been rumours of an increased subsidy for the Abbey as well as governmental assistance for other

[1] *Plays and Players*, February, 1963.

important theatrical groups in Dublin and in the provinces. The Irish theatre is certainly in need of financial support, but it is even more in need of an official appreciation of vital drama and its importance to the cultural life of the community. How far will the Government go in removing the Abbey Theatre from the control of a reactionary directorate? To put it into really competent hands would amount to surrendering control over it; yet there is no other real solution. In a televised broadcast on November 8, 1963, Sir Tyrone Guthrie hinted at a willingness to help the Irish theatre, provided he had a free hand. How rarely does so brilliant a producer go a-begging. Who would be better able to reorganise the Abbey Theatre, with the support of Hilton Edwards, Micheal MacLiammoir, Jim Fitzgerald and a half-a-dozen others who distinguish Irish theatrical life at the present time?

Serious Irish magazines have had a rough time because the Irish Catholic clergy fear ideas more than they do, say, music, in which ideas are implicit. It is significant that the only cultural achievement to the credit of the free Irish State are the Radio Eireann orchestras.

The Irish cultural climate has a deceptive softness which lulls the suspicions even of the much-tried writers. In 1924, Yeats helped a group to found a magazine, *To-Morrow*, and told them that his aim was 'a wild paper of the young which will make enemies everywhere and suffer oppression . . .' He wrote provocatively in the first issue: 'We proclaim that we forgive the sinner, but abhor the atheist, and we count among atheists bad writers and bishops of all denominations.'

Yeats' justification of 'atheist' as applied to Bishops would seem to lie in their virtual denial of a principle which informs the whole of life, for he goes on to ask if the Bishops believed that the Holy Spirit should manifest itself in decoration, architecture and daily manners. 'What devout man,' he inquired, 'can read the pastorals of our hierarchy without horror at a style rancid, coarse and vague, like that of the daily papers?' Yeats affirmed his belief in immortality, and asserted that a real act of creation is possible only when the artist believes this 'with all his blood and nerve'. The decline of art, he thought, followed from the corruption of this religious principle, and showed itself in a substitution of photography for creation. By implication he attacked the Churches for their lack of faith in the human mind, thus undermining life and art: for 'new form comes from new subject matter, and new subject matter must flow from the human soul restored to all its courage, to all its audacity'.

Nothing could dismay the Irish clergy more than the prospect of the human soul 'restored to all its audacity'. For, as time was to show, the clergy were opposed even to a modest reinstatement of human reason. The second and final issue of *To-Morrow* caused an outburst of indignation, as it contained two stories which gave offence in Protestant and Catholic quarters; one by the wife of a distinguished historian, Professor Curtis of Trinity College, Dublin, dealing with intercourse between white women and black men; and a story by Lennox Robinson – *The Madonna of Slive Dun* – about a servant girl who believed herself pregnant of God. The Provost of Trinity College and the Rev T. A. Finlay, S.J., both members of the Advisory Committee to the Carnegie Trust Fund – of which Robinson was secretary – threatened to resign as a result of Robinson's story. This incident, which Lady Gregory describes in her *Journals*, was one of the first real trials of strength between the Anglo-Irish writers and Irish Catholic officialdom. The outcome led Thomas O'Donnell, a Catholic member of the Advisory Committee, to conclude that the 'most priest-ridden people in Ireland are the ex-Unionists'.

Ireland To-Day (1935–1937) was of a quite different order, inspired by a moderate rationalism. Its editorial staff was mainly Catholic, but the magazine was liberally representative of all intelligent opinion in the country. Its scope was wide – social, economic, national and cultural – and it aimed, as one contributor put it, at 'cool and purposive self-criticism'. Its reasonable approach was quite new, removed at once from the extravagant idealism of the great Irish writers as from the narrow bigotry of patriot and puritan. The main contents of one issue convey the range of its inquiry: 'A Foreign Commentary'; 'Ireland and the European Chaos'; 'Archaeology and History'; 'The Slum Problem'; 'The Unpopular Front'; 'The Spread of Industry'.

The main problem which faced *Ireland To-Day* was to define the principles of Eire's reconstruction as contrasted with those current in its European environment. One can only commend the progress made in this respect, and deplore the folly of the clergy who put the magazine out of circulation. For this type of social analysis is indispensable, as the clergy are now beginning to realise. *Ireland To-Day* was essentially Catholic in its attempt to assert the supremacy of reason over feeling and force. Indeed, it produced one of the best Catholic social syntheses which came out of modern Ireland, 'The Unpopular Front' by Edward Sheehy (April 1937). But the clergy did not want a synthesis, but rather evasion and repression, the fruits of which have now become bitter to their taste.

The editors of *Ireland To-Day* were not cautious enough, if, indeed, extreme caution could finally have saved the magazine. It was objected, for instance, that one of the contributors, Dr Sheehy-Skeffington, had leftist sympathies. But what finally angered the clergy and led them to press for the removal of the magazine from the bookshops, was the publication of articles criticising Franco's part in the Spanish Civil War. Apparently, articles had also been invited in his defence, but it so happened they were not received.

The collapse of *Ireland To-Day* meant a defeat for Catholicism since it was a blow against sanity and realism. The great Irish writers had badly shaken faith in the human reason; the Catholic revivalists, victims of both puritanism and nationalism, had no use for it. The failure, therefore, of *Ireland To-Day* to assert rational standards led to their defeat. After 1937, the cultural light went dim in Ireland, like the lowering of a lamp.

The Bell appeared in 1940. Its stated policy, at any rate, was anti-rational. Explaining this policy, its editor, Sean O'Faolain, wrote in the first issue that '*The Bell* stands . . . for life before any abstraction . . . abstractions are the luxury of people who enjoy befuddling themselves methodically.' So much for rationalism, Catholic or otherwise. According to Dr O'Faolain, Ireland's real destiny lay in herself. 'Our only job,' he wrote, 'is to encourage life to speak.' This was taking the mystique of nationalism further than it was taken by Yeats and AE, both of whom had definite ideas about the form life should take. Indeed, until his death in 1935, it was AE who was the chief mentor of the nation, giving the Irish, as Herbert Howarth remarked, 'their first acquaintance with conscience', that is, with social conscience. Sean O'Faolain's *laissez faire* policy suited the clergy who were willing to wait for life to speak, since they were able to ensure that it would have little coherent to say. Fortunately, O'Faolain was not too consistent in his anti-intellectualism, as is evident from some of the fine editorials; and when he took up a firm position – as on the question of censorship – he was most effective. *The Bell* was the strongest rallying platform for Irish writers and critics until it went out of publication in 1956; it was edited by Peadar O'Donnell from 1946. It is rumoured to have had the support of an unidentified patron, a supposition which would help to explain its long term of life.

In the nineteen forties, a progressive contraction of the national mind showed itself in the absence of moral purpose. This is evident in *Envoy* (1946–1951), edited by John Ryan, whose narrow field of interest – a Review of Literature and Art – indicates the limits imposed on literature by a rapid cultural impoverishment. Not, of course, that a purely literary magazine has not its place, but, in Eire, lay magazines are apt, in view of the need for moral rearmament, to engage on as wide a front as possible. The same considerations apply to *Irish Writing* which first appeared in Cork in 1947, edited by David Marcus and Terence Smith. In December 1954, when it seemed that this magazine would have to go out of circulation, it was taken over by S. J. White and appeared in Dublin for a few years as a precarious quarterly. Irish cultural life suffered a big loss with the collapse of *The Dublin Magazine* (1923–1958). This was a liberal journal of a more academic type, offering a quarterly review of literature, science and art. It ceased publication with the death of its editor, Seamus O'Sullivan.

Such were the principal magazines which derived from the Irish literary tradition, and which illustrate its decline. There are two other magazines, however, worthy of mention, one of which still survives:

The *National Observer* (1959–1960), a monthly Journal of Current Affairs, was edited by Alexis Fitzgerald, and was the most profound expression of the Catholic social revival. It was inspired by the younger members of the *Fine Gael* party, and attracted a group of able critics, which included some university teachers, such as Professor M. A. McConaill and Kennedy F. Roche.

The National Observer attacked ultra-nationalist ideas and sought to show their conflict with those of Catholicism. Its frank criticism of contemporary conditions and attitudes was too much for the incipient liberalism of the clergy who, as yet, did not wish to be reminded of the constructive work of Fr Walter MacDonald, which the *National Observer* was trying to continue (October–December 1960). Nor did they, as yet, relish a sympathetic approach to the Anglo-Irish writers and a rehabilitation of Sean O'Casey (April 1960). And, of course, to read sharp lay criticism of a philosophical work by a clerical author was too much for clerical conceit (July–August 1960).

The *National Observer* ran into trouble with some of the elders of the *Fine Gael* party, especially with General Mulcahy who resented its criticism of the language revival. In the last issue of the journal, the editors appealed for £500 to ease the burden of the editorial work. Apparently, they did not get it; and so, for the lack of this small sum, there failed the best attempt to date to strengthen the intellectual character of Irish Catholicism.

Hibernia, a liberal Catholic magazine, has had a chequered career, and managed, remarkably, to survive from 1935 when it was founded. It was first edited by Peter O'Curry who went over to the *Standard* in 1948. It then fell into the hands of Basil Clancy who sold it to the *Kerryman* in 1951, buying it back again in 1954. Its position was strengthened with the Catholic revival, and its directorate was enlarged in 1959 when it was incorporated in a company. The new directors included Charles MacCarthy and some lecturers from University College, Dublin – Jack Walsh, Geoffrey Hand and Jack Watt. This magazine, critical and lively, works for more rationalism and realism in Irish Catholicism, and has the support of many of the clergy.

The cultural struggle in Ireland was mainly urban and narrowly based, depending on a small number of inspired and dedicated individuals. Outside Dublin the going was harder because of cultural backwardness and the stronger inhibiting controls of the clergy. Some of the more significant provincial achievements were the Wexford Festival, organised by Dr Tom Walsh; the nucleus of a professional ballet in Cork, formed by Miss Denise Moriarty; and the choir of St Mary's Cathedral, Cork, organised by the late Aloys Fleischmann. The growth of theatrical life in Cork city owes much to James Stack, a producer who has worked under great difficulties since the late thirties in a city where the control of the clergy is far more rigid than in Dublin.

Such patronage of culture as was to be found in self-governing Ireland came mostly from industry. Patrons of the calibre of the late William O'Dwyer of Cork city were rare, but business firms have done much to assist culture. An example of these too little-acknowledged acts of kindness is that of the Esso Petroleum Co. which is giving generous support to the Athlone Drama Festival. The firm with the finest tradition in this respect is Guinness and Co., which George Moore extolled in *Parnell and his Island*.

Before the rural drama movement began, cultural life in the Irish country towns found its highest expression in the work of Gilbert and Sullivan and the more sentimental operas and operettas. The songs of Thomas Moore represented the popular level of Yeats' 'romantic Ireland'. These songs were, as Frank O'Connor remarked, the 'only real education that the majority of the Irish people got during the nineteenth century and after'.[1] Their nostalgic poignancy expressed the longings of a frustrated people for a dream world of youth and fantasy, as in that favourite of Frank O'Connor's mother:

> I saw from the beach when the morning was shining
> A bark o'er the waters move gloriously on;
> I came when the sun o'er the beach was declining,
> The bark was still there but the waters were gone.
> Now such is the fate of life's early promise,
> So passing the spring time of life we have known;
> Each wave that we danced on at morning ebbs from us
> And leaves us at eve on the bleak shore alone . . .

In Ireland, as elsewhere, however, popular taste moved either up to a more disciplined appreciation or – and for the most part – down to a vulgarised conception, as in the rhythmic obscenities of many of the 'pop' singers.

The real point about Irish culture is not that the area of ignorance is wide – that is true of most countries – but that the field of awareness has been restricted by the clergy. In *Hail and Farewell*, George Moore quotes Fr Tom Finlay as saying of Maynooth that 'after a hundred years of

[1] *An Only Child*, Macmillan, London, 1961.

education it has not produced a book of any value, not even a theological work'. Early in the century, Fr D'Alton noted that 'while there has always been plenty of talent, the number of Maynooth men who have become authors is small'.[1] It hardly convinces to explain, as he does, that Maynooth professors are too busy to write.

D'Alton thought that the Irish clergy would write more if Irish publishers showed more enterprise, and if the clergy did not 'encounter discouragement' at home. Irish publishers have, no doubt, some excuse for their lack of enterprise, since injudicious publications would mean a lack of valuable patronage. And it is evident that the discouragement with which the clerical authors meet comes from within the Church. The novels of Canon Sheehan, a parish priest in a County Cork town, were widely popular in Ireland; and his work was for many their only experience of the serious novel. Highly praised by Leo Tolstoy, Sheehan did not escape the suspicions of Maynooth and his fellow priests who sent one of his novels to Rome for assessment.

The Rev J. C. O'Flynn's interest in Shakespearean drama was regarded with amused contempt by his fellow priests, even if they enjoyed the wide variety of his fine impersonations. His influence on the dramatic life of Cork, however, was such that there is hardly a single Cork actor or producer today who does not owe much to him either directly or indirectly. Yet, the only serious bit of recognition he got was when, shortly before his death, the BBC featured him in a televised broadcast in the Spring of 1961.

Fr O'Flynn was too early on the Irish scene to benefit by the more sympathetic attitude of the Irish Catholic Church to drama; for, at the time of his death, drama had become not only a major national preoccupation but also a distinctive clerical pursuit. In the early sixties, the priest was establishing himself both as producer and dramatist. Yeats' *A Pot of Broth*, superbly done at the Athlone Festival of 1962, was the work of a priest. There must be scores of priests trying their hand at drama at the present time. Two plays by clerical authors were submitted to the North Cork Drama Festival in 1963, one of them, *The Survivors*, a remarkably fine one-act.

Needless to say, the cultural efforts of the Irish clergy suffer from defects inevitable in cultural work so long distrusted. On April 2, 1961,

[1] *History of Ireland*, Half-Vol. VI, p. 496.

the Rev D. Murphy suggested at the opening of the North Cork Drama Festival that the Irish theatre had a 'tremendous part to play in the Spring [of Irish humanism]'. He thought that Irish dramatists could find a suitable model in the film *Going My Way*. What Irish dramatists would think of so shoddy a model would probably be unprintable. Yet, even in Ireland, one can come across interpretations of a Catholic humanism which show a deep sense of its individualistic requirements. The Right Rev D. Lamont, Bishop of Umtail, made such a plea at Blackrock College on July 3, 1960:

> Our present requirements are men [he said]. The world, if it is to be saved from chaos, needs men – men of stature, as God intended them to be; men conscious of their creaturehood and proud and responsible for their position at the peak of it; men who are good citizens of this world and prospective citizens of the next; civilized men, balanced men; men who instinctively guess at the true value of things; men with the depth to see them, with personal conscience, with selflessness, idealism and a sense of law; men of sturdy individuality to stand up against the thoughtless opinion of the common herd; men of goodness, men of God.

CHAPTER X

Isolation

A CATHOLIC and isolationist Eire is a contradiction in terms, as Walter MacDonald saw, but as did few others, even up to as late as the mid-sixties. This shows how blind the Irish Catholic Church is to the international nature of the religion it professes, and how a fear of life – European life, in particular – has led to a basic distortion of Catholic social philosophy. Indeed, Eire's new positive external policy owes far more to economic realism than it does to Catholic idealism; and, as this chapter will show, the Irish clergy, writers and people have as yet only a very limited sense of a supra-national human ideal, or intuition of human universalism. The raising of the Green Curtain is prompted not so much by a conviction that the Irish are Europeans, as by the realisation that Eire cannot feed and clothe itself without the help of Europe.

Ireland was not always oppressed by a jealous sense of its own special and unique character seen as threatened by contact with the outside world. It was far otherwise in the early centuries when Irish missionaries were instinct with a sense of Europe's life and needs, and when they made a valuable cultural as well as spiritual contribution to Europe.[1] One of the great international figures at the beginning of the Christian period was the heresiarch, Pelagius (c. 360–420), who stressed the independence of the human contribution to the Christian life. This Christian-humanist was representative of Irish Catholicism which, until the nineteenth century, was mainly marked by a duality of forces, divine and human.

Between the thirteenth and nineteenth centuries, the Irish had all they could do to keep their own spiritual fires burning. The missionary life was resumed when Ireland became self-governing, but, by then, Jansenism and ultranationalism had undermined the human element in

[1] *A History of Medieval Europe: 476–911*, M. Deanesly, 1956, pp. 468–72.

Irish Catholicism, cutting religion off vitally from life at home and abroad. For this reason, the contribution of humanism to European life and spirituality was depreciated, and its evolution through Greek, medieval-Catholic and modern humanism largely ignored. Hence the break of modern Catholic Ireland with the European tradition, and the point of Christopher Hollis' comment that Irish Catholicism is 'oddly unintellectual and little interested in the movements of the Catholic mind in the world at large'.[1] Hence also the concentration of Irish missionaries in the remote mission fields – Korea, China and Africa – where conversion involves a minimum of humanistic development. This was the position in modern Ireland until the middle of the twentieth century when the Irish Catholic Church began to see the inadequacy of this dehumanised Catholic concept, and to glimpse the importance of a vital human element in religion, which linked it essentially with the European tradition, and on the destiny of which its survival mainly depends.

Ireland was isolated, in particular, from the growth of modern humanism, so that today she is largely ignorant of the distinctive nature of the European environment into which she is progressively moving. True, Ireland sends missionaries to English-speaking countries, such as England, America and Australia. But these do not differ much in their cultural equipment from the others. Evelyn Waugh comments on the 'simple' Irish missionaries; and this stricture applies to the Irish priests in England as elsewhere. The difference between them lies not so much in the intelligence as in the will, connoting only more self-sacrifice for those who undertake the materially onerous missions. The Irish priests in England are, for the most part, unconsciously and unashamedly naive, and behave as if working in a sophisticated English environment is little different from working in an immature Irish country parish. The presence – sometimes the predominance – of Irish emigrants among their congregations contributes to the illusion of identity.

In recent decades, it is hard for the Irish Catholic Church to avoid seeing the spiritual importance of Europe. The central significance of the conflict between Rome and Moscow is shown by the fact that it now dominates the missionary problem everywhere. By its extension,

[1] *Along the Road to Frome*, Harrap, 1958, p. 216.

indeed, Eire has been largely cut off from her main mission fields; and conditions in Africa indicate a similar outcome. An attempt to come to grips with European life has been a striking feature of Catholic Ireland since the mid-fifties. Before that time, a consciousness of Europe was practically confined to radical Ireland which operated outside and in opposition to Irish clerical influence, that is, to the Anglo-Irish writers and the revolutionary political movements.

The nationalism of the great Irish writers was not narrow. Of them it can be said, as Richard Ellman says of Yeats, that 'Ireland is his symbol of the world.' The concern of Yeats and AE with Celtic divinities did not exclude recognition of a universal pantheon in which the Celtic gods had their own place. AE and George Moore made a pilgrimage to places of druidic interest in Ireland; but then Moore accompanied Martyn to Bayreuth to hear Wagner's music, and to pay their respects – at least on Moore's part – to the Teutonic gods.

Yeats and AE worked to integrate Irish myth and legend with those of the East, and showed no regional prejudice, even if they sensibly believed that native material could be used more effectively. 'The Ireland-picture and the world-picture merged in their theology', writes Herbert Howarth. It was a world rebirth that Yeats and AE envisaged, and it was their vain hope that Ireland would play a major role in shaping the new world.

Joyce's material is strikingly restricted in view of his extended sojourn on the continent. But it is clear that he intended his work to have a general reference, and that his relationship with Dublin was a microcosm of his relationship with the world. Like Yeats, he believed that 'one can only reach out to the universe with a gloved hand – that glove is one's nation, the only thing one knows a little of'. But if the artistic material should be local, Joyce believed that the interpretation should be universally valid, and the form of art the best provided by world models. Joyce was sharply critical of the regionalist tendencies in the national movement. In *The Day of the Rabblement*, he criticised the Abbey Theatre for failing to look outside for literary models, contending that the native ones were inadequate. Joyce feared that Ireland would become an 'afterthought of Europe' – a fate, indeed, which overtook her.

The work of Synge and O'Flaherty, though based on Irish life, does

not lend itself to an exclusively national interpretation, appealing rather
to the common energies of nature everywhere. Indeed, Synge objected
vehemently to Irish isolationism: a fact which is all the more remarkable when one considers that, like Joyce, he was little given to comment-
ing on his work or on his views. In an unpublished letter he wrote that

> this delirium will not last always. It will not be long – we will make
> it our first hope–that some young man with blood in his veins, logic
> in his wits and courage in his heart, will sweep over the backside of
> the world to the uttermost limbo this credo of mouthing gibberish.
> This young man will teach Ireland again that she is part of Europe . . .[1]

The world outlook of our writers had little influence on the people
who, outside Dublin and a small provincial intelligentsia, read little of
the new literature. Hugh Lane might try to introduce the work of the
French Impressionists to Dublin, but apart from a liberal and educated
coterie, he got little for his pains. There was little sign of Catholic
realism in the national revival. Apart from Walter MacDonald, there
were few to stress the need for a positive Catholic attitude to European
culture. Tom Kettle's conviction that 'if Ireland is to be a new Ireland,
she must first be European', anticipated by half a century the feeble
beginnings of an Irish Catholic internationalism. What perhaps of
tangible Catholic value came out of the literary revival was the
establishment of Palestrina and eighteenth-century polyphonic music in
the Church music of Dublin, due to the efforts of Edward Martyn.

Ireland's strongest links with the outside world were political, based
on ties with Britain and the Commonwealth. Even the liberal outlook
of the Irish Parliamentary Party, however, could hardly be called
international, since it merely envisaged Ireland as part of the British
Empire or Commonwealth. It was from the left or radical position
that a world sense emanated, as from Wolfe Tone and, later, James
Connolly. He alone among the conspirators saw the 1916 Rising in
world terms. He anticipated that

> Ireland may yet set the torch to the European conflagration that will
> not burn out until the last throne and the last capitalist bond and
> debenture will be shrivelled on the funeral pyre of the last war lord.[2]

[1] D. H. Greene and E. N. Stephens, *J. M. Synge*, p. 263.
[2] C. Desmond Greaves, *The Life and Times of James Connolly*, p. 284.

Oddly, it was in the direction of communism, not fascism, that the extreme Irish nationalists first moved when baulked at home. True, the bonds between Irish nationalism and socialism were strong enough, due to the influence of Connolly. The Connolly Clubs in Britain today, in which the Irish play an active role, are palpable evidence of his sowing. Lord Attlee once highly commended the Irish contribution to British socialism.[1]

What the Irish did for socialism in America is not so marked, apart from the influence of Connolly himself. It is not as negligible, however, as suggested by the *New York Sun* which, at the time of Connolly's arrival in New York, claimed that 'in the United States of America all efforts to enlist Irishmen or men of Irish ancestry in the Socialist movement have failed'. The *Weekly People* retaliated by publishing a list of thirty-three Irish S.L.P. men. Evidence of a socialist bias can also be seen in the Irish-American organisations inspired by a revolutionary nationalism, as among the variety of Freedom and Prisoner Aid Committees which gave such valuable aid to the I.R.A. at home. Such, for instance, was the James Connolly I.R.A. Club of New York founded by Commandant Patrick O'Mahoney whose body was brought to his native Kerry and interred with ceremony in 1961.

The embracing of communist ideas by some of Mr de Valera's Irregulars was remarkable, no doubt, for it ran counter to so much that was traditional. The explanation lies in the rapid growth of anti-religious sentiment, as well as in a hatred of parliamentary forms. This developed naturally during the years when the extremists voluntarily excluded themselves from the *Dail* and impotently watched the shaping of democratic institutions. But what precipitated the move to the left was the decision in 1927 of Mr de Valera and his followers to enter the *Dail*. This left the 'incorruptibles' angry, weak and leaderless, disposing them to move further to the left and ally themselves with Soviet Marxism which was then making short work of priests and parliaments.

The late twenties and thirties was a period of intense activity for the socialist elements in Labour and the I.R.A. Delegations left Ireland almost yearly to attend meetings organised by the Third International. A Communist Party of Ireland came into existence in 1928, as well as

[1] *The Labour Party in Perspective*, Gollancz, 1937, p. 28.

an Irish branch of the Anti-Imperialist League. In the early thirties, the I.R.A. programme was a thinly camouflaged Marxism, as Professor James Hogan explained in a contemporary study, *Could Ireland Become Communist?*[1] And, indeed, the I.R.A. leaders soon became the driving force behind the new movement, even if they had only the shaky backing of the rank-and-file of the organisation. So close was the contact between Irish sympathisers and the Soviet authorities, that Ireland was the first European country to establish a branch of the European Peasant's Committee in Galway, shortly before the Berlin Congress (March 1930) authorised the new development. By 1932, Ireland merited a special section in the Soviet classification of foreign areas in which communism might be developed; until then it had been lumped with Great Britain. By the mid-thirties, Ireland had no less than seven organisations subordinate to the Third International, as well as a semi-communist I.R.A. and *Cumann na mBan* or female branch of the I.R.A.

Though more advanced than in Connolly's time, the Irish revolutionary situation in the thirties was not ready for a popular communist movement, though, at that time, as Professor Hogan claimed, Irish labour was more open to communist influence than was British labour.[2] Marxist aims affronted the Catholic and individualist preferences of the vast body of the people, in spite of dedicated and intelligent leaders, such as Peadar O'Donnell, Sean MacBride, George Gilmore and Hannah Sheehy-Skeffington. Indeed, it is a paradox that this powerfully organised movement left so little trace upon the national mind. The Irish communist leaders showed their hand too openly, as in public addresses; in the I.R.A. paper, *An Phoblacht*; as well as in a statement of aims in a booklet entitled *Constitutional and Governmental Programme of the Republic of Ireland*. This was indeed the most comprehensive and coherent social programme ever put forward by an Irish political group.

The most ambitious venture of the Irish communists was their attempt to organise an agrarian revolutionary movement through *Saor Eire* (Free Ireland) in 1931. It met with marked initial success, but fell away when it was condemned by the Irish Catholic Church and when its Marxist aims were exposed. This unsympathetic public

[1] Printed by Cahill & Co., Dublin.
[2] Hogan, *ibid.*, p. 134.

reaction had a sobering effect on the Irish communist leaders who henceforth behaved with more caution; and the revolutionary movement took on a more subtle and underground character.

The so-called Fascist movement of General Eoin O'Duffy, an ex-police commissioner, made a wider appeal than did the communism of the I.R.A. Founded in 1933, it was inspired, in part, by continental fascism, pursuing a vaguely defined corporate ideal, and adopting a blue shirt as uniform. It was also inspired, however, by the need for organised defence against the I.R.A. who were threatening public meetings and freedom of speech; and it grew out of the Army Comrades Association founded in 1932 to that end. It became a constituent element in the United Ireland Party, and was closely associated with the pro-Treaty faction which had been dislodged from power by Mr de Valera in 1932. Many of its leaders were Catholic and conservative, and came from the upper middle classes from which the pro-Treaty group and its successor, *Fine Gael*, got so much support. The Blueshirts were harried by the de Valera Government and by the I.R.A. As a result of this and of internal dissensions, the movement broke up in 1936.[1]

Because of their defence of free speech, the Blueshirts may as well be called anti-fascist as fascist. They made a last gesture in sending a force about eight-hundred strong to Spain to aid General Franco. They were reinforced by a new movement, the Irish Christian Front under Patrick Belton, one-time member of de Valera's party. These were practically the only foreign volunteers Franco got, and they enjoyed some prestige on that score.

Closer to the spirit of fascism was Mr de Valera's *Fianna Fail* party, though it had no overt links with the continental movement, no clearly defined fascist ideology, and lacked those superficial trappings – a distinctive shirt, massed meetings and a blatant propaganda – to identify it with that movement. Yet, in essence, its character was the same. It had its hero-leader (*An Taoiscech*), de Valera, and the party machine worked to achieve his total supremacy. In an era of increasing bureaucracy, it was not difficult to plant *Fianna Fail* nominees in political and civil administration, from which even the judiciary was not free. Mr P. McGilligan, speaking in the *Dail* on July 19, 1962, said that it was a 'disgusting argument' to contend that the salaries of the judges should

[1] See T. P. Coogan, *Ireland Since the Rising*, Pall Mall Press, 1966, pp. 79–85.

be raised in order to attract the best men, pointing out that 'there were good men who had never been approached and, so far as the present system went, they never would be'.

The I.R.A. were divided as to whether they should send a militant body to aid the Republican forces in Spain. Frank Ryan, who was prominently associated with the Irish communist movement, was in favour. Sean Russell opposed it on nationalistic grounds; and it was finally decided that I.R.A. members might go as volunteers. About 200 men left under Frank Ryan. They saw hard fighting; and those who returned from Spain proved to be some of the most virulent and anti-religious of Irish revolutionaries.

The division of the I.R.A. over the question of organised help for the Republicans in Spain was intensified when an alliance with Nazi Germany recommended itself to many in the movement. A loss of drive and effective leadership was one result of this, as was shown during the forties. Nazi agents made contact with the I.R.A. in Britain during the thirties, and together they worked out plans for sabotage and the disruption of the British social services. The bombing outrages were a premature result of this collaboration. The I.R.A. figured in the Nazi war plans, especially during the first year of the war when an invasion of Britain was under consideration.

Nazi exploitation of the I.R.A. was limited, however, by rivalry between the German secret services, as well as by defects in the I.R.A. Hermann Goertz, the ablest of the Nazi agents in Ireland, could make little headway with the I.R.A. leader, Stephen Hayes, and soon came to suspect him of being an informer.[1] Nor did anything come of the Nazi attempt to send Sean Russell and Frank Ryan to Ireland to reorganise the I.R.A. Russell died on April 9, 1941, in a submarine taking him to Ireland, and the submarine returned to Germany with Frank Ryan. Ireland's main value to the Nazis was as a centre of espionage, especially in the North where information regarding ship and troop movements was transmitted to Germany through a station on Rathlin Island.

The conservative Irish, unlike the radical, saw little to concern them in the Second World War, failing to appreciate the Nazi threat to freedom and Christianity. Only one Irish member of the *Dail*, James Dillon, publicly protested against Irish neutrality. Mr de Valera saw

[1] *The Jackboot in Ireland*, Sean O'Callaghan, Alan Wingate, 1958.

the Nazi expansion simply as another example of German imperialism as shown in the First World War. From such a standpoint, the war was none of Eire's business; and, in any case, de Valera was opposed to any alliance with Britain which he claimed was keeping Ireland divided.

The position Mr de Valera took laid the basis of Irish neutrality which was to embarrass successive Irish leaders. It had the full backing of the Irish people, cynically glad to be relieved of responsibility. Even the growing threat of communism did not alter Mr de Valera's neutral stand, in spite of the full Irish awareness of the anti-Christian nature of Marxism. In 1949, Mr de Valera refused Irish membership of N.A.T.O. The contradiction in Catholic Eire's neutral policy was bound to reveal itself in time, however; and external criticism of that neutrality was not without effect, such as that made by Winston Churchill and Cordell Hull, U.S. Secretary of State.

Eire's external policy is so bound up with the problem of partition that a brief review of that problem is necessary. Up to 1955, the Irish saw political unity in an external and mechanical sense, that is, as dependent on British goodwill; and efforts to unify Ireland took mainly the form of appeals to, and propaganda against, Britain. This view wore thin, however, for the good reason that the North's decision to remain outside the Dublin Government is clearly its own, and not to be changed by Britain. A new approach was needed; and Ernest Blythe had been urging that the problem was a domestic one, requiring vital adjustments between the Irish communities. In April 1955, a study of partition appeared which suggested that some of these adjustments were external, requiring Eire to join N.A.T.O. and to rejoin the Commonwealth, so as to make common ground with Northern Ireland.[1] On July 12, Liam Cosgrave, Minister for External Affairs, recommended in the *Dail* that a more co-operative external policy would make a contribution to unity. In subsequent years, the external aspect of the partitition question assumed great importance in realist circles in Eire, especially as some began to realise the anomaly of Irish Catholic neutrality, and many to see that Eire's material dependence on the outside world demanded external associations.

What came closest to a Catholic approach to Irish separatism is best

[1] *Divided We Stand*, Michael Sheehy, Faber & Faber.

found in the *Fine Gael* party. It was this party which opened the attack when a member of a coalition government. On April 2, 1956, Premier John Costello, immediately on his arrival from an American tour, launched a strong, if oblique, criticism of Irish separatism. During subsequent months, spokesmen of his party – Liam Cosgrave and Declan Costello – continued to strike this new note whose theme was, in the Premier's words, a criticism of Eire's tendency to see itself as 'a small island and not as the centre of a very historic moral empire'. It was the tragedy of this party – which formally declared an Irish Republic in 1949 – that it failed to sustain its traditional sense of the importance of our links with the external world. This was its central weakness, and led to a rapid decline of the party when its main rival, *Fianna Fail*, under Mr Lemass, adopted a positive external policy which *Fine Gael* did little to support.

The clergy were also becoming uneasy about Irish isolation. They could not altogether miss the implications of a solemn papal plea 'in the name of religion, civilisation, or human feeling . . .' that Western countries should unite in defence of Hungary. In the spring of 1957, Cardinal D'Alton, in an interview with the *Manchester Guardian*, suggested that, in the interests of unity, Eire should join N.A.T.O. and rejoin the Commonwealth – a suggestion he put forward not 'as a churchman but as a citizen'. Was there some covert Catholic motivation behind the Cardinal's suggestion? It is doubtful. By and large, the outlook of the Irish clergy is inspired more by regional feeling than by a Catholic sense of human identity.

This regional outlook is evident in an otherwise fine study of Patriotism by Dr Philibin, Bishop of Clonfert: the text of a lecture he gave to the Social Summer School in Mount Melleray in 1957. While the Bishop admirably points to the need for nationalism to concern itself with the community rather than with the State, he fails to establish the universality of humanity. He does say, in passing, that the 'brotherhood of man is a bigger reality than the distinctiveness of nations,' and refers to those thinkers who 'can foresee no real tranquility or order in the world until it [a narrow nationalism] is subordinated to a wider allegiance'. In practice, however, the Bishop's preoccupations are mainly national. Thus he appears to support the State's language revival and anti-partition policies. He refers to the 'transformation effected in the life of the country and the outlook of the people', even though 'several portions of the ideals aimed at are still unrealised'. But of the world and our links with it, the Bishop has little to say. His main hope is for an Irish 'economic rebirth'; and, indeed, the Bishop played a part in the present industrial revival, suggesting to the civil service economist, Kenneth Whitaker, in 1957 the need for a plan of industrial development. This plan, inviting foreign industrial management and investment in Eire, was put into operation in 1958.

Attempts to rationalise Eire's place in an expanding world show how hard it is to revive a broad human ideal weakened by a protracted regionalist outlook. In his study, *Uniting Ireland* (1958) Donal Barrington deals with the international background of the partition problem. He sees that traditional Irish nationalism is too narrow to permit of unity, and suggests that it should be extended so as 'to meet the needs of a society of men of different origins and different religions'. This could be done, he thinks, 'by drawing on the general civilization which grew up around Christianity and the English-speaking world'. But, as has been pointed out, Eire has made much use of ideas to be found in the English-speaking world. The only European idea official Eire would have nothing whatever to do with was liberalism; and this could have done much to unify Ireland. Mr Barrington makes no reference to this significant omission. Nor does he make any reference to the astringent human outlook of the Irish Catholic clergy, which was the main reason why liberalism was repulsed.

It is a conventional and not a real marriage of Irish and European ideas which Mr Barrington has in mind; a marriage in which the dowry – Irish unity – is the decisive consideration. This must first be secured; it must precede the so-called cultural embrace. Thus Mr Barrington states that 'it is unrealistic to speak of going back to the Commonwealth again except as part of a scheme for uniting Ireland'. But surely it is realism – the need to align ourselves with our principal market and to have a secure place in an economic confederation – which dictates our return to the Commonwealth; whereas unity emerges merely as a by-product of such a return.

In the late fifties, the Green Curtain began to sag, and views of the outside world were opened up for the Irish people who were by this time – apart from holiday trips abroad – largely indifferent to the offer of extended political and cultural horizons. The growth of official liberalism, however, led to the founding of a variety of progressive societies, such as the Dublin Institute of Catholic Sociology, and the Christus Rex Congresses which began in 1955. To open up the outer world there were the Dublin Drama Festival (1958) and, in Cork, International Film and Choral Festivals.

It was economic pressures rather than a Catholic idealism which contributed to a European outlook. Rising emigration and a progressive weakening of Eire's agricultural exports in the British market made for a sense of material dependence and these were reinforced by trends towards European economic integration. As J. M. Dillon, leader of the *Fine Gael* party, put it in the *Dail* on January 18, 1959, 'the whole illusion of national self-sufficiency has blown up'.

Mr Lemass, who became Premier in 1959, was well adapted to exploit the new realism in economic outlook. In contrast with Mr de Valera, he yet possessed hardly less formidable qualities – ruthlessness and a cynical intelligence. His colleagues were disconcerted by a change in leadership which substituted economic statistics for ultra-nationalist ideals. Lemass kept the party together, however. Losing a job to maintain a principle is a rare event in Irish politics, as when Mr Patrick Norton resigned from the Labour Party after its advocacy of extreme socialism in October 1967.

Mr Lemass eased the personal control of his party, which Mr de Valera had rigorously enforced, though it was mainly the progressive members who were allowed to air their views. One of the first rebels was H. Boland – an ex-minister of the party – who on July 7, 1959, sharply attacked Irish neutrality in the *Dail*, urging that 'Eire should not leave a gap in the Western defence of Europe'. From this time on, there were frequent reassessments of Eire's responsibility in the East-West conflict, the effect of which was to suggest that in Premier Lemass' words, 'we were clearly on the democratic side'.

Mr Lemass knew that if Eire could not live apart from Britain, the Commonwealth and Western Europe, then it must join them. But to act openly on the basis of such logic would not have suited the extremists even in his own party, much less the I.R.A. The first years of his premiership were spent in conditioning Irish opinion towards a realistic view of Eire's position. He made no secret of his aim to strengthen external relations, especially with Britain, but he refrained from defining too clearly what he was really after – membership of the Commonwealth and of N.A.T.O. He defended his external moves to the extremists by pointing out that they would help to achieve political unity at home; an argument the extremists could not easily refute.

Eire's participation in the work of the United Nations was one means by which Mr Lemass made the Irish world conscious. In 1960 the Irish Government responded to the U.N. request to send an Irish contingent to the Congo. The immediate reaction to this showed Irish immaturity, and also showed how much work Lemass had cut out for him if he hoped to find public support for his external policy. For the Irish reaction suggested that the Congo crisis was providentially inspired for a display of Irish military genius. 'One would think,' commented Rawle Knox in the *Observer* (Irish Rediscover the Congo) that 'Ireland was the United Nations at least as far as the military side was concerned.'[1]

The Irish were quickly sobered, however, as events in the Congo demonstrated the complexity of the situation into which they had rushed. The experience was an enlarging one, nevertheless, as Irish responsibilities increased with the appointment of General MacKeon to the command of the U.N. troops in the Congo, and Dr Conor Cruise O'Brien to a post in the U.N. administration of the Congo. The Irish adventure, which began on a note not far from farce, soon acquired a note of tragedy, especially when Dr O'Brien attacked Britain and France for supporting financial interests which, he claimed, were stiffening the resistance of the rich Katanga province against U.N. efforts to integrate it in the Congo.

Dr O'Brien's Congo mission and its unhappy outcome was conditioned by the policy adopted by the Irish Department of External Affairs. Eire was admitted to the U.N. in 1955; and, until 1957, the Irish delegation was mainly concerned with airing grievances about partition. It then decided to play a more active role in world affairs, while still remaining neutral. This role suited a liberal like Dr O'Brien who, while keenly interested in world affairs, had divided sympathies on

[1] July 31, 1960.

the East-West conflict. Dr O'Brien acquired much influence in the Department, and became a close adviser of Mr Frank Aiken, Minister for External Affairs.

The liberal line taken by the Irish delegation at the U.N. was little to the taste of anti-Soviet countries, especially America, as also to that of the American Catholic hierarchy. They were disconcerted by a series of Irish resolutions which might just as well have emanated from the British Labour Party as, for instance, on the need to discuss in the U.N. the question of communist China's membership of that body; on the creations of 'areas of law' in highly disturbed regions; and on the need to restrict the spread of nuclear weapons. Dr O'Brien was regarded – as he himself suggests in *To Katanga and Back* – as the main architect of Eire's policy at the U.N. The part he played was highlighted by his conflict with another senior member of the Irish delegation, Eamonn Kennedy, whose stand was more orthodox Catholic or anti-neutralist.

Suspect by the Western powers, Dr O'Brien found some favour with the anti-Western. His ambiguous position contributed (he suggests) to Hammarskjoeld's choice of him for the post in Katanga (*op. cit.*, pp. 39–42). In Katanga, however, Dr O'Brien had much to do with some of the Western countries which distrusted him; and this, no doubt, contributed to make his position in Katanga finally untenable. Part of Dr O'Brien's misfortune lay in the fact that he was associated with Catholic Ireland, from which the Western powers naturally expected a foreign policy more consistent with Eire's frequent condemnations of 'godless communism'. Indeed, it is a paradox that the Irish Government trusted so much to the guidance of a man who could see no great difference in the limitations on freedom in Marxist and some communities in the West:

> I was well aware [he wrote] of the harsh limitations on personal freedom in the Soviet Union, yet I doubted if I would feel less free in the Soviet Union than in South Africa or Portugal, or Spain, or French Algeria, or Guatemala, or Southern Rhodesia or in many other places which are thought to be part of the free world. (p. 34)

Evidently, as the case of Dr O'Brien implies, religion and politics in Ireland are not all of a piece: religion is one thing, politics another. The politics of the Irish clergy is either ultra-nationalistic or it is crudely and naively Catholic. This second type of approach was illustrated by the critical attitude of many of the Irish clergy to the support which the Irish Government gave to the U.N.'s Congo policy. Dr Browne, Bishop of Galway, objected to the use of Irish Catholic soldiers to force Catholic Katanga into the arms of a Soviet-biassed Congo Government.[1] He had much praise for the missionary achievements of the Belgian colonists, omitting to note, however, that they did little for the political education of the native people. He also praised the civilised temper of the rebel province, shown in the treatment of prisoners, as compared with the massacres of religious and others by the Congolese soldiers. A comparable line of criticism was taken by some Catholic laymen, as by Senator Quinlan and Kennedy F. Roche of University College, Cork.

Dr Browne's reasoning has little essential relevance to the question of U.N. intervention in the Congo, which was the result of an invitation by the Congo Government to help maintain order. The main cause of disorder was the secession of Katanga; and this the U.N. sought to remedy. The ideologies of the contending groups were no real concern of the U.N. To be swayed by such considerations as the Bishop advanced would result in a partisanship which would defeat the purpose of the U.N. As the main instrument for the creation of world order, the U.N. performs a profound Catholic function which should not be endangered by ill-judged criticism.

The use of Eire's soldiers in the Lebanon and the Congo enabled Mr Lemass to put a better face on Irish neutrality, suggesting that 'we could make our contribution to a better, more secure and permanent foundation for peace as effectively outside N.A.T.O. as within it'.[2] A few months earlier, Declan Costello provided another argument in support of military neutrality, pointing out that the 'techniques of modern warfare have greatly reduced the importance of this island,' and that the 'West does not really need an Irish base to complete an effective plan of Western Defence'.[3] The main concern of Irish policy, he stated, is 'to maintain the existence of this state as a national entity'. Thus, in fact, he

[1] At Galway, November 21, 1961.
[2] December 1, 1960.
[3] *National Observer*, July–August and September 1960.

placed the needs of the Irish state before 'our predominantly Christian beliefs [which] place us among the implacable foes of communism'. In this way is even one of the most Catholic of Irish politicians caught in a confusion between Catholic and ultra-nationalist ethics.

What Messrs Lemass and Costello left out of their calculations in Western defence is the moral factor; that belief in Western ideals which, in so far as it is vital, holds the West together. It is this faith which provides the real *raison d'être* of a defence, that is, demonstrates the existence of something worth defending. True, one may see N.A.T.O. as a bulwark against communism rather than as a support of Western ideas; and this is, in fact, how no small numbers tend to see it. But an organisation built on fear rather than on faith cannot be strong, and is more in need of moral than of material support. Eire's membership of N.A.T.O. would contribute a quota of confidence in Western ideas, showing Eire's willingness to fight for them: just as it would strengthen America's resolve to defend the West by providing some more evidence of Western faith in its own values. President Kennedy expressed confidence in the West's cause, but 'only if we demonstrate our strong convictions in it'. After all, even the weapons and organisation of defence depend on moral energy, on the existence of those who care enough to put time, energy and money into them. Why should America especially be expected to carry this burden? And why should Eire not prove that it cares, instead of limiting itself to hypocritical assertions of sympathy with Western ideas.

The case for Eire's rejoining the British Commonwealth is a strong one, and can be defended by much the same arguments as those used to support membership of the Common Market. One is stronger inside an economic confederation than outside it, especially if one happens to be vitally dependent on it. Eire's material and social dependence on Britain is considerable, as time has shown: even in numbers alone, over a million Irish have emigrated to Britain since 1922. The Irish in Britain enjoy many of the advantages of Commonwealth membership; and Anglo-Irish affairs still remain in the hands of Commonwealth relations. It is only elementary prudence to safeguard and increase such advantages. By virtue of her ambiguous position vis-à-vis the Commonwealth, Eire managed to escape the net of Britain's immigration restrictions, but not the 15% surcharge on imports which Britain imposed in 1964, and which had a 'severe' effect on the struggling Irish economy.

Premier Lemass was well aware of the material cost of that anti-British feeling which keeps a reluctant Eire loitering on the Commonwealth's doorstep; and on at least two separate occasions he made strenuous, if covert, attempts to get Eire inside the door. The first was revealed in a pattern of events between December 1960 and the following March. There was a debate in the House of Lords on December 14 when a plea, supported by several speakers, was made for better Anglo-Irish relations, and when Lord Wyndlesham hoped that the discussion might 'start up certain thoughts which might be helpful in time'. In the *Guardian* on January 8 there appeared an article by Lord Pakenham – a confidant of the Irish Government – suggesting that Eire should be invited to join the Commonwealth. This was followed in due course by Princess Margaret's visit to Ireland, and later by a visit of Dr Ramsay, Archbishop of York.

The hope that underlay these calculated events was suddenly shattered by the brutal shooting of Constable Anderson in Northern Ireland on January 27. Vice-Premier MacEntee might declare in London shortly before Constable Anderson was shot that 'we have a vast stake in Britain's welfare and in her peace and prosperity', but the I.R.A. made it clear that they would retaliate harshly if Eire made any move towards Britain. What was intended to be the high point in these moves towards an Anglo-Irish *rapprochement* was the visit of the Canadian Premier, Mr Diefenbaker, to Dublin in March. Little was made of this event in the troubled capital, discomforted by extremist tactics, and no doubt by the insistance of die-hards like President de Valera that Irish unity must be an absolute condition of Commonwealth membership. It was later in this year that the Government took strong measures against the I.R.A., which brought them to their knees early in 1962.

It is noteworthy that there exists in Eire no small affection for British royalty, which may be wondered at in the light of history. It was perhaps the wish to exploit this popular liking which lay behind Princess Margaret's visit which had, however, to be handled with caution because of the I.R.A. It is this fanatical minority, rather than the easy-going majority, who are apt to dictate the manner of our public expression regarding Britain. This prejudice was evident in what is, in

fact, an official organ, *Radio Telefis Eireann* – as in its refusal to feature
Princess Alexandra's wedding and, later in 1963, in the cutting of the
Queen's presentation of the Cup at Wembley to the Irish Captain of
Manchester United; and, what was even more remarkable, the omission
of the royal presentation to Tommy Wade at White City in July.
There is little popular relish for this type of bigotry in Eire, as
Senator T. Mullins implied when he urged in the Senate that such
cuts should not be repeated, if only 'to prevent bad language on the
part of the viewers'.

While making overtures to Britain, Mr Lemass sought membership
of the Common Market. This was the most openly acknowledged and
widely accepted of his external projects. Since it was undertaken on the
assumption that Britain would also join, one would have expected
more opposition from the extremists, though *Sinn Fein* complained
about being 'frog-marched' into the community. It came as something
of a shock to the Irish people when Eire's application was adjourned for
examination; a response which reduced the complacence of a people
who had come to regard external associations exclusively from the
viewpoint of its own willingness to join them.

The economic and political situation in Eire at the time was such as to
provide little basis for Irish optimism regarding entry into the Common
Market. Eire's political eligibility could be improved by joining
N.A.T.O. Mr Lemass threw out a feeler when, on February 10, 1962,
Mr O'Morain, Minister for Lands, read a carefully written speech
recommending that Eire should join N.A.T.O. The reaction was unfavourable, challenged as the suggestion was by B. Corish, the Labour
Leader, and even by the *Fine Gael* benches. Indeed, it caused something
of a crisis in the *Fianna Fail* party itself. Messrs Aiken and MacEntee
upheld the traditional refusal to join N.A.T.O. as long as Ireland was
divided. Judging the opposition too great, Mr Lemass blandly denied
in the *Dail* that they, the Government, had any intention of joining
N.A.T.O.

Mr O'Morain's speech illustrates Mr Lemass' oblique technique in
introducing changes of policy. The literal meaning of what was said or
done took second place to their implications; and the reading of the
Irish political scene became something of an art. No Irish politician, for
instance, would, in 1962, raise in cold blood the question of allied

bases in Eire. But on April 24, Robert Briscoe, the wandering Lord Mayor of Dublin, told the World Affairs Council in Los Angeles that Ireland would grant military bases to the United States in return for Irish unity. Mr Briscoe stressed the importance of America's role in the East-West conflict, and pointed out that in the event of an American defeat, 'all the small nations would go overboard'. Since any question of American intervention in Ireland is a patent absurdity, the intention and effect of Mr Briscoe's speech could only be to draw attention to Eire's responsibilities in the ideological war.

Neutrality was the main issue between Mr Lemass and the traditionalists. Mr Lemass cleverly graded, in a positive direction, his successive assertions that, as a democratic and Catholic community, we were not neutral. Each assertion was defended in terms of the previous one, so that the progressive change in foreign policy resembled that children's game which requires you to change your position without being caught changing it. Mr Lemass made a particularly long jump, however, during his tour of the Common Market countries in October 1962, stating at Bonn – when challenged on Irish neutrality – that 'our reason for desiring to join [the Common Market] was primarily political . . . we were making no reservations of any sort, including defence'. On his return to Dublin Mr Lemass informed a very critical *Dail* that 'I did not say anything at Bonn that I did not say already'. No doubt what Mr Lemass said at Bonn may be seen as a logical inference from his oft-repeated statement that Catholic Ireland cannot be neutral in the East-West conflict. But his Irish audience saw this statement as a mere platitude.

Mr Lemass played the Catholic card in the neutrality game with great effect, catching his opponents between their academic profession of a Catholic, and their vital adoption of an ultra-nationalist, political ethic. When Mr Lemass returned from Bonn, he claimed that he had 99% of the people behind him. He was lucky, indeed, if he had the support of 1% of the people whose concern with the Common Market – to the negligible extent to which they were concerned at all – was purely economic, and was entirely out of sympathy with its political aims. Yet, though there was, in fact, little or no positive support for Mr Lemass' policy of political engagement in Europe, nobody had the courage to challenge publicly his assertion that as a Catholic nation we were committed. Any attempt to do so was met with cries of 'Red'; and it was this taunt which halted Dr Noel Browne when he jibed at Mr Lemass that he was turning the East-West conflict into a 'holy war'. Even those closest in spirit to Mr. Lemass' stand, the *Fine Gael* party, gave him little support. Shortly after Mr Lemass' return from Bonn, Mr Richie Ryan, a member of the *Dail*, was assuring a *Fine Gael* meeting at the Mansion House, Dublin, that neutrality was 'honourable', and exposing Mr Lemass' tactics which stressed our involvement abroad and our non-involvement at home.

Neither Mr Lemass nor his opponents wanted to clarify the ideological basis of their disagreement. Mr Corish asked Mr Lemass in the *Dail* 'what were the special circumstances which prevented our joining N.A.T.O. in 1959?' Mr Lemass replied casually that these were 'wellknown'. Mr Corish did not pursue the matter. For while to do so would have embarrassed Mr Lemass by showing that he was no longer ultra-nationalist, it would have incommoded Mr Corish by showing that he refused to take a Catholic stand on the neutrality issue.

The liberal movement inspired by Pope John occurred when the Irish clerical revival was half-a-dozen years old, and this provided a helpful background to Irish efforts, strengthening the hand of the liberal clerical faction. The Irish Catholic Church had lived too long in isolation, enforced and voluntary, to play any worthwhile role in the Catholic world movement, but this movement naturally reinforced Irish trends towards external co-operation, especially in the field of economy. Even as early as 1962, Dr Murphy, Bishop of Limerick, urged that 'when we seemed about to enter E.E.C. we needed to gather together our economic forces of men and money . . . If we did not do this [he warned] we shall drag along as the lame duck of Europe.'[1] By the mid-sixties, the Irish Catholic Church largely accepted the view that the 'economic rebirth' envisaged by Dr Philibin demanded foreign associations. The Irish people had come passively to accept this view; they had, in fact, little or no say in the matter. The only time the Irish public reacted with sympathy to foreign events was when Hungary revolted in 1956; perhaps this awoke echoes of their own plight in 1916.

Eire's growing interest in external life was welcomed abroad; and,

[1] At Limerick, March 11.

no doubt, contributed to President Kennedy's visit to Eire in June 1963, when he did what he could to strengthen the positive tendencies in Eire's foreign policy. It also resulted in a tribute from the *Time* magazine – in an issue of July 12 – accompanied by an acute assessment of contemporary Irish life.

While Eire's place in outside associations remained in the balance, Mr Lemass took advantage of the breathing space to build up Irish industry and – more important – to make it competitive by introducing a 10% tariff each year. He expected to be in the Common Market by 1970, in spite of the fact that Britain's entry met with sharp set-backs, as that administered by President de Gaulle in 1963 and 1967. Mr Lemass' bias towards the continent was probably due to the fact that joining E.E.C. would meet with less opposition at home than would joining Britain and E.F.T.A.; and, indeed, there was talk of 'going it alone' should Britain's application fail. Nevertheless Mr Lemass was well aware of the advantages of a British alignment: the closeness of Britain; its manifest goodwill towards Eire; and the importance of Anglo-Irish trade and of the industrial structure to which it had given rise; and he never ceased trying to improve Anglo-Irish relations.

It was early in 1965 when Mr Lemass made his second serious effort to bring Eire and Britain into closer step. This he did, however, by working simultaneously towards London and Belfast, for stable Anglo-Irish relations depend essentially on coming to satisfactory terms with both. But this was the first time in the history of the Republic that an Irish Government took such an obvious and sensible course.

In Mr Lemass' second, as in his first, overture to Britain in 1960–61, we are left to guess the background moves which resulted in tangible events. The second episode began early in January with the visit of Princess Margaret and Lord Snowdon to Eire. Unlike her previous visit, this one met with opposition from the I.R.A., as if they had an inkling that something was afoot. Trees were felled to obstruct her movements, and there was a large explosion in the region of Abbeyleix House where she was staying. Several members of the I.R.A., involved in these incidents, were charged, and their trials were marked by bloody riots. It was against this incongruous background that the conciliatory moves were made.

On January 14, Premier Lemass visited Stormont at the invitation of the Northern Premier, Captain O'Neill, to discuss 'possibilities of practical co-operation'. Though there was, Mr Lemass stated, no question of surrendering 'basic national aims', it would seem otherwise to judge by the strong Northern response to his visit. For it was a cardinal point of Northern policy, as a senior member of the North Government, Mr Edmond Warnock, pointed out, that there was to be no meeting with Eire's leaders 'unless it was as equals with each regarding the other as a fully sovereign and legitimate government'.

Captain O'Neill came to Dublin on February 9 – the first visit of a Northern Premier since 1921 – and this was followed by visits from other Northern ministers. And, indeed, on February 10, Mr Lemass conceded in the *Dail*, regarding his Northern visit and its implied recognition of the Northern Government, that 'if by recognition is meant approval, I do not regard it as implying this'. On February 2, the Nationalist Party took over from the Northern Labour Party as the Official Opposition. This move was rightly seen by *Sinn Fein* as 'helping to give the North an image of a democracy'. But, indeed, the significance of what was taking place was only too obvious to the extremists; and Hugh McAlteer, brother of the leader of the Nationalist Party in Northern Ireland, described Mr Lemass' visit as the 'greatest betrayal since 1916'.[1]

The tactical recognition of Northern Ireland and the settlement of the vexatious partition issue was another great achievement for Mr Lemass. In the Republic's elections of April 1965, there were no *Sinn Fein* candidates; though this did not mean that the ideal of political unity lacked strong support, even in high quarters, such as in President de Valera and Mr Aiken. If there was anything in this achievement to regret, it was the manner in which it was done – the tacit rejection of a traditional ideal without open admission or explanation – and a consequent sense of betrayal felt by the extremists. This deviousness marred an administration in many other respects statesmanlike.

As Dublin and Belfast reached closer understanding, so did Dublin and London, as shown not only in a closer collaboration between the Governments, but in an unwonted exchange of civilities. On February 23, the remains of Roger Casement were returned to Ireland – 'another step', commented Mr Lemass, 'towards the establishment of

[1] At Trinity College, Dublin, February 3.

178

the closest and most friendly relations between the two countries'. The British Premier, Mr Harold Wilson, was guest of honour at a St Patrick's Day banquet at the Irish Club in London, to which a representative of the *Belfast Telegraph* was also invited.

The fruit of the Anglo-Irish negotiations resulted in the establishment of a Free Trade Area between Britain and Eire in an agreement of December 14, 1965. The last remaining British protective duties on Irish industrial goods were abolished, and Eire benefited by a direct participation in British agricultural subsidies. In return, British industrial exports were to have free access to Eire; a yearly 10% reduction of Irish tariffs would result in their complete disappearance by 1975. Thus was renewed a natural and historic trade association, making for Anglo-Irish economic integration, and uniting the destinies of both counties whether within or without the Common Market. It was also a prudent move for Eire in its hopes to join the Common Market, forcing its industry to become competitive. This Free Trade agreement is the most important politico-economic development in the history of free Eire – a marked achievement for Mr Lemass and Mr Wilson.

The closer ties between Dublin, Belfast and London, naturally aggravated the extremists on both sides of the Border; and the year 1965 was marked by much political unrest – riots, bomb throwing, sporadic shooting. In Eire this opposition was petulant and ineffectual, as expressed, for instance, in the blowing up of Nelson's Pillar in Dublin. In the North, opposition was more grave and seriously threatened the O'Neill regime. It centred round the fanatic personality of the Rev Ian Paisley, Moderator of the Free Presbyterian Church of Ulster, who was imprisoned for three months for unlawful assembly at a rally of the Presbyterian Church in Belfast. Such extremism, however, lost its *raison d'être* after the virtual acknowledgment of the Northern Government by Eire, though extreme nationalists tried to keep alive the ideal of political unity. The strength of Northern moderate opinion which helped to keep Captain O'Neill in office owed much to the preparatory work done by a group of Northern liberals, which included Brian Maginess, John Sayers, Editor of the *Belfast Telegraph* which was the platform of the liberal movement, and Sir Graham Larmor, an ex-president of the Northern-inspired Irish Association which has worked patiently for improved relations between the Irish communities.

Towards the end of 1966, Mr Lemass relinquished the leadership of his party to Mr Jack Lynch. It was a regrettable resignation of the most effective political leader free Eire has so far produced. In the politico-economic field his achievement was remarkable; a *tour de force* of magnitude, since it was really a one-man job, done with little effective support from any quarter. No doubt it was not unwelcome to the clergy frantic at the loss of their congregations, and willing to go to any lengths (except education, of course) to keep them at home. His achievement reflects on the essentially autocratic character of the Irish political system which stands or falls by the quality of its leadership. That Mr Lemass could so flagrantly ignore widespread opposition (which he treated with a barely concealed contempt) is an aspect of the immaturity of a people who, until recently, were never encouraged to grow up.

Popular Irish interest in politics was renewed in the late sixties by the students of the National University who revived the revolutionary tradition which had been attenuated by the pacificism of de Valera and the realism of Lemass and Lynch. With the stress on Connolly rather than on Pearse, Irish undergraduates were brought into line with those in the outside world, reflecting the wide-spread anti-American bias especially regarding America's role in Vietnam, which the Irish Government supports. This sympathy with the forces of Marxism and revolution found a powerful advocate in the *Irish Times* which derided President Johnson's view that the war in Vietnam is a 'war of morality'.[1] The radical trend in Irish undergraduate opinion suggests a popular swing to the left, which may finally reverse the moderate tendencies in Irish politics since Mr Lemass became premier.

[1] *Irish Times*, February 14, 1968.

CHAPTER XI

The Individual, the Welfare State and the Church

IT IS OFTEN SAID that the Irish Catholic clergy want ignorant people so as to remain top-dogs and lord it over their congregations. There may well be some truth in this, but a more significant explanation is that the clergy see backwardness as a condition of Catholic loyalty; or did, at any rate, until recently. Consequently, their bugbear is education. The only important occasion when the Irish Catholic Church interfered publicly with the Irish Government was on an educational issue, when, in 1948, Dr Noel Browne, a Minister for Health in a Coalition Government led by Mr John Costello, introduced as part of a Health Bill educational training for all mothers. The Irish Catholic Church vetoed the Bill which was then dropped by the Government.

The Health Bill was on the lines of the British National Health Service legislation. It aimed principally at reducing the high infant mortality rate which was then in the region of fifty per cent higher than in Britain and Northern Ireland. The Irish hierarchy objected that the pre-natal instruction embodied in the Bill would lead to the spread of practices – such as birth control – which are opposed to the moral teaching of the Catholic Church. As Dr Browne gave an assurance that such education under the Bill would conform strictly to Catholic teaching, the clerical objection amounted to little more than the reactionary assumption that education is unacceptable because of the risks implicit in it. In point of fact, Pope Pius XII later advocated pre-natal instruction, a course of which is now being given in Dublin.

It is true that the clergy objected to Dr Browne's Scheme on another score. As it offered free maternal care to 'all' mothers and 'all' children, regardless of their means, the hierarchy rightly claimed that this was opposed to Catholic individualism, transferring to the State an obligation which primarily belongs to the individual and the family. Some British critics of the Welfare State have made the same point, which, in Henry Fairlie's words, means that 'the State should do what the people cannot do themselves, no more . . .'[1] It is hard to believe, however, that this objection of the hierarchy was intended seriously because, if so, why did they not object to the Childrens' Allowances which, under previous legislation, are also given to all parents?

Any real objection to Irish socialism ought surely to express itself in a condemnation of the general trend of Irish Government policy which is clearly marked by the growth of State management as against private initiative. It is precisely this feature which impressed American critics who remarked on the paradox that a Catholic government 'has gone further towards nationalisation than even Britain's socialists advocate'.[2] But there has been no general condemnation by the Church of socialist policies. Such criticisms as are made are, as a rule, of a general character. Such, for instance, was the address by the Rev James Kavanagh on *The State and Economic and Social Policy*. Fr Kavanagh condemned the 'arid materialism' of socialism and the 'State idolatry' of totalitarianism, but characteristically left it to his listeners to infer that he was dealing with Eire.[3]

The difficulty of the Irish Catholic Church is that it cannot condemn socialism effectively unless it advocates individualism. Its dilemma is that it refuses to accept either. It is opposed to socialism on doctrinaire, and to individualism on hidden Jansenist grounds. Thus, when the hierarchy condemned Dr Browne's scheme, the bishops made no real attempt, by an appeal to the public and the medical profession, to ensure that the benefits of the scheme would be provided by voluntary activity. The hierarchy did later acquiesce in a modified State Health Scheme, which shows that the Scylla of socialism is to be preferred to the Charybdis of individualism.

It was mainly because of its harmful effects on the Irish emigrants that the Irish clergy began to modify their reactionary attitude to criticism and thought. Estimates vary a good deal as to the extent to which Irish emigrants in Britain lose their religion. It is put at between twenty

[1] *Time and Tide*, January 13, 1961.
[2] *Time*, July 12, 1963.
[3] At a Christus Rex Congress in Galway, April 26, 1962.

and twenty-five per cent by the Bishop of Cork. Halliday Sutherland quotes an official of the Legion of Mary as saying that twenty-five per cent were 'worthy Catholics', twenty-five per cent 'unworthy Catholics', and fifty per cent gave up their religion.[1] In *Vive Moi* Sean O'Faolain quotes an English Catholic bishop as saying that sixty-five per cent of Irish emigrants 'stopped practising their religion'. The losses were big enough at any rate to induce the Irish Catholic Church to create in England a missionary group to help the stragglers and to bring back those who had strayed from the fold. Telling disclosures must lie behind such a change in policy, for until the mid-fifties it was usual for the Irish clergy to contend that Irish emigrants were little short of lay missionaries.

A distressing feature of Irish emigration is that many of the emigrants are so young. One in five are under eighteen years, a fact which led Fr Owen Sweeney, ex-director of the Irish Centre in London, to call for legislation 'to control the emigration of children'.[2] According to Fr Sweeney, loneliness is the main reason why emigrants 'lapsed'. It is certainly one of them, for the Irish emigrant meets with little welcome or understanding from the Catholic community in England. The piety evident in the Church is not conspicuous in the street where the Catholic eye is cold and indifferent. This callous lack of concern reflects particularly on the substantial body of educated Irish in England who make little effort to meet so poignant a challenge. This body is more successful than the uneducated in keeping the faith – as they understand it.

Irish backwardness is mainly a feature of rural life where the inhibiting control of the clergy is most complete. It is the rural community which provides the bulk of the emigrants, that 'export of raw labour' which the Rev Dr Cusack sees as 'one of the most urgent problems confronting the country at the present time'. It is rural life which offers the clearest evidence of social breakdown. Here the parish priest is the dominant influence, the mainstay of reaction; a man who is himself 'just about as well-informed as a well-informed peasant', as Liam O'Flaherty noted in his *Tourist Guide to Ireland*.

[1] *Irish Journey*, p. 166. 'W.C.' hears Mass on Sundays and goes to Holy Communion once a month; 'U.C.' goes to Mass and Holy Communion at Easter.
[2] May 1967.

The loss of faith by Irish emigrants in England is due, in part, to the constraints under which they live in Ireland, especially in rural Ireland, constraints which conditioned them to the practice of religion out of fear of priestly and public censure. Life in the 'valley of the squinting windows' may easily turn what should be a private devotion into a public performance. In Ireland, whatever one's beliefs, it is more convenient to go to church than not to go; for a refusal to go means public gossip and criticism; appeals from relations and friends; disputes with the clergy; possibly even the endangering of one's employment or promotion. One result of this is a great deal of hypocrisy in the practice of religion, especially in the rural areas, the extent of which only God alone knows. It is easy to understand the sense of liberation which comes to Irish youth in London or Manchester, where he (or she) can do just as he pleases; and it is evident that here only a genuine religion can save him from the influence of an environment where formal religion counts for little. The sad thing is that the Irish clergy exploit these social constraints, adopting methods – such as reading publicly the amounts the parishioners pay in dues – which degrade rather than ennoble. In this one may find further evidence of their failure to see the human mind as vital and responsible, and the spiritual life as a genuine and generous acceptance of grace by the human spirit.

Rural Ireland has been most unhappily conditioned. Historically, the Irish farmer has been the pawn of arbitrary British rule, at the mercy of government and landlord. Consequently, he has lacked an opportunity for self-expression. He was even without the political experience of the urban dweller who had the urban council under the Local Government Act of 1898. The farmer had to be content with the county council, no parish councils being set up under the Act. Against such a background, it should not be hard to guess the outcome of a paternalist Irish government policy and a clerical policy which, until recently, aimed at keeping the people ignorant.

The approach of the Irish Catholic Church to the rural problem is typified by that of Dr Lucey, Bishop of Cork and Ross, the most forceful and energetic of clerical sociologists. The Bishop's many pronouncements on social questions – made mostly in the form of addresses at Confirmation ceremonies throughout his diocese – provide a rare opportunity of observing the Irish clerical mind at work. It is very instructive. It may be objected that there are more liberal bishops in Ireland than the Bishop of Cork, but it is reasonable to assume that, basically, the views of the Bishop of Cork are representative enough of those of the body of the Irish Catholic hierarchy. It must be remembered, however, that the Bishop of Cork has tried, with what ever degree of success or failure, to deal publicly with the Irish social problem; a compliment one can pay to not all of his colleagues.

Dubbed by the politicians as the 'prophet of doom and gloom', the Bishop has, since 1954, constantly drawn attention to the 'catastrophic' rural decline, and insisted on the need for social measures to check it. So far, however, he has shown a reluctance to counter it with an individualist policy. On the contrary, he has constantly pressed for a State solution. Indeed, the present industrial revival owes something to the Bishop's efforts. The Bishop is not too happy, however, about making the State responsible for the decay of rural life. His instinct for Catholic orthodoxy has led him to intersperse his appeals for State action with other appeals directed to the community itself. So far, these have been ineffectual, for the Bishop shies away from any form of vital individualism.

The Bishop has often enough criticised the bureaucracy of Irish Government which has squeezed out popular life, leaving it like a used orange. 'You can starve out private enterprise as well as buy or force it out of existence,' he complained, 'but the result is the same, a socialistic economy and we are certainly heading for that at the present time.'[1] Yet he has done little to ensure a loosening of the State's stranglehold on the community. The industrial policy he favours has, in fact, intensified state controls. He has not, except within narrow limits, sought to improve education. He has not advocated rural co-operatives. He has not even encouraged popular rural movements like *Muintir na Tire* and *Macra na Feirme*.[2] He has, indeed, shown a clerical distrust of such movements.

Dr T. Morris, Archbishop of Cashel and Emly, a former Recording Secretary and energetic advocate of *Muintir na Tire* noted 'that community organisation was not simply a freak, was a proposition that was

[1] At Cork, February 10, 1956.
[2] See the Bishop's Minority Report in the Reports of the Commission on Emigration, Dublin, 1956.

gaining recognition . . . It was reassuring [he said] to find experts from abroad who readily classified *Muintir na Tire* as an Irish form of community development.'[1] Who, one wonders, is responsible for the idea that a simple rural organisation, founded in 1937 by a Catholic priest, Canon Hayes, should still be considered a 'freak'. The Archbishop went on to say that he was 'confident that the community postulate would figure more largely in our social thinking'. Whom is His Grace seeking to convert – the clergy or the people? One of the biggest obstacles to the progress of *Muintir na Tire* was the clergy themselves; and much of Canon Hayes' time was spent in persuading parish priests to give support to the movement. For this purpose he was glad to use a recommendation from Pope Pius XII who wrote to him in 1954 that

> In order to promote the practice of justice and charity in each one's immediate surroundings, *Muintir na Tire* fosters the spirit of neighbourliness and self-reliance, and it inspires individuals to devote themselves to the good of the community even at the cost of personal sacrifice.

It is strange, indeed, that the backing of a Pope is not sufficient guarantee of a social movement in Catholic Ireland, and that foreign experts are needed to confirm anything so elementary as that *Muintir na Tire* is 'an Irish form of community development'.

Typical of the Bishop of Cork's approach to the rural problem was his appeal to the government to set up an industry in the West Cork islands, asserting that a 'few thousand would make the difference between decay and development'.[2] The Bishop, it seems, does not realise that rural depopulation is the result of an organic breakdown of the rural mind due to small-mindedness and ignorance. Consequently, he does not see reform as something to be achieved through spiritual means – through education – but through material reorganisation. This is exactly the position adopted by the socialists. It is not as if the Bishop lacked a solution along Catholic or co-operative lines, whose success Denmark and East Canada have amply demonstrated.

The Bishop objects to rural mechanisation. Industry may have

[1] At Cashel, August 15, 1960.
[2] May 27, 1954.

machines but not agriculture. This curious attitude shows the cultural insensitivity of the clergy who deny the use of machinery where it would do least harm. The Bishop defends his opposition to rural mechanisation on the grounds that it is not economic. 'Mechanisation as such adds nothing whatever to the production of the land', he stated cryptically, and advised farmers to find out by experiment 'how much cheaper human labour is in reality', that is, in economic terms.[1] The logic of such a view would take us back behind the horse-drawn plough to the spade and fork. The Bishop went on to add that what sealed the case against the machine was that it was an 'imported' commodity. The Bishop seems to be thinking in pre-industrial terms which have, unfortunately, little relevance today. National self-sufficiency is a dead letter; and imports of machinery needed to make farming competitive are indispensable.

The Bishop may well be right in contending that Irish farming is over-mechanised, that 'the farmer has too much money put into machinery most of which is lying idle most of the year'.[2] But why has the farmer put so much money into machinery since he is slow to invest otherwise in his farm? Is it because he is tight-fisted and will not pay the labourer a decent wage? Farm labourers are leaving Ireland at the rate of 5,000 a year. In that case, over-mechanisation is the price he has to pay for his own shortsightedness. Or is it because the inefficiency of Irish farming makes it impossible for him to pay a good wage? In that case, the answer is to educate the farmer until he can create a co-operative organisation on which efficiency finally depends. The Irish farmer will not share machinery; he must own what he uses. It is the small-holders who suffer most from this lack of organisation – they are leaving their farms at the rate of 10,000 a year – and it is the elimination of the small-holder which specially worries the Bishop. But the Bishop is averse to making any criticism of the farmer himself. Indeed, he thinks the Irish farmer 'neither lazy nor inefficient'.[3] By what standards is he judging – pre- or post-industrial? Does he think the Irish farmers are efficient in the sense that the Danes are, or that they need to be?

The Bishop of Cork's appeal for individual action does not really

[1] At Cork, June 29, 1956.
[2] At Kilmichael, Co. Cork, May 30, 1960.
[3] At Ballyroe, Co. Cork, June 29, 1956.

envisage an educational programme or any organised effort such as that required by a co-operative movement:

> What I would like to stress [he wrote] is the value of individual effort. It is much easier for a thousand individuals to provide employment for an extra man than it is for the State or an organisation to provide factories employing thousands . . . The obligation to provide work is not primarily the Government's, it is the property owners'. And it rests not on big business alone but on all according to their means.[1]

But if the obligation to provide work is not primarily the Government's, why does the Bishop appeal mainly to the Government to provide it. He suggests that since the Government has made itself, in fact, mainly responsible for social well-being, it is up to the Government to find a solution:

> . . . emigration is neither by an act of God nor by the choice of the people. It is by force of circumstances which the State could and should alter, particularly now that we have a government of our own, that has taken to itself so much of the country's economy.[2]

But this is really no way out. The Bishop knows that Catholic individualism demands that the individual should shoulder his full measure of social responsibility, and that his failure to do so must impair his moral energy and initiative. It is true that many Catholic publicists see the Church as neutral between different political systems. Dr Herlihy, the Bishop of Ferns, stated that 'the Church was bound to no particular form of human culture, not to any political, economic or social ideology'.[3] Pope John XXIII in his encyclical *Pacem in Terris* suggests that no political system is undesirable if it benefits the people. The Catholic social position is, however, more truly stated by Pius XI in *Quadragesimo Anno*:

> It is indeed true, as history clearly proves, that owing to changed circumstances much that was formerly done by small groups can nowadays only be done by large associations. None the less, just as it is wrong to withdraw from the individual and commit to the group

[1] *Blarney Magazine*, Summer 1957, p. 17.
[2] At Ballinasloe, Co. Galway, August 15, 1958.
[3] In Dublin, June 19, 1966.

what private enterprise and industry can accomplish, so too it is an injustice, a grave evil and a disturbance of right order, for a larger and higher association to arrogate to itself functions which can be performed efficiently by smaller and lower societies. This is a fundamental principle of social philosophy, unshaken and unchangeable . . .

The Bishop thinks that the Government 'could and should' revive rural society. But how? Hardly through the provision of extra material assistance, since Irish agriculture is already heavily subsidised by the State – over £50 million a year. The Bishop's main suggestion is the provision of new industries. But the recently established industries do not really effect the rural problem at all. These industries are mainly for export and include *inter alia* a shipbuilding yard, an oil refinery; the manufacture of cranes, sewing machines, refrigerators, transistor radios; motor car and cycle assembly. What have these to do with the rural community? Are they not simply a stop-gap, an artificial urban development, designed not really to keep the people on the farms but to hold them in the towns, and so prevent them from emigrating. The Bishop seems content enough with this. 'Is it not better,' he asked, 'that we should have our people in a German factory in West Cork than in an English factory in Lancashire; working for a foreigner at home than working for a foreigner abroad?'[1]

The Bishop has no liking for foreigners – except as employers and tourists. He objects to the alien resident. There have been many such who have bought properties especially along the coastal districts, as in the West Cork area. The Bishop referred derisively to 'nests' of foreigners.[2] He notes, possibly with some justice, that foreigners are more punctilious about insisting on their property rights than are native owners. He deplores the fact that 'every farm taken over means one emigrant more for England, one Irish family less for the parish'. Such considerations, however, hardly justify the Bishop in advocating what amounts to a boycott of resident aliens. 'People should let them see,' he urged, 'that they are not wanted. Farmers should be patriotic enough not to sell to the foreigner, even though it

[1] At Cork, November 20, 1960.
[2] At Skibbereen, April 29, 1962.

means resisting a tempting price.' Such sentiments seem incongruous in a Christian bishop, of whom more might be expected than mere patriotism. The Bishop may possibly regard 'nests of foreigners' as centres of contamination, despoilers of native innocence, but if so, there is not much he can do about it without violating Christian charity. It is an irony of Irish clerical social policy that in making rural Ireland a cul-de-sac for the native Irish seeking life, it has also made it a refuge for escapists from abroad.

The important fact remains that the rural decline is mainly the outcome of clerical and not of Government policy. True, the Government might try to revitalise the rural people by educating them, by giving them a sense of initiative and responsibility. But would the Bishop of Cork back them if it did? It is very doubtful. Education is the last resort of the Irish clergy: they have to be driven to it. Indeed, they are being driven to it, but so slowly that educational improvements lag far behind real needs. It is notorious that secondary education is much less advanced in the rural than in the urban areas. The number of children receiving secondary education in Eire is the lowest percentage of any population in Western Europe, and the expenditure per child is the lowest obtaining in most of the progressive countries in the world. Northern Ireland, for example – an area less than quarter the size of the Republic – spends twenty-two million pounds on education as compared with nineteen million in the Republic.

The Bishop of Cork got round to education by 1960, after six years of intensive concern with the rural problem. He is chary of vocational and technical instruction which is the most vital branch of Irish education. This, he thinks, should not be available to the rural worker between the ages of fourteen and eighteen because it disorientates him from the land.[1] It may well do so in a situation where rural life is stagnant, and the prevailing wish of the young is to gain a proficiency which will enable them to get a job in industry, or to emigrate. In the present circumstances, rural youth is apt to emigrate anyway, and its lack of technical education means that it must join one of the lowest strata of Britain's labour force. The Bishop of Cork's qualified view of technical instruction is not entirely shared by the hierarchy. Dr Staunton, Bishop

[1] At Dunmanway, Co. Cork, May 22, 1960.

of Ferns, made a strong plea for technical training which would help people to 'develop the skill and craftsmanship now necessary to build our place in the world'.[1]

The Bishop of Cork said of primary education in the rural areas that it is 'worse than defective – it is positively baneful in a number of ways'.[2] The only significant criticism he makes of it, however, is that it is 'bookish and urban'. This is quite true, no doubt. Rural education has little distinctively rural about it, and serves to orientate the mind of rural youth towards urban life and employment. Conscious of this, the Government is thinking of introducing 'more general teaching of nature study into the schools'.[3] This is not its only serious defect, however. There is also a fanatical language policy which aims to make Gaelic the spoken language and the medium through which other subjects are taught. This has a retarding effect on students who, in rural areas, usually leave school at the age of fourteen.

The Bishop of Cork sympathises with the Gaelic Revival, and is 'all in favour of maintaining compulsory Irish, as we know it, in the schools . . .'[4] Yet the clergy are well aware how defective is teaching through an imperfectly understood language, and have long forbidden the teaching of Christian doctrine through Gaelic to English-speaking children. No doubt, the study of the Incomprehensible through the medium of the incomprehensible is an irony which is too much even for the clergy. Dr Lucey, apparently, sees nothing amiss in a Christian bishop urging a regional language at a time of social expansion when its effect must be to separate communities. He noted that it was not only the duty of a bishop to 'help people to be Christ-like and to save their souls . . . he must also have a thought for temporal values'.[5] But surely what temporal values suggest at the present time is an international language which would help to eliminate the national hate which divides communities, and create a sense of human identity.

The success of the Gaelic Revival the Bishop sees as depending on the Gaelic-speaking areas, whose decline is shown in the Ballingeary parish.

[1] At Wexford, June 9, 1959.
[2] At Kilmurray, Co. Cork, May 5, 1960.
[3] Programme for Economic Expansion, 1958, pp. 21–2.
[4] At Ballingeary, Co. Cork, May 1, 1956.
[5] *Irish Times*, January 11, 1964.

There, he pointed out, the numbers of baptisms fell away as follows: 270 in 1845; 109 in 1856; 57 in 1925; and 35 in 1955. To halt this decline, the Bishop suggests a 'factory with compulsory Irish'. It would be hard to think of anything less inspired.

On occasion, however, doubts have assailed His Lordship about the orthodoxy of the Gaelic Revival, and given some hint of the spiritual dichotomy which exists in Eire today. At Bandon on April 13, 1958, the Bishop charged the State with a misdirection of energies inspired by ultra-nationalist ideas, and with a failure to fulfil its Catholic function, namely, 'to promote the peace and prosperity of the country'. But the Bishop's unease about ultra-nationalism – like his doubts about socialism – has so far reached no critical point. He goes on tolerating, even accepting, both in practice.

To say, as does the Bishop of Cork, that rural education is 'bookish and urban' is not to say that it is the right education in the wrong place. Irish education is of little value either in town or country, creating neither thought nor sensibility. T. J. McElligott, himself a teacher, describes the stultifying mentality which conditions Irish education, and how a chronic fear of vitality has banished independent minds from the schools, thus making for an overall conventionality of outlook:

As matters stand [he wrote] the secondary schools are scared of ideas, scared of discussion, scared of simply being different. Because of this, people of independent views with the courage to make known such views are few, and the disappearance of such sources of spontaneity and independence must have a cumulative effect on the climate of political and intellectual life which it is almost impossible to overestimate.[1]

It is easy to subvert a system of education by reversing the process implied in the Latin root of the word. This changes a slow, organic process of expansion into one of compression by superimposing on the mind undigested facts and conclusions – a technique popularly known as 'cramming'. Dr Philibin commented on book-learning in our schools which 'often means no more than a facility in memorising coupled with speed and accuracy in writing down what has been memorised'.[2]

[1] *Irish Times*, October 26, 1961.
[2] At Kilkee, March 31, 1961.

This memorative process was described by Professor John O'Meara as 'dishonesty and fraud', leading the students to 'shirk issues, to practise a measure of deceit, to admitting to tedious, unintelligent and frustrating occupation'.[1]

If the schools are to create some real thinking, both the teachers and students need more latitude, more time to discuss subjects and to develop vital, personal attitudes. It was the 'impersonality' of the Irish system of education which the Rev Denis Hickey, Lecturer in Philosophy at the Servite Priory, Co. Tyrone, criticised at a social Study Conference in Carlow on August 8, 1967. He saw that the system lacked 'creativity' and was one 'in which Socrates would have been a poor teacher'. This is because the method of teaching is informative rather than questioning, memorative rather than analytical. Examiners should insist on originality, on ideas that show individual judgment, and are not mechanically taken from teacher and text book. Examinations are pivotal. The schools will provide the kind of knowledge examiners want, whether vital or conventional. Where there is any doubt about this, the schools will use a 'cramming' system which gets more immediate results.

The Irish people see education as a means for getting jobs. Few care about what is taught, or how it is taught. Apart from showing resentment about the compulsory study of Gaelic, the public ignore what is going on in the schools. This apathy is the result of a past in which to criticise education was one of the surest ways of becoming suspect by the clergy. More freedom to criticise in recent years has so far failed to find much public response; and it is ironic to observe some of the more liberal clergy trying to awaken a public conscience once so carefully put to sleep. In the *Sunday Independent* some years ago, the Rector of Mungret College, Rev G. Perrott, S.J., made a courageous appeal to parents:

The question I would like to ask is this – are you Irish Catholic parents getting the education you want for your children? And if not what are you doing about it? If you are not getting the education you want, you should be parading the streets with placards and the slogan 'Give us back our children'.

There is too much hesitation among parents in this matter . . . Parents are too slow to criticise either the schools or the State. They

[1] At Waterford, February 17, 1961.

are slow to criticise the schools perhaps because they are conducted by religious or priests for the most part. And they are slow to criticise the State because perhaps so many of them depend on the State for their livelihood. If that is so, we are in a serious condition. We talk of the tyranny of custom. We could also talk of the tyranny of system. We need organisations to bring the parents together. We want to hear the parents.

Even a sound primary education is not enough for Irish rural society whose needs are really greater than the urban, since rural life demands a profound reorganisation. It will need great effort on the lines of the People's High School in Denmark to change the backward farmer into a member of an organic community. The real need is for a vision large enough to integrate farming not merely into Irish life but into a rapidly changing world environment. This can come only from liberal studies – such as the arts, literature and history – with which the Danes have for long wisely supplemented instruction in the material techniques and the principles of co-operative farming.

In a profound assessment of Irish religious education, Fr Brendan O'Mahoney noted that the 'main defect of religion in modern Ireland lies in the sphere of education'. Professor O'Mahoney pointed out that Catholic principles make little or no impact on Irish education, whether at the primary, secondary or university levels.[1] And, indeed, recent educational reforms have little relevance to Catholic principles, or indeed, to vital social principles. So it is with the post-primary day school scheme, promulgated in May 1963, to cater for children between the ages of twelve to sixteen years. Mainly academic and scientific in character, these schools are likely to guide the young, not towards the land, but towards the secondary and technical school. When introducing the scheme, Dr Hillary, Minister for Education, stressed that 'since we are on the threshold of industrial expansion, the time has come for a firm step towards technical instruction'. It looks as if the educational needs of rural society must wait on the passing of the Government's obsession with urban life and manufactures.

The Irish Government envisages a large expansion in secondary and higher education, evidenced, for instance, in the provision of free

[1] *Irish Times*, December 13, 1967.

secondary education for all Irish children, as also in the decision to introduce 'free' university education in October 1968. A Report of the Commission on Higher Education, published in August 1967, recommended the establishment of New Colleges – a kind of superior secondary school run on academic and vocational lines – which would increase the number of those in receipt of higher education to a total of 26,000 by the mid-seventies, that is, fifty per cent more than the figure for the mid-fifties. In a quantitive sense, the new Irish reforms are impressive, but how they reflect on the more important issue – the quality of education – remains to be seen.

The rot in Irish education may be seen in the state of the universities which, as Professor John O'Meara frankly admitted in the *Irish Times* (April 8, 1968), exercise little influence on the course of Irish life. There are exceptions, no doubt, such as the frankly critical Michael Viney of Trinity College, Dublin, Professor John M. Kelly of University College, Dublin, and Professor Aloys Fleischmann who has worked so tirelessly and thanklessly to raise the musical standards of Cork city. The natural tendency of university life to stagnate in comfortable isolation has been aggravated by a preference for appointing safe mediocrities to teaching staffs. These make careers rather than scholarships their main concern, so that academic life has degenerated into feuds and rivalries whose venom recalls Christopher Hollis' dictum that the 'only sort of politics that are even worse, more bitter and unscrupulous than service politics are academic politics.'

It hardly surprises that Irish university teachers had only a limited influence on undergraduates when they took the bit between their own teeth in the late sixties. An inept or dishonest teacher makes for a restive pupil especially when honesty of thought and expression is on the increase. The vital trend in Irish undergraduate opinion is radical; as shown, for instance, in the intemperate challenge which Logos – a Catholic student society in University College, Dublin – repeatedly offered to Dr McQuaid, Archbishop of Dublin, during 1967-68.

The question of who controls Irish education has often been argued. The Bishop of Cork may well be right in claiming that 'the Church has little enough direct control in Irish education'.[1] But would he be willing to admit that it has considerable indirect control? The greater part of

[1] At Kilmurray, Co. Cork, May 5, 1960.

secondary education is managed by religious orders, by the Christian Brothers and nuns. Professor O'Meara referred to a view current in the teaching body that the 'clerical and religious owners of the majority of the secondary schools were responsible for arranging that the secondary teaching career be unattractive in the beginning so that lay people be discouraged from entering, and so leave the field mainly to the religious'.[1]

The growing part which religious orders are playing in Irish education has been causing unrest among lay teachers who see their livelihood or promotion threatened. Some years ago, the Irish National Teachers Organisation took a determined stand in a dispute with the Marist Brothers in charge of Ballina national school on the question of the promotion of lay teachers. Conditions of 'cold war' existed for a number of years between the religious and the lay teachers in the school, followed by a strike of the lay teachers. The dispute was even referred to Rome, and the outcome was a compromise.

In regard to the primary schools, the parish priest acts as school manager. He appoints the teachers to the school, subject to the sanction of the Department of Education. The Department decides educational policy, the curriculum and the method of teaching. Then there is the teachers' trade union, I.N.T.O., whose influence, according to the Bishop of Cork, 'though not channelled in any statutory form, is all pervasive'. Thus Irish education is shaped by three bodies, the State, the Church and I.N.T.O. Where among them lies the responsibility for a system of primary education which, according to the Bishop of Cork, is 'worse than defective', and a system of secondary education which, according to Dr Philibin, does not educate at all?

There is no hard and fast answer to the above question. It poses the characteristic difficulty of defining Church influence on Irish life. In theory, the Department of Education is responsible. The Department is, or was, notoriously reactionary. Up to 1961, writes T. P. Coogan, 'the Department's job was conceived as little more than a plumber's'. Recent ministries, however (under Hillary, Colley, O'Malley and Lenihan), have been active, as evidenced in the first serious educational reforms since the establishment of the Irish Free State. The vitality of the Department of Education really depends on the growth of Irish

[1] At Waterford, February 17, 1961.

clerical liberalism, in regard to which Departmental policy may be seen as a measure or index.

As yet, the teachers have little effective freedom. They work under the Department of Education and in conjunction with the clergy and religious bodies. The Bishop of Cork claims that their influence is 'all pervasive'. But one wonders what it pervades, apart from the teachers' private circles. The Bishop is no doubt right in contending that they can be dismissed only for 'grave faults'. But there are other ways of bringing the teacher to heel; ways of making life difficult for the critic or rebel. P. V. Carroll describes the treatment in *Shadow and Substance*. Dr Lucey implies that the teachers are free to speak their minds publicly. It would not seem so, to judge by the difference between their private and public utterances. It would, indeed, be too much to expect that the teachers would be more outspoken than the secure university professors who keep such a discreet rein on their tongues. It is significant that the teachers have not criticised education as trenchantly as the clergy have done in recent years. This is hardly because they know less well the defects in the system they operate. Nevertheless, the teaching bodies in Eire are not without courage, and may perhaps make a better claim to integrity than most other public bodies. They were the first to warn, in 1941, of the dangers of teaching through the medium of Gaelic.

The Bishop of Cork is hardly justified in implying that educational policy may be left to the Department of Education. True, he does suggest that I.N.T.O. be given a statutory standing and so, by implication, some say in the shaping of educational policy. But the responsibility of the Church goes much further than that. Without doing violence to its own teaching, the Church cannot continue to tolerate the chauvinism of the Department of Education which ejects into the schools a prejudice that distorts, as it poisons, the student mind. With this in mind, presumably, Dr Philibin warned that 'it is unjust to the young to make a country's story a mere propaganda weapon to influence their minds in a particular direction'.[1] Many of the schools, especially those run by Christian Brothers, see it quite otherwise, and enthusiastically implement the Department's perverted policy. For this reason alone, there is much to be said for using lay rather than religious teachers, and for subjecting all teachers to a test of political orthodoxy.

[1] *Patriotism*, p. 5.

Nor, finally, should the clergy continue to indulge their own irrational fears of the human mind, which have turned the schools into agencies for the coarsening of the human spirit. It is odd that the outspoken Bishop of Cork should be more puritan than some of his less eloquent colleagues. His strength of mind, however, is not matched by a sense of logic; and one wonders how long it will take him to realise that only an individualist stand is orthodox. At Rosscarbery he complained that 'we pay lip service to private enterprise and free competition. We might do better if we went over to them in practice, but that is not for me to say'.[1] Why is it not for the Bishop to say? Is not Catholicism individualist? And does not the Bishop, by implication, put aside socio-political neutrality in criticising socialism. If socialism is wrong, what then is right?

[1] May 7, 1961.

CHAPTER XII

The Wasted Island

AFTER MR DE VALERA got into power, little was heard of and little vital done for the rural community which, indeed, suffered severely during the Economic War with Britain (1932–38) over the land annuities. Neglected by the politicians and repressed by the priests, a rural decline was inevitable.

It was most clearly shown in the fishing industry. There are, at present, about 1600 sea fishermen. Early in the century, there were, according to AE, over 31,000 in the whole island. It is the failure of this most colourful industry which has done so much to depopulate the barren areas in the South and West of Ireland where, in some districts, every second house is uninhabited and entire villages practically wiped out.

As far as population went, the Irish Government managed only to stabilise between 1922 and 1952 a decline which had been going on for over a hundred years. During these thirty-odd years, the excess of births over deaths was just sufficient to offset the rate of emigration. Between 1950 and 1960, however, emigration rose steadily, resulting by 1960 in a loss of 144,000, bringing the total population down to 2,814,700. This distinctively rural loss was widely distributed, most marked in the North-western region, least marked in the Leinster or Eastern area.

The decline of rural society has been aggravated by the bias of industry towards manufactures using imported raw materials. True, appreciable progress has been made, especially in the production of sugar, canned foods and processed agriculture produce. The Irish Sugar Company is the most successful of these enterprises, with its subsidiary processing industries (Erin Foods) which have given a strong lead in this field. But there has been no consistent attempt to use native raw materials. Thus, farming has lacked the support it could have had from an industrial growth allied to the land.

In 1958, Mr Lemass, Minister for Industry and Commerce in the de Valera Government, set about industrial development to stop the population decline, as well as to improve Eire's balance of external payments. Quick results, though, were to be sought in industry, not agriculture. Even in industry, experience had shown the inadequacy of native ability. Few industries established under native government had made good, as did Sunbeam Wolsey of Cork. Most of them were content to relax behind high tariff walls and produce inferior and high-priced goods. In 1958 the Government passed an Industrial Development (Encouragement of External Investment) Act enabling it to offer valuable grants and concessions to aliens setting up industries in Eire.

This External Development Act was the most spectacular social development in modern Ireland. By September 1960, 189 new industries were established under the Act, an example of voluntary colonialism in an industrial sense. With Britain, Germany and America in the lead, the variety of nationals involved in this expansion was outdone only by the variety of manufactures; and the people in the Irish towns and villages made acquaintance with modern industrial techniques.

The main defect in the new industries, however, was their haphazard character, and the general failure to relate them to native raw materials. This, and the flagrant ignoring of the principle of specialisation, was the most objectionable feature of Eire's industrial development – a predominantly agricultural country, with few industrial resources, placing such an exaggerated emphasis on industry. And, indeed, it was not long before a profound unrest began to show itself in the agricultural sector which, though heavily subsidised, found itself in a relatively weak position. This led to a revolt of the farming community during 1967-68 when the National Farmers Association adopted a 'no rates' campaign and road blockades to try and force the Government to give the farmers a say in shaping agricultural policy.

The decline in emigration in the sixties does not warrant too optimistic an inference as to farming conditions in Eire. While rural depopulation is continuing, it is conditioned by the actual decline itself. The flight from the least productive areas diminishes, as these areas become progressively abandoned. 'Emigration, as ordinarily talked of,' wrote Peadar O'Donnell, 'is no longer the problem of the West which has now reached the more advanced stage of decay where the houses which sent out flight after flight of emigrants in the past are now being abandoned.'

A singularly low marriage rate is symptomatic of the Irish rural decline. Indeed, the backwardness of the Irish rural mind is shown in the reluctance of parents to surrender the title to a farm. 'Boys' of forty years of age are still tied to parental apron strings, unable to marry or undertake the management of a farm. It hardly surprises that the average age when the Irish marry – 28 years for men and 26 for women – is the oldest of any nation in the world. Michael Owen Fogarty, President of the 12,000-strong *Macra na Feirme*, sees this conflict between the young and the old as 'one of the greatest problems in rural Ireland today', and he can find no solution except through a raising of the general level of prosperity which would make it possible for the old to retire in comfort.[1]

The delayed marriage of the oldest son often reduces the marital prospects of his sisters who usually depend for dowries on what is provided by the brother's wife. Desertion of the farm is not surprising under such circumstances. Boys and girls who have few prospects of farm or dowry are educated for the professions or the civil service, or they find work in the towns as domestics or shop-assistants. Unfortunately for the efficiency of agriculture, it is not uncommon for farmers to educate the brighter and leave the dullards on the farm.

The girls in rural Ireland have long come to realise that what they want in terms of marriage, security and freedom, is more likely to be found in England. Their hopes of the outside world are fed by its exciting reflections in the cinema and television, as well as by reports from their emigrant friends. The result is, in some districts at any rate, the almost total disappearance of marriageable girls.

Lack of opportunity is not the only important restriction on the rural marriage rate. There is also male indifference to marriage, as Fr O'Brien complained in *The Vanishing Irish*. The Irish farmer is unromantic, spending his leisure in the pubs and not in amorous dallying along the leafy lanes. Sport or booze exhaust his interest in the outside world, since politics has largely ceased to stir his imagination. Indeed, one suspects that some farmers would dispense with the institution of marriage

[1] *Sunday Independent*, May 13, 1962.

were it not that a wife is a valuable part of a farming economy. True, rural organisations are at present doing a good deal to change this apathetic outlook, creating a more sociable atmosphere and a livelier interest in the economics of farming.

The sexual apathy of Irishmen – highlighted by the impressionability of a minority – is one of the more obscure manifestations of Irish inertia. Yeats suggested in his *Autobiographies* that it is the result of a national outlook so compounded of hate that it 'dries up nature and makes for sexual abstinence'. The fact that it is found in men rather than in women in Ireland suggests that its cause lies among those impersonal influences to which men are more subject; hence to be an outcome of puritanism leading to cultural frustration and to an atrophy of sexual energy seen as ugly and destructive.

Marital inertia is not confined to the Irishmen at home. It extends also to the Irish in America, Canada and Australia. The marital decline was traced to the latter part of the nineteenth century and associated with the post-Famine emigrants from Ireland.

The Famine (1845–9) was the most intensive of Ireland's historic shocks, making for a national sense of bitterness and despair. Some see in it the cause of the sexual devitalisation of Irishmen. It is true that, before the famine, the Irish were maritally prolific, when the country was, according to Disraeli, more densely populated than China. One can still sense in the people of the South and West a residue of that despair which would appear to owe much to the Famine. It shows itself in a resigned mentality, a fatalistic apathy which shrinks from change as it does from experimentation; hence a wariness about marriage which is the most exacting of all personal experiments.

Despair and anger were the contrasted responses of the Irish people to their harsh destiny. The anger gave a stimulus to revolutionary nationalism. But it was really the Irish Americans who kept the fires of political hate at a white heat, for they were apt to subside at home, as in the period following the death of Parnell. In the light of this, it is not hard to understand the morbidities of the Irish American, subject to a double hate – puritan and political. And, indeed, his outlook, as described by the American contributors to *The Vanishing Irish*, seems even more morbid than that of the Irish at home, just as the population decline among the Irish Americans is more striking.

The effect of sexual indifference on the Irish marriage rate is made worse by an irresponsible attitude towards marriage. The Irish do not see marriage as a duty. Their attitude is opportunist; and too often they do not find marriage opportune. True, the short summer of Irish male romanticism is remote from the period of harvest when the Irish can afford to marry. Recent socio-economic changes, however – especially the industrial development of the towns – are making early marriages more feasible.

It is not an admiration for celibacy which keeps Irishmen bachelors, as Fr O'Brien suggests in *The Vanishing Irish* (pp. 88–9). If Irishmen choose to be bachelors, it is not usually with any intention of depriving themselves of such sexual pleasures as may come their way. An ideal of sexual purity, to be vital, presupposes some faith in the essential goodness of the human mind. But Irishmen tend to lack this, and see in sexual excesses the more or less inevitable outcome of human corruption. 'It is high time,' urged Oliver Gogarty in the Senate, that 'the people of this country found some other way of loving God than by hating women.' This cynical view of woman can be found in Patrick Kavanagh's *The Great Hunger* where the romantic reality is coarse and devitalised. This reality is even more forbidding in the country towns, conditioned as it is there by a combination of prudery, commercialism and snobbery. Frank O'Connor describes this obnoxious mentality in *The Holy Door*.

The clergy have a celibate ideal. It is wholly ascetical. Joyce could see himself as a 'knight' of the Blessed Virgin in this renunciatory sense. Sex can be denied with moral point, but not used creatively with moral point. The distinction is significant, and indicates the absence of an Irish Catholic humanism. Irishmen justify – unconsciously at least – their abstention from marriage on the grounds that it involves a shabby sex element which no sacramental character can quite overcome. Dr Conway, Titular Bishop of Neve (now Cardinal Conway), complained that 'public opinion has been for the most part silent . . . about the shameless exploitation of sex in many modern novels, films and television programmes . . .'[1] But surely it is hard to expect from the Irish public, conditioned to see sex as ugly, much in the way of indignation when business men exploit sex. In recent years, the Irish clergy have been at

[1] At Carrigart, April 20, 1960.

pains to try and correct this sordid impression and to present sex in a more favourable light.

The barriers to marriage, especially in rural Ireland, place a heavy strain on the young who are denied a vital means of biological and social expression. Indeed, the scene is here set for a chaotic form of sexual life which the clergy are never tired of condemning, and of which Synge wrote '. . . if I were to tell you . . . all the sex horrors I have seen I could a tale unfold that would wither up your blood . . .'[1]

Such sexual repression helps, no doubt, to explain why the incidence of mental disease in Eire is the highest of any country. According to the findings of Dr. Dermot Walsh, the treated rate of Irish psychiatric patients was 10·82 per 1000 of the population during the period 1955–1959, as compared with 5·65 in the U.S.A. and 3·32 in France. It is significant that Northern Ireland comes next to Eire with a rate of 7·43.[2] The incidence of the disease in Eire is highest in the western, south-western and north-western seaboards.

It is in respect of mental illness that Eire has done much to modernise her thinking and practice; and there is taking place at present a revolution in the Irish treatment of mental disease. The institutional centre of the new scientific approach is the St John of God Hospital in Dublin, and its first organised expression was the publication of a series of lectures given in this hospital during October 1961.[3] The Conference was under the patronage of Dr McQuaid, Archbishop of Dublin. Nothing shows so clearly as this book – in which half the contributors are priests – the salutary change in Irish clerical thinking effected over a few years.

The public houses rather than the mental hospitals, however, provide a better guide to the presence of mental disease in Ireland. The Irish are a tough peasant people who can put up a strong fight against frustration. They are also a religious people who can interpret this frustration as inevitable in this 'vale of tears' and see human resignation as meritorious. A belief in the compensations of the after life has kept many Irish –

[1] Greene and Stephens, *J. M. Synge*, pp. 157–8.
[2] *Psychiatry (British Journal)*, January 1968.
[3] *The Priest and Mental Health*, edited by Rev E. F. O'Doherty and Dr E. D. McGrath, Clonmore and Reynolds, Dublin, 1962.

especially women – outside those grim institutions whose barred gates are at present being unlocked in accord with a more humane therapy. It has also saved many of them from suicide, that deliberate decision to end an experience which seems no longer to have either pleasure or point. The Irish suicide rate – 2.5 per 100,000 of the population – is one of the lowest in the world, as compared, say, with 19.1 in Denmark. But as was remarked in an essay in *Time* (November 25, 1966), this figure may be considered too low in a country were 'suicide comes under strong religious censure, [and where] there are compelling reasons for relatives, doctors and coroners to report it as an accident or a heart attack'.

While faith in an after life helps one to cling to the present world, the clinging may prove a severe test of endurance, and so generates a need for some form of relief. Intoxicating drink is the Irish anodyne. A fondness for drink, like religion and patriotism, unites and characterises the Catholic Irish. It is evident everywhere, in city, town and country; in all social classes, rich and poor, educated and ignorant; and, in recent decades, in women as well as men. It is no less evident in the emigrant, as in U.S.A. where surveys show that the Irish, or those of Irish extraction, account for 50% to 80% of alcoholics.[1]

Irish drinking is heaviest in the country towns where addicts excuse themselves by saying, 'There's nothing else to do.' The clergy themselves are apt to share in this 'good man's weakness', and turn a blind eye on Irish drinking habits. No doubt, the new freedom, and the satisfaction provided by materialist pursuits will reduce Irish frustration and, as a result, the volume of drinking. Besides, Ireland is fast losing her fine spiritual intuition, a vital sense of transcendence, the frustration of which accounted for so much of the excessive drinking of her best sons.

The use of drink as a means of escape leads inevitably to alcoholism, and Dr P. D. McCarthy, Assistant Medical Director of the St John of God Hospital, stated that 'at a conservative estimate' there are 70,000 alcoholics in Eire, that is, 23 per 1000 of the population – a higher incidence than in any other race, except perhaps the Red Indians. *The Priest and Mental Health* provides a general review of the problem of alcohol in Eire. It points out that this has long been recognised by

[1] Michael Viney, *Alcoholism in Ireland*, pp. 7–8. Reprint from *Irish Times*.

sociologists and psychologists, as by Bales who attributed Irish drinking to stresses in the Irish social structure. The contributors emphasise the conclusion that, in the words of the Rev Professor Riordan, 'drinking is very often a symptom of a deeper personality problem or disorder', and conclude that preventative means alone are not adequate to deal with it. They suggest the need for a more positive human approach, such as that provided, in a simple and direct way, by Alcoholics Anonymous. This is indeed the radical weakness in the Pioneer Total Abstinence Association (founded in 1938) – the most important clerical social movement in modern Ireland inspired by Fr Mathew – which seeks to cure Irish drinking habits while leaving their cause – human frustration – intact.

Few marriages and many emigrants mean Irish devitalisation. These reduce Irish vitality both in quality and quantity. For over a hundred years it is the best who have gone. D'Alton complained early in the century that 'more than three quarters of those who go are between the ages of 15 and 35'. This leaves a preponderance of the old and very young, the lethargic and the unfit. It is true, however, that the low marriage rate is partly offset by a high birth rate per family – four children being the average size of an Irish family.

CHAPTER XIII

The Irish Social Conscience

IN VIEW OF the negative social policy of the Irish Catholic Church, it hardly surprises that Irish Catholics have little sense of social responsibility, and are, as a rule, cynically indifferent to social and ideological issues. Thus it is with the Irish at home and abroad. The Irish clergy see the Irish Americans rather than the Irish in Britain as exemplars of the pious Irish emigrant. No doubt, Irish transgressions in America are obscured by distance as well as by the sentimentally pious and chauvinistic outlook of the American Irish.

The Irish in England are a different kettle of fish, belonging to a more recent exodus, and critical of faith and fatherland. They appear to leave the Church in greater numbers. Their censorious attitude to Irish conditions is obnoxious to official Ireland; and when their behaviour results in public censure – as witness the appreciable numbers of Irish who have been deported from Britain – the Irish Church and State are affronted by the implied rebuke. Yet, whatever be the social liberties which the Irish in Britain have taken, they can hardly compare with those taken by the Irish in America.

True, there is no disputing the Irish contribution to the basic religious, as distinct from secular, outlook in America: as priests, nuns and teachers, the Irish have exercised a great influence towards the preservation of Christian values. Yet, they have made no significant moral contribution to the shaping of America's social environment. On the contrary, their social influence has been either radical or downright corrupting. Tammany Hall, their best-known creation, does them little credit: an organisation which, though not perhaps lacking in a certain loyalty and imaginative sympathy, was nevertheless based on self-interest and graft. The perverted political instinct of the Irish American later found expression in McCarthyism – a destructive combination of cynicism and hysteria which sought to justify itself by an attack on a public evil.

In fairness, it must be said that not much was to be expected from the Irish in America, especially from the bulk of those who emigrated during the nineteenth century. They were wretched and backward, the product of appalling Irish conditions. Many of them congregated in the slums of American cities – as did other nationalities such as the Italians and Jews – happy with their kind and the shared memories of the old land. They were faced with the problem of adjustment in a young and brash country-in-the-making which admired a rugged individualism. It was the first generation, however, who were really caught between the pull of American life and the diminishing appeal of racial memories they but dimly understood. Some of them joined the street gangs which were the vulgar expression of that go-getting spirit in the American environment. 'The first gangsters were Irishmen, the Molly Maguires . . .' wrote John O'Hara. These gangs formed the breeding ground of an organised criminal element which became a distinctive feature of American life.

The Irish Americans gained a strong foothold within the agencies of law and order, in the police force and in politics. For them, however, the line of demarcation between law and outlawry was blurred; and there was established a certain alliance between the politicians, the police force and the criminals, which laid the basis of a sinister tradition which Americans are now finding it hard to break. This triple alliance was embodied in Tammany Hall which, in Kenneth Allsop's view, was the 'earliest classical pattern of the American political machine . . . an apparatus for the exercise of power, privilege and commercialised patronage on an unprecedented basis.'[1] Though the Italians and, especially, the Sicilians were to gain an ascendancy over the Irish in the field of organised crime in America, they never achieved the same measure of political control, the same integration of crime and politics.

Frederick M. Thrasher, investigating street gangs in 1927, noted that most of their members were 'children of parents one or both of whom are foreign-born immigrants. Polish, Italian and Irish furnish many more gangs than might be expected from their population groups . . .' Mr Allsop explains that the Irish, Sicilians and Jews had in common a European background in which 'self-preservation had depended on

[1] *The Bootleggers*, Hutchinson & Co., 1961, p. 217.

fighting and a clannish solidarity against an internal enemy'. (p. 255) It is significant to note the predominantly Catholic as distinct from Protestant composition of the groups, and to see in this a defective moral sense in the field of social relations; a defect which is all the more remarkable in view of the fact that American gangsters with a Catholic background often retained a strong religious sense. Referring to the Polish-American gunman, Hymie Weiss, Mr Allsop comments that he 'conformed to the traditional Catholic Italian-Irish gangster pattern in remaining throughout his career of murder and indiscriminate dishonesty devoutly religious – he wore a crucifix round his neck nearby his armpit holster and carried a rosary in his pocket'. (p 87)

The Irish-American gangster, apparently, was not quite as socially amoral as Catholic emigrants from other countries. For while he was willing to engage in the most varied skulduggery, including murder, he drew the line at exploiting women. So it was with Dion O'Bannion and the O'Donnellys of Chicago, who – writes Mr Allsop – 'being more consistent Catholics than the Sicilians, they abhorred prostitution and would not dabble in brothel-keeping'. (p. 58) Apparently Irish Jansenism, with its special emphasis on sexual morality, had left its mark. It may be noted, in passing, that, in recent years, the Irish in Britain have not been so scrupulous on this point.

The growth of organised crime in America was the outcome of a breakdown of liberal humanism and the Catholic social ethic. An undue stress on individual freedom, combined with a strong faith in the value of material growth, opened the way to crime in a country which much admired worldly success and was little concerned with the morality of the means used to win it. On the Catholic side, an atrophy of the moral sense in human relations expedited a criminal breakthrough to affluence and notoriety by the socially depressed immigrants. The fact that the Irish and the Sicilians went far towards reducing some major American cities to a state of banditry indicates deep moral flaws in both the American environment and in the emigrants. It is in its search for those flaws that Mr Allsop's fine study is most revealing, especially in the section dealing with the 'Anatomy of a Gangster'.

The Irish political system has no little in common with the Tammany Hall regime. Both were inspired by racial consciousness which, though strongly influenced by Irish Catholicism, was significantly devoid of a sense of social justice. The absence of this sense of an elementary Catholic ethical precept indicates just how defective was Irish clerical influence on the Irish outlook, in spite of continuous indoctrination.

Reference has already been made to the manner in which social justice in Ireland was subordinated to political needs as they stemmed from the state abolutism of Mr de Valera. While he was in office a system of political patronage (adopted perforce by the other political parties) was extended over the entire compass of Irish life; into civil administration through the country and urban councils and administrative committees of all kinds; into the life of the community through nation-wide cells or *cumainn* which built up support for the party by the exercise of party influence on behalf of its members. In this way, Irish political parties became mere 'benefit' societies, to use an expression which Carl Wittke applies to Tammany Hall.[1] One may doubt whether, as Lt.-Gen. Costello suggests, this political mentality was 'imported' from Tammany Hall, but the General is right in his assessment of the socially devitalising policy it engendered: 'Vote right and vote often and the Government will dispense manna for you.' (At University College, Cork, December 3, 1967.) This close-knit organisation, based on self-interest, has helped much to provide a popular support for the Irish political system, in spite of widespread cynicism regarding Irish politics. It has also helped to exclude new blood and leadership which is at a disadvantage in opposing such well-entrenched and well-organised groups.

There is no doubt that the absolutist party system was the most corrupting force in Ireland, undermining the people's faith in public honesty and justice. The most oft-quoted of popular maxims is 'it isn't what you know but who you know'; or to put it in the racy language of the chorus in James O'Toole's *Man Alive*:

> Without pull in Holy Ireland
> Though you saint or scholar be,
> You don't stand a bloody earthly
> With Selection Committees.

Yet the Irish Catholic Church largely ignored the acutely demoralis-

[1] *The Irish in America*, Louisiana State University Press, 1956.

ing influence of the Irish party system, presumably because it served to weaken popular vitality and growth, making the people mere puppets to be jerked by the party leaders over whom the clergy felt they could exercise effective control. It is a rarity to find clerical criticism of this system, as that of the Rev T. Cosgrave who complained that the 'system of political patronage is an eyesore, democracy is discredited by it'.[1]

Up to the late sixties the dynastic character of Irish politics was largely unaffected by Premier Lemass' energising policies. The rank and file of the party members continued to be recruited mainly from the families of the original members of the *Dail*, or where this was impracticable, from popular personalities, especially in the field of sport. Thus, in by-elections held during 1964-5, no less than three widows of retiring members were elected to the *Dail*, while in the general election held in April 1965, the *Fine Gael* party reinforced its ranks with two famous hurlers, Willie Rackard of Wexford and Donie Nealon of Tipperary.

As might be expected, Irish political life was at its best when it allowed a voice to the Anglo-Irish who alone showed any vision and sanity in a Catholic system inimical to both. This enlightenment was practically confined to the Senate between 1922-1928 when it had a strong Anglo-Irish representation which included Yeats and such distinguished spokesmen as Sir Horace Plunkett, Alice Stopford Green, Andrew Jameson, former Chairman of the Unionist Party, Sir John Keane and Lord Glenavy, a former Lord Chief Justice of Ireland.

At most points, the Irish Catholic social ethic shows evidence of weakness and neglect, seen, for instance, in rural organisations which quarrel jealously in spite of a profound need for unity. It is no less obvious in Labour-Capital relations which are so bitter and divisive that Eire is now one of the most strike prone countries in Europe. Perjury is common in Eire. 'When one reads evidence of court cases,' remarked the Bishop of Cork, 'it is hard to escape the conclusion that perjury is a sin often committed among us.'[2] Robbery in a crude sense – where money or goods are taken at once and concretely – hurts the Irish conscience.

[1] At Kilnemona, Co. Clare, April 1959.
[2] At Crosshaven, March 31, 1967.

But the subtler forms of unjust acquisition – as in overcharging and giving an unfair return for wages – are seen as only fair in a relentless economic struggle. The outlook of many Irish Catholic business men is utilitarian, combining a profession of charity with an exploitation of their employees.

State taxes are treated as purely penal. Even the timid of conscience will smuggle without scruple. Nor is it likely that those making fortunes out of illegal traffic across the Northern border declare their ill-gotten gains in the confessional.[1] Most striking, however, is the wholesale evasion of the income tax code by those, such as business, professional men and farmers, whose incomes are not easily determined. This has placed those with readily ascertainable incomes, such as State employees, in an unjust and difficult position. The remarkable fact, as Paul Blanshard pointed out, is that the Irish clergy connive at this fraud, treating infringements of the tax code as penal, not moral.[2] The argument of the clergy seems to be that since wholesale fraud exists, in fact, the individual is justified in treating the particular charge made on him as exorbitant; thus overlooking the consideration that, in exonerating the defaulters from blame, they help to perpetuate an unjust charge on a minority.

Irishmen see little wrong in living merely for themselves. In Ireland, the term vocation has only a religious connotation. In the secular field, the Irish follow those careers which they find profitable, and not those for which they are naturally adapted. This is not seen as reflecting on a professed obligation to develop their own talents and to give of their best to society. Archbishop Temple's view that to choose a career on selfish grounds is the 'greatest single sin that a young person can commit' is incomprehensible to the Irish. The moral of Christ's choice of carpentry as a career is entirely lost in a community obsessed with the idea of bourgeois respectability. The rush on the professions has produced a crop of misfits – of priests, doctors, lawyers, and teachers – many of whom would be better employed 'snagging turnips', as Myles

---

[1] In a Sunday sermon in a South-east London parish during July 1966, a priest admitted that the pattern of confessions gave some support to those who held that the Church was only concerned with the Sixth and Ninth Commandments. He also admitted that sins against justice were rarely the subject matter of confession.

[2] *The Irish and Catholic Power*, Derek Verschoyle, 1954, pp. 178–9.

na Gopilin suggested. So profound, indeed, has been the social failure of Irish Catholicism that those who live outside convent or monastery are mostly in a moral wilderness. Life for them is, in Honor Tracy's brilliant summary: 'Mass in the morning, vacuity during the day, oblivion at night; religion, inertia, alcohol.'[1] By the late nineteen sixties, however, the Irish Catholic Church had come far towards an understanding of its main weakness which is – in the words of Fr Brendan O'Mahoney – 'its lack of a developed and contemporary social consciousness and therefore, of a social conscience'. (*Irish Times*, December 13, 1967).

[1] *Mind You, I've Said Nothing*, Methuen, 1953, p. 64.

CHAPTER XIV

Ireland Today

UP TO THE LATE FIFTIES, the Irish imagination mirrored, for the most part, a Western image of life, in spite of efforts to assert a native image. By the early sixties, the Irish had begun to accept the Western image. Such acceptance could not be long postponed in view of the poverty of the native image. This poverty became evident in the Irish reaction to the challenge of television and the Common Market, as well as in a victory for outside inspiration, especially in the fields of drama and popular entertainment.

Neither priest nor politician in Eire had much liking for the challenge of television. For the first time, the Irish Government had to hold the active attention of a wide audience. How was such attention to be held – with native or foreign programmes? Neither solution appealed. Foreign programmes were suspect because they were believed to express an alien culture; native programmes because there was little vital native culture; and in so far as it existed, it could not be readily used.

Television poses a great challenge. Keeping a large audience on its toes for several hours a day is no mean feat. All the organ stops have to be used; and Eire's cultural prejudices and inhibitions made this difficult. These limitations may be classified as propagandist and anticultural.

The *Radio Telefís Eireann* Authority has been under great pressure from the revivalists and, to an extent, from the clergy. Edward J. Roth, first director of *R.T.E.*, complained that 'we do not have to be reminded about these [the claims of the Gaelic language] continuously'. He pointed out that since the *R.T.E.* was obliged, by statute, to become self-sufficient as soon as possible, programmes must have a wide appeal. He warned that a recent survey of *Radio Eireann* listeners showed that 'programmes in Irish received about the lowest ratings'.[1]

1 April 7, 1961.

Eamonn Andrews, first Chairman of the *R.T.E.* Authority, dealt with the claims of religion at a Catholic Social Study Conference at Gormanstown Castle on August 6, 1961. He wisely suggested that the 'most effective religion on television is one which comes from a climate of thought, a background of philosophy, a reflected way of life . . .' But this is precisely where Irish Catholicism is weak. Of formal religion, it has plenty and to spare; but of religion as reflected in a vision or way of life, it has little to show.

The essence of propaganda lies in the mere assertion of an idea, without an appeal to reason, feeling or reality. Such an assertion springs from a belief based on an uncritical faith which resents the doubts raised by an inquiry into its rational basis or application. Irish Catholicism is of this kind and is, consequently, only of limited value to television. A propagandist treatment of religion, however, is apt to cause a profound popular frustration, a deep unconscious need to have conventional standards subjected to critical analysis. Irish Catholicism could achieve star status on television if the members of the hierarchy were willing to subject themselves to public criticism in the robust manner in which British television conducts such enquiries. That *R.T.E.* has come a long way in the challenge it offers to public personalities can be seen by a comparison between the discreet handling of Ernest Blythe by Proinsias MacAonghusa in October 1964 and the exacting questioning of Monsignor McCarthy by John O'Donoghue (January 1968) concerning the lack of governmental supervision of funds entrusted to clerical managers for the upkeep of schools.

Ultra-nationalism came under growing attack in *R.T.E.*, in spite of a Government policy nominally favouring its aims. One of the most stimulating of *R.T.E.*'s programmes was a debate on the Language Revival on January 15, 1965 – the very day on which the Government White Paper on the Gaelic Revival was published. Such frank criticism of a traditional and sacrosanct ideal gave the public an extraordinary experience; and the comic force of Joe Lynch's satirical sallies gave him more popular reputation than did his fine acting roles.

The most outspokenly critical of *R.T.E.*'s early programmes was 'Broadsheet' which was in the hands of a competent group which included Brian Cleeve, John O'Donoghue, Brian Farrell and John Skehan. On occasion, the frankness of this programme obliterated the distinction between public and private discussions in Eire; and one felt one was eavesdropping on Dublin intellectuals in one of their favourite bars. Apparently, this boldness was too much for the reactionaries, and 'Broadsheet' was discontinued in the Autumn of 1963. In its stead was substituted an innocuous programme called 'Newsbeat'. Nevertheless, the best of *R.T.E.*'s early programmes came under the headings of educational and critical. Such were 'On the Land' – dealing with practical farming; 'Headlines and Deadlines', critical of Irish regionalist attitudes; 'Radarch' and 'Signal', the first a Catholic, the second a Protestant, programme along documentary lines.

R.T.E. has a strong contemporary sense; so strong, indeed, as to cause a hiatus with the past, even with the immediate past. This seems due to a wish to obscure the fact that present liberal-realist policies are a profound departure from tradition. This, of course, limits an under-standing of present trends, and leaves unexplained the great release of national energy into the social and cultural fields since the mid-fifties.

Sensitive to the charge of illiberalism, the clergy try to meet it by finding some excuse or scapegoat to explain social backwardness. Thus the outcome of a discussion by 'The Professors' (November 2, 1964) was that there was no force in Eire inimical to Irish writers, even though Professor T. Desmond Williams made the significant point that it was only after 1922 that the Irish writer became an exile. On the other hand, Peadar O'Donnell put the blame on pietistic lay bodies when Hilton Edwards charged the Church with censoring the stage.[1] It shows how well the clergy have covered up their tracks when such a veteran writer as Peadar O'Donnell – one of the most suspect by the Church – can miss the source of repression. For it is, of course, naive to suggest that groups of pietistic mollycoddles could dictate clerical policy. They can, it is true, be more fanatically narrow than the clergy them-selves, but they could not possibly remain in existence without clerical support.

The most effective way to show that the Irish are free to criticise is to allow them to do so; and *R.T.E.* came into existence when this freedom was on the increase. Yet, until late in 1967, this freedom was more apparent than real. There was much discussion but its quality was poor. Ken Grey, television critic of the *Irish Times*, when asked to

[1] December 25, 1964.

comment on *R.T.E.*, remarked on the 'large numbers of nonentities encouraged to talk their heads off.'[1] Cathal Og O'Shannon commented on the absence of honesty in the Irish as compared with the English in answering questions.[2] Also, there are ways of reducing the risks of public discussion: by keeping the time for discussion short; by choosing a chairman who will slant the discussion; and by selecting speakers from the ranks of the immature, the discreet, or the not-too-bright.

Irish youth, growing up under a more liberal regime, are the least mentally inhibited of the Irish today; and, in the early years, 'Teen Talk' was the freshest of *R.T.E.*'s critical programmes. The teenagers got little help from a panel of adults who – with rare exceptions like Angela MacNamara – showed less good sense than the teenagers themselves. To the charge of nepotism – one of the most pernicious of Irish social sins – made by a teenager, Liam MacGonagle, a panel member, suggested that showing a preference in public life and appointments for one's family and relations was natural, inevitable and of no particular importance.[3]

In 1967 *R.T.E.* reasserted its early critical spirit evident in 'Broadsheet'. Programmes such as 'To-morrow's People' – a more mature version of 'Teen Talk' with Bunny Carr as chairman – showed more honesty of approach and comprehensiveness in the inclusion of touchy Irish issues – the Church, education, family regulation, politics. This was even more evident in 'Seven Days' whose daring drew strong protests from within and without *R.T.E.* With other programmes, such as 'Celtic Challenge', 'Inside Europe' and 'Person in Question' – interviewing public personalities – *R.T.E.* achieved a high degree of maturity which reflected on the growth of the official Irish outlook. There were also some fine documentaries such as Jim Sherwin's study of alcoholism, 'The Lonely Disease' (December 1967).

In spite of its much improved performance, *R.T.E.* is not really free, being permitted only 'to nibble at the grass of freedom', as Eamonn Andrews declared at University College, Cork, on October 30, 1967. *R.T.E.* is really under the control of the Government which is itself under strong pressure from the clergy and the extreme nationalists.

[1] December 1, 1964.
[2] *Ibid.*
[3] April 16, 1965.

The Government uses *R.T.E.* to advance its own (*Fianna Fail*) interests, a fact which contributed to a crisis in *R.T.E.* in February 1968, when the survival of the 'Seven Days' programme was endangered. But, indeed, Irish political parties have no wish to expose their glaring weaknesses; and, according to John Healy, the Chief Whips of the main political parties entered into a 'secret agreement' with *R.T.E.* to limit that exposure.[1]

Restriction on *R.T.E.*'s freedom shows in the poor quality of the 'Late, Late Show' which, even in the competent hands of Gay Byrne, is often dull and sometimes in bad taste. First-rate personalities are uninvited (or unwilling) when there are official reservations about public criticism. Lack of money also lowers *R.T.E.*'s standards, ruling out expensive programmes. Thus, live plays are rare, and new native plays – of the calibre of Eugene McCabe's *A Matter of Conscience* – rarer still. *R.T.E.*'s films are mostly old and valueless. Advertising – *R.T.E.*'s main source of funds – is appallingly fatuous, with little of the imagination evident in Esso advertising. *R.T.E.* should be run at public expense. This would not increase by much the risk of State interference, since *R.T.E.*, as it stands, is a State organ; it would be enabled, rather, to exploit more fully that freedom of expression which a growing official liberalism permits.

Critics of Eire's cultural struggle might well concentrate on *R.T.E.*, where that struggle finds its sharpest definition. The choice of *R.T.E.*'s directors betrays the Government's wish to keep television under its control. In 1963 Mr Roth was followed by Kevin McCourt, a business executive; and he was followed in March 1968 by Thomas Hardiman, an engineer. Obviously, the director of *R.T.E.* should be an outstanding personality with a broad liberal culture. This type of culture is not to be found in those fanatical language revivalists at present members of the *R.T.E.* Authority. The resignation of Eamonn Andrews in 1966 was *R.T.E.*'s most serious loss. But what man of spirit could be expected to withstand the tedium of accountants and the lunacy of language absolutists.

It was the language revivalists who were most disturbed by Mr Lemass' wish to join forces with Western Europe. They sensibly

[1] *Irish Times*, March 7, 1968.

decided to accept the inevitable, and even expressed the hope that Gaelic would benefit by the challenge posed by the continental languages. The challenge was a critical one, however, and moved the revivalists to embark on an expensive nation-wide 'Save the Language Campaign' in 1964. But, by then, it was generally obvious that there was little chance of realising the constitutional aim of making Gaelic the first official language.

A Report of a Commission on the Restoration of the Irish Language – whose members were largely in sympathy with the revival movement – was published in the Spring of 1963, and clearly showed the failure of the forty-year-old language policy. It suggested that the only people who took the trouble to learn the language were students who needed it to pass examinations and to be eligible for public posts. In spite of pressures and aids – such as special 'forcing schools' set up in the Gaeltacht – as well as incentives – extra money for schools teaching through the medium of Gaelic, and extra marks for examinees answering through the medium of Gaelic – the Commission's account of the results is almost uniformly disappointing. For example, in the *Dail* and Senate, from which a lead might be expected, the Commission noted that the 'space occupied annually . . . by speeches in Irish is still less than two per cent'.

Under strong pressure, however, the Government issued a White Paper on the Irish language on January 18, 1965, promising to press forward with the Gaelic Revival. But its treatment of the subject was so ambiguous as to leave serious doubts as to the Government's sincerity in its declared intention to create a bilingual Ireland. The White Paper noted that Gaelic was of little value as a means of communication outside the Gaeltacht, and that English was of increasing value 'as an international language in communications, trade and tourism, and as a means of participating in world affairs'. It suggested that the language revival might impede political unity, referring to the 'existence in the country as a whole of communities whose historical backgrounds differ, but who have all a valuable contribution to make to the development of the nation'. Coming from an official source, the notion that life in Eire might benefit as a result of a synthesis with that of the North was most revolutionary.

At all events, a Gaelic Revival without a significant cultural content is of little value; and Sean O'Faolain is hardly right in seeing its failure as due to a triumph of materialism over idealism:

> We foresaw the new Ireland as a rich flowering of the old Ireland [he wrote], with all its own simple ways, pieties, values, traditions. Only the old men went on thinking like this; men like President de Valera. The younger . . . hardheaded men . . . want a modernised country, prosperity, industrialisation, economic success. These ambitions have, for years, been demolishing the bridge with the past . . .[1]

The Catholic revivalists never really offered anything which could meet vital human needs. If they were on the side of the simple ways, these were far too circumscribed, too naive, to provide a worthwhile life under modern conditions. The Irish people could hardly avoid ending up making money because they never really got a chance of making anything else.

It is of interest to observe the similarity between Irish Catholic and what *Time* magazine called 'Gaelic-Puritanism'. The attitude of both to life is negative, largely indifferent to social and cultural values. One believes in the formalities of religious ritual, unconcerned with their positive influence on human outlook; the other in the efficacy of the language itself without any definable reference to what people think and feel, to historic or contemporary philosophy. The Language Revival is a logical manifestation in the cultural field of Catholicism in the religious field. The survival of the language absolutists consequently depends on the survival of Catholic puritanism. The growth of a Catholic social philosophy – as hinted in the Government's White Paper – will automatically undermine the present Gaelic Revival, revealing its adherents as inimical to life and to orthodox Catholic teaching. This sane approach to Gaelic finds popular expression in the Language Freedom Movement.

Pope John's energising policy inevitably had its effect on Ireland, though the response of the Catholic hierarchy – as distinct from that of the younger priests – was formal rather than enthusiastic. The

[1] *Vive Moi*, p. 114.

result was that the new movement made only a limited impact on the Irish community as a whole. The educated laity were only marginally affected, while the uneducated were dismayed by the many changes introduced into a system which they felt to be absolute and unchangeable. It would take time before the new ideas penetrated the reluctant Irish clerical consciousness and the apathetic public consciousness.

The most positive effect of the Roman movement in Ireland was in improved relations between the Churches. Hitherto Irish Protestants held distinctly aloof from the national life, feeling rightly that any critical suggestions they might make would be resented by Irish Catholics. The Roman movement led to increased participation of Protestants in the life of the community, evident, for instance, in R.T.E. and in friendlier Catholic-Protestant relations. Referring to these during October 1966, Dr Simms, the Protestant Archbishop of Dublin, stated that

> We are happy that relations have improved so much. I think our Church should have a mood of reconciliation and understanding of others' point of view and a readiness to help towards any peacemaking that can be done in our country.

Indeed, it was the Irish Protestant rather than the Irish Catholic, who reacted more vitally to the change in Roman Catholic policy; a fact which is understandable in regard to a minority whose relations with the Catholic majority have been uneasy and frustrating. Besides, Anglicanism, in general, has shown an unhappy awareness of its complete isolation from Rome; a certain wish for some recognition from the historic centre of Christendom. No doubt, the new movement will modify the Irish Catholic attitude to Protestants, an attitude summed up by George Moore when he said of the pious Edward Martyn: 'He thinks I am damned and he doesn't care.'

One cannot but sympathise with present Irish clerical efforts to create a more positive human outlook. We are not here dealing with an arbitrary attitude, a mere perversity of view, but with a fundamental distortion of vision which – as is claimed in this work – insinuated itself widely into post-Reformation Catholicism. No doubt, the consequences of this were socially and culturally disastrous, but a distortion of vision can occur in the best regulated societies. It is no help – indeed, it is a hindrance – that a tainted view of the human mind found a basis in the Catholic unconsciousness rather than in the Catholic reason. This is because one is less aware of its presence; because it is part of an instinctive reaction, an element in the emotional-imaginative attitude, which only time and a rigorous critical examination can eradicate. Such a predicament certainly merits deep sympathy. It can also benefit, however, from shock tactics – a sharp confrontation with the conflict between Catholic theory and practice, as well as with a stark description of the tragic outcome of the actual social policy of the Church.

It is to be hoped that the Irish Catholic Church will soon produce some vital social ideas. In an address at Maynooth College on August 19, 1966, Cardinal Conway stressed the 'vital role' of priests in adjusting themselves to modern needs. What are these needs? They hardly lie in an industrial programme which will create attitudes and conditions inimical to Catholic ideals of simplicity and honesty. Irish youth can rot in an Irish industrial town as in an English; and it is only too evident that they are fast aping the less desirable aspects in the outlook and behaviour of their foreign counterparts, as the Rev Simon O'Byrne insinuated in an address to teenagers at Knock Shrine in Co. Mayo on September 17, 1966. There he referred to

> the rapid increase in teenage crime in Eire over the past nine years. Among those over 14 years of age and under 17 there were . . . 1,889 indictable crimes and 789 were with violence.

(Referring to those between 14 and 21 years he said that more than 75 per cent of all problems concerned the sixth and ninth commandments.)

Education is pivotal in a liberal Church programme. True, educational reforms are in the air – Cardinal Conway has heralded such reforms – but will they remain there? It looks as if Maynooth – whose graduates make up two-thirds of the Irish Catholic hierarchy – must find a place for social and cultural studies, even if the demands of its present curriculum restrict such studies to selected groups of students who show aptitude in one or other of the social fields. This is important if only because the clergy set themselves up exclusively as moral guides, distrusting lay contributions to social problems. Even in England, according to George Scott, the word 'intellectual' is a favourite term of disparagement as applied by bishops to middle-class educated Catholics.[1]

There is reason to believe that the Irish Catholic clergy are not lacking in ideas to deal with the modern problem, a fact which is evident from the Maynooth magazine, *The Furrow*. But the application of these ideas is constrained by the overall conservatism of the Catholic hierarchy. Of the mentality of Maynooth itself, T.P. Coogan writes that

> Any liberal-tempered, modern-minded layman . . . will find in Maynooth as lively and critical a collection of clerics as exist anywhere in these islands. Such men are waiting until the old guard passes on. They do not say in public the things they say in private, their reason being that they do not want to cause schism or even hurt the feelings of the older men.[2]

As Mr Coogan suggests, however, this waiting policy has its dangers in a situation where time is of paramount importance in getting to grips with the Irish spiritual problem.

It is a promising sign that Maynooth is providing facilities and courses to meet the requirements of the laity as well as the religious. At a meeting in Maynooth on August 22, 1966, the Rev James Mackey stressed the need to

> bring the body of the clergy under university influence because universities were still the key centres of higher education . . . Fifty years ago the incorporation of Maynooth into the Irish university system had been a most imaginative step, but it would be folly to rest now in the belief that the development in Maynooth has kept pace with development in the other Irish universities.

This is no doubt true but, judged at a vital level, the results of Irish university education are not impressive. Relatively few graduates achieve any real cultural distinction, a fact which is mainly due to the heroic qualities required for free and honest expression. Besides, discussions in Irish universities are inspired more by what Dr Mackey calls the 'thought patterns of the age' than by Catholic concepts.

Catholic thought patterns are a profound need in Ireland whose life

[1] *The RC's*, Hutchinson, 1967, p. 235.
[2] *Ireland Since The Rising*, p. 224.

has been impregnated with humanist views and attitudes. Such patterns cannot emerge, however, unless modern humanism is closely studied, and its ideas contrasted with those of Catholicism. This is especially necessary as Ireland draws closer to its European environment which, up to the present, the Irish have neither the wish nor the ability to understand. This is obviously a task for the schools, ecclesiastical and otherwise; but it is one which they will be slow to undertake. Even in England where the humanist challenge is more immediate, George Scott notes of the seminaries that 'the works of the twentieth century philosophers are neither studied nor mentioned'.

If the Church is to be an enlightening influence on Irish life, the standard of clerical preaching must be raised; and – in spite of the demands which the routine of parish duties makes on the clergy – a much larger allowance must be made for the intellectual needs of the laity. That parish priests, even in England, place little emphasis on such needs emerges from the account of an ex-priest, George Long, in *All I Could Never Be*. A high standard of sermon may require that competent preachers are used solely for preaching in different parishes. The present standard of Irish clerical sermons is deplorable. When the clergy can be heard and understood, what they have to say is usually conventional and platitudinous, and suggests little of the profound crisis of Christianity in the modern world.

One suspects that Irish bishops are chosen for their piety and discretion – admirable virtues, no doubt, but inadequate in a situation which demands imaginative perception and intellectual ability. It is regrettable that, with the exception of Dr Philibin, the Irish bishops show limited evidence of such qualities. No doubt the Church suspects such qualities, not only in the layman but in the clergy themselves. Hence the ambiguous position of the Irish Catholic hierarchy who are at once revered and ignored; potent in the ecclesiastical sphere; inept and despised in the social world which they are now naively trying to shape. In this situation, the critical Catholic layman finds himself in an unhappy position, caught between the suspicions of a sincere but intellectually limited clergy and the need to express his criticisms of a religion which leaves little mark on his social and cultural environment. Writing of America's Catholic bishops, Daniel Callahan sums up the dilemma of the critical Catholic layman:

If the bishops are not yet fully alive, neither are they quite dead. They know the pressure is now on them, and that it is growing. No man in a position of authority easily gives up those habits of company loyalty, defensiveness and isolation which got him authority in the first place. But that is precisely what the bishops are being called upon to outgrow. No doubt, many see this demand as posing a terrible dilemma. Yet it is hardly more terrible than that felt by their critics. For how can one tell sincere, hard-working, well-intentioned men that they may be wrong? That they must run risks? That gradual progress is not fast enough?[1]

The attitude of the Irish clergy to the outside world is changing from an uncritical rejection to an uncritical acceptance. Just as the clergy in the past tried to close the Irish mind to European influence, the tendency now is to expose it to the same influence with little sense of discrimination. This change is manifested at present in two main ways: in the attitude to outside works of literature and art, and to the 'pop invasion'.

The Irish clergy now show some tolerance of foreign literature and art. In the clerically-controlled Y.M.C.A. hall in Cork, for instance, the Everyman Group have been presenting plays by writers such as Beckett, Anouilh, Albee . . . with the strong support of Robert O'Donoghue of the *Cork Examiner*. This is a revolutionary change, indeed, in a city where Mairead ni Grada's *The Trial* and Richard Johnson's *The Evidence I Shall Give* were vetoed by the clerical authorities during recent years. Perhaps the clergy feel that not much is to be lost by presenting modern dramatists to small audiences with only a limited ability to understand what these dramatists are saying.

This problem in communication was illustrated, at a national level, when *R.T.E.* featured *The Tea Party* by Harold Pinter during March 1965. This was the first time that the bulk of the Irish saw a really modern play; and the reaction – even of the intelligent and educated – was mainly one of bewilderment and disgust. That Mr Pinter was expressing an interpretation of life – and a not untypical one outside Ireland – was lost in a sense of arbitrary corruption and pornography.

The Irish are untrained to deal with modern works of literature and

[1] *The Atlantic*, April, 1967.

art, unable to see in them a serious statement of faith or lack of faith. The Irish view is conventionally theological, not vitally intellectual and artistic, a defect which – as has been suggested in this work – is not confined to Irish priest and layman. This artistic failure means that the therapeutic value of modern literature is largely lost, disposing the Irish to take its cynical and corrupting elements at their face value. With the relaxation of censorship, this is one of the most serious educational problems which face the Irish Catholic Church. It demands a vital approach to literature, a modernisation of outlook, and an understanding of the decline of humanism, which leaves the modern writer without the mainstay of an ideal in terms of which to interpret and reorganise a disintegrating life. Such a reform would find a natural beginning in a study of the modern Irish writers, especially Joyce and Yeats.

Irish interest in 'pop' music grew rapidly in the sixties, dominating the entertainment world. Its most distinctive manifestation was the Showband, of which there were several hundred in the country by the middle of the decade, spreading like the pimples of an ugly rash over the entire community. This mass movement caused, one suspects, some unease among the clergy, for *R.T.E.* did not feature the Showbands until the middle of 1963, and eased out of them during 1966.

Though the 'pop' music and mentality is an import into Eire, it is not without some sympathetic basis in the Irish mind, evident in some original features of the Showband itself. True, as Patrick Kavanagh noted, 'vast numbers of young folk take part in it without realising its dark connotations'. One can see these unfortunate innocents swaying with vacuous expressions, as if under mild hypnosis, as they listen to 'pop' music in *R.T.E.* programmes; while, with equal fatuity, a panel of adults discuss the merits of the latest 'pop' records.

One can sympathise with the modern adolescent who turns away in disgust from the gross materialism of the life he is offered, a life which, under a veneer of Christian and humanist pretensions, lacks an ideal which unifies as it raises the human mind above a scarcely disguised go-getting self-centredness and cynical opportunism. The adolescent may well react to such a world in a variety of ways; in a vengeful destructivism; in suicide; in drugs; in an escape through an hysterical abandonment to his gross instincts; in a naive attempt to create a life of freedom and simplicity, symbolised by such terms as the Beautiful People or the Flower Children.

To Christians with a sense of human dignity it must seem odd that the Irish clergy can look on the world of 'pop' without some sense of Yeats' intuition that the 'ceremony of innocence is drowned'. Their complacence is understandable only when one realises that they do not see man as they profess to see him, but as a corrupt creature whose natural capacities limit him to the mundane, the trifling and the sordid. Thus the mature Joyce saw man; and the 'pop' world finds a fitting place in his literary universe with its coarseness, mediocrity and sexual-egotistic motivation. Or one can see it in sympathy with the work of another Irishman, Francis Bacon, whose vision of a degraded humanity enables us – as the *Observer* put it – 'to feel a shock of recognition about our society'.

Joyce contended that life imitates art; but it is rather that art, penetrating to the form underlying contemporary trends, embodies the shape of things to come. The artist cannot enlarge on the actual potential of life unless he uses a system of ideas which makes enlargement possible. On the Catholic system Joyce deliberately turned his back. So did the Irish Catholic Church – in effect at least – for it found man no more lovable than did Joyce, and obstructed any attempt to enlarge his heart and mind. It is hardly surprising then that what the Irish clergy made out of the real Ireland should resemble the literary picture of it which Joyce painted.

If Catholic Ireland kept her faith in God, she lost her faith in man. It was the clergy rather than the people who succumbed to historical pressures; and the clergy were in a position to shape the course of Irish life. Yet it was just possible that the people might have asserted themselves against the clergy – given a leader. Only Joyce had the stature to fulfil this role; and he spent too long under the dark penumbra of clerical influence. Did the Irish fail in their responsibility to meet the challenge of history?

Those who believe in Christian providence may well think that an extended historical discipline was intended to isolate and temper the Irish mind for some worthwhile role in the modern world; and, indeed, the discerning Anglo-Irish writers had some intuition of this. But, up to the present, there is little evidence to support such a view. On the contrary, Catholic Ireland has been largely, in fact, on the side of the enemies of religion in its relentless attack on human individuality and responsibility; for, if man is made in God's image, it is no less true – from an operative human standpoint – that God is made in man's image. It is hard to avoid the impression that Catholic Ireland's failure is symbolised by James Joyce whose awful presence overshadowed the birth of the free Irish State, over whose threshold he was perched like Poe's raven with its cryptic refrain, 'Nevermore'.

APPENDIX

Censorship

THE WESTERN VIEW of man is torn between the pessimism of the Christians and the optimism of the liberal humanists. One is all out for control and repression, the other for freedom and expression. The Christians are reluctant to trust the human mind, while the liberals place an excessive faith in its ability to benefit by an unregulated experience. The outcome for both groups has been unhappy. Liberalism is giving way to a highly disciplined environmentalism or socialism, while Christian society is largely without any sense of direction, ethically or aesthetically.

The Christian rebels are usually affirmers of life, reacting from a view which is disparaging. Joyce, Moore and O'Flaherty are Irish-Catholic examples. Dylan Thomas and D. H. Lawrence are Protestant types. During the trial of *Lady Chatterley's Lover* at the Old Bailey, Richard Hoggart described Lawrence as a puritan, which he defined as 'a man who felt a profound sense of responsibility to his own conscience'. Lawrence would be better described perhaps as an anti-puritan who was concerned with the human mind rather than with the human conscience. He wanted to liberate the human mind – especially the unconscious part of it – from the rigid controls of a Protestant and non-conformist ethic. Some Protestant dignitaries were themselves aware that these controls were too rigid. Dr Cosmo Lang, Archbishop of Canterbury, sought to loosen them when he urged the London Diocesan Council for Rescue Work to

> liberate sex from the impression that it is always to be surrounded by negative warnings and restraints, and to place it in its rightful place among the great creative and formative things.

Sex is not, taken in itself, 'creative and formative' as Dr Lang contended, since it gives only an illusion of unity which is, in fact, an intensification and extension of the ego. That is why, as the psychoanalyst, Eric Fromm, pointed out, current sexual freedoms in no way contribute to a true sense of 'aliveness' or 'richness of experience'. Sex is creative only when combined with sympathy which leads to a real identification with the person loved. This sympathetic or moral force, however, is also suspect by Christians; and the result is the moral isolation of the individual – 'every man is an island'. In such circumstances, one is apt to welcome any breakthrough; and it is here that Lawrence offered a solution – if only an apparent one – with an ethic which depended mainly on sex as an integrating force. 'Beggars can't be choosers,' and even the Bishop of Woolwich, the Rt Rev J. A. T. Robinson, came in on the side of *Lady Chatterley's Lover*, contending that Lawrence 'saw through to the natural goodness of creation at this point in a way that Christians have often failed to do'.[1] Dr Fisher, Archbishop of Canterbury, was justifiably critical of the Bishop's defence of Lawrence's book but, on the other hand, the Anglican Church had failed to provide the Bishop with an alternative or more complex interpretation of the romantic aspect of the man-woman relationship.

George Moore remarked in *Hail and Farewell* that 'Irish Catholics have taken their morality from English puritans'. But, indeed, this they did not need to do, having acquired a puritanism of their own from Jansenism. This is evident in Irish literary censorship (as well as in film censorship). For that censorship is not really concerned with the morality of literature. True, the Censorship of Publications Act of 1946 does enjoin on the censors to consider the 'literary, artistic or historic merit or importance, and the general tenor, of the book'. But its real point of inquiry lies not with aesthetic values but to determine whether a book is

(a) indecent or obscene, or

(b) advocates the unnatural prevention of conception or the procurement of abortion or miscarriage or the use of any method, treatment or appliance for the purpose of such prevention or procurement.

Thus, the censors are not really concerned with the interpretation of the writer, but with whether his work is indecent, that is, 'suggestive of,

[1] *Observer*, November 13, 1960.

230

or inciting to, sexual immorality or unnatural vice or likely in any other similar way to corrupt or deprave'.

The test of indecency is made narrower still when books are banned from a reading of isolated passages, marked by anonymous Catholic bodies who send suspect books to the Censorship Board. To what extent this still occurs is hard to say. Comments made by some members of the Censorship Board on Edna O'Brien's novels (all five of which are banned) suggest a close knowledge of and even some sympathy with them.[1] Edna O'Brien's work is sincere, however, in spite of its preoccupation with sex.

A major concern with sex in censoring literature suggests a moral approach divorced from an aesthetic. A concern for the good of man (morality) is obviously defective when the censor lacks an appreciation of the beauty of man's work (aestheticism).[2] Such a moral approach is not concerned with the general conception of a work, with the vision of an author who interprets sex in a particular way, and uses it as one of a number of elements which go to make up his interpretation. Hence the absurdity of banning Kate O'Brien's *The Land of Spices* because of a single direct reference to homosexuality. This narrow moralistic approach to literature and art is typical of most censorship bodies, such as the American League of Decency.

Even with a genuine Catholic literature, this crude ethical approach is likely to result in its rejection because, on any realistic reckoning, sex is a powerful force and must, in modern times, find a large place in creative work. But when the literature derives from modern values which attach a primary creative function to sex, then this literature must seem specially repugnant to the puritan censor. In such circumstances, it is almost impossible for the puritan moralist to distinguish between literature and pornography. The difference is to be found in the purpose or conception which inspires the work, but this is something about which the puritan moralist is not concerned, and about which he is not qualified to make a judgment.

George Moore rightly contended that literature and pornography are quite separate, pointing out that

[1] *Irish Times*, December 14, 1967.
[2] See Maritain's *Art and Scholasticism*, Chap. IX, Art and Morality.

real literature is concerned with the description of life and thought about life rather than acts . . . The very opposite is true in the case of pornographic books.[1]

There can, however, be some ambiguity with so-called serious work where, for instance, talent is combined with an absence of real inspiration, and where this is made up for by the adoption of some spurious and sensationalist approach calculated to make an appeal to what is base in the human mind. According to George Orwell, the art of Salvador Dali falls into this category, combining a fine talent for drawing with an outlook which is a 'striptease act conducted in pink limelight; a record of fantasy, a perversion of instinct; a solution of a bankruptcy of inspiration by a descent "into wickedness"'.[2] This does not mean, however, that Dali's work should be banned. Orwell rightly saw Dali as a phenomenon whose work implies serious criticism of the life that produced him, and deserves study in order to discover the spiritual defects in his social milieu.

The Bishop of Cork has come out strongly on Irish literary censorship, but what he has to say does little to clarify the distinction between literature and pornography. He deplores the fact that

> our Censorship Act . . . is represented to the world at large by our liberals, anti-Catholics and pornographers as a censorship destroying all real freedom of expression. The suggestion is that the Church controls it, and uses it to suppress not only free discussion of religious matters, but to keep both the faithful and the unfaithful in literary and artistic ignorance as well. In a word, it is used to suppress whatever would broaden the people's outlook and endanger their Catholic way of life.[3]

This passage may appear to suggest that the Bishop's view of censorship is liberal, but in fact this is not really so. One may note the significant grouping of 'liberals, anti-Catholics and pornographers', which suggests some kind of alliance between them. In point of fact, it is the Irish writers who have done most to attack pornography and cheap

[1] Joseph Hone, *The Life of George Moore*, p. 152.
[2] *Decline of English Murder*, Penguin Books, 1965, p. 20.
[3] At Bandon, May 6, 1962.

literature. One may note also the reference to the assumption, on the part of critics, that it is the Church which controls Irish censorship. This is the old, familiar question. One may ask, however, if the Church is satisfied with it or not. The Bishop has some criticisms to make of it, but these hardly reflect on the quality of its performance.

The Bishop of Cork denies, in effect, that the real purpose behind Irish literary censorship is to repress cultural life. That this is its purpose, however, is the view of the majority of those engaged in cultural work in Eire. The Censorship Board has come under sharper attack than any other Irish institution. Even the public despise it, treating the banned list more as a guide to what they should rather than should not read.

Obviously, there is some basic difference between the popular and clerical view of literature. In the passage just quoted, the Bishop, in referring to 'literary and artistic ignorance', accepts by implication some artistic standard. Indeed, he strongly recommends 'good papers and good books'. But what does the Bishop mean by a 'good book', apart from the Bible and the lives of the saints, which he recommends?

Speaking on the same subject later in 1965, the Bishop of Cork took up a more satisfactory position, conceding that 'good' reading includes books about life, and not only about the good side of life:

Life has its seamy side too. And so any reading true to life will give us the bad as well as the good in life. Only when it presents the bad, it must present it for what it is, namely, as but part of life and an objectionable part at that. What is wrong is not the description of what is degrading or evil but the glorification of it, or the condonation of it . . .[1]

This is fair enough and applies to all serious writing. But what happens when there is disagreement about what is good and bad in life – when humanist writers often regard as good (sex, for instance), what Catholic theologians see as bad?

For the most part, modern literature cannot be called good in a Catholic sense, since the ideas which inspire it are mainly anti-Catholic. But if the works of Joyce, Genet, and Lawrence are not 'good', ought a serious and intelligent Catholic to read them? This is the basic issue on which the clergy and the writers (and people) differ, however instinctive

[1] At Drimoleague, Co. Cork, May 3.

their attitudes may be. The Liberal-Catholic argument amounts to this: that in the conflict between Catholicism and humanism, it is indispensable that Catholics understand the nature and evolution of humanism; and to this end Catholics should read the works of humanist writers. How can there be an effective Catholic defence – much less an effective Catholic attack – if Catholics do not know what humanist writers are saying? This need has contributed probably to the disrepute into which the Roman Index has fallen. In February 1966 Pope Paul abolished the Curia office which judges writings for the Church's index of forbidden books (the first catalogue of which appeared in 1559), radically liberalising the Church's attitude to literature.

Most of the books the Irish read today come from Britain and America. If the Irish were pressed as to why they read these, they would answer that there was little else to read, and that they wanted to know what was going on in the outside world. The Irish clergy have never openly quarrelled with this implicit attitude, but they leave one with the impression that the people would be better off without the art and ideas which come from abroad. A simple and naive mentality is their ideal, recalling the criticism of a liberal Catholic prelate that the 'Church has too long been organised with the simple, the uneducated and semi-illiterate in mind . . .' which Monica Furlong quotes in a review of the opening of the Ecumenical Council in the *Sunday Times*, October 7, 1962.

The Irish people tend to see the humanist novel for what it is; the clergy see it as Satan-inspired. This means that they deny to humanism a moral purpose, integrity and a coherent development. From such a standpoint, there is no significant difference between literature and pornography except in the degree of evil, pornography being the exploitation of human depravity for the sake of money, and literature its exploitation for the sake of corruption. Speaking of the temptations of the flesh, the Bishop of Cork noted at Bandon that

we shouldn't have them thrust upon us at every bookstall and street corner . . . by those who want to make money out of our weakness, namely, the purveyors of dirty pictures, dirty papers and dirty reading generally. These people, of course, never admit that they are in pornography just for what they can make out of it, or just because

234

they are corrupt themselves and cannot keep their viciousness in. Instead they profess to be artists, scientists, realists, littérateurs, anything that will trap the unwary into their net of viciousness and smut.

Yet though the clergy can appear, as in the above passage, to condemn modern literature, they remain somewhat ambiguous. They carefully avoid any reference to a specific writer (whether to praise or blame), and there exists a doubt as to whether they are warning against literature or pornography. No wonder the Irish attitude to literature is chaotic.

In point of fact, the Irish people read anything on which they can get their hands. They read serious work because they think they ought to; and they read pornography because the clergy suggest, by implication, that this is no worse than literature. The Bishop of Cork is aware of this popular irresponsibility, for which he blames the Censorship Act because, by it, 'people are lulled into a false sense of security . . . the Censorship Act is substituted for a censorship of conscience'. But the real explanation is that the Irish literary conscience remains undeveloped, and is confused by defects in the clergy's own outlook on literature.

At Bandon, for instance, the Bishop suggested that offenders against the Censorship Act should be heavily fined or imprisoned; and that the trial of such offenders should be by jury. This, he pointed out, 'would give the common man, in the person of the jury man, the say as to what they think bad or not bad'. Here we come again to our old friend, the butcher's boy, who out of the unerring instinct of his simple heart, will tell us whether Joyce's *Ulysses* is literature or pornography.

The same simple ideal was put forward by Dr McQuaid, Archbishop of Dublin, on February 17, 1963. When speaking to the members of the National Film Institute, he told them: 'I am confident . . . you will continue to uphold the ideals of good ordinary people.' It should be evident surely that an effective Catholic simplicity today must be of an evolved kind; not the natural simplicity of the village idiot, but the mature simplicity of a Maritain or a Pope John. Yet, in opposing a highly sophisticated humanist culture, Dr McQuaid puts his faith in a psychological immaturity which he seems to regard as a Catholic ideal; for he assured the members that 'if you had not standards of Christian reverence, you should not be regarded as uneducated, illiberal, in-experienced'.

Obviously the best censors of literature and art are the writers and artists themselves, as well as their established critics. For the real purpose of the moralist is to find out whether a work is genuinely inspired or not; whether it provides a sincere and vital interpretation of life; and those with cultural training and experience are best qualified to do this. The irony is that those who should be on the Irish Censorship Board are precisely those responsible writers and critics whose work the Board holds under suspicion if not actually banned. It should be no less evident that a work should not be banned without due consideration of the critiques to be found in responsible newspapers and journals outside Eire.

The Irish clergy have shown a greater fear of literature than they have of the trashy novels and magazines which clutter our cheaper bookstalls, even though their inspiration is both anti-Catholic and anti-cultural. This lenient view of work written largely for profit, led Arland Ussher in *The Face and Mind of Ireland* to conclude that 'censorship is maintained primarily for the purpose of baiting the intellectuals'. It would be truer perhaps to infer that the censors distrust less the frivolous work whose purpose is not to educate but to entertain; and, indeed, the Irish clergy show a tolerance of smut and vulgarity when it is used to amuse. Some years ago, Dr Murphy, the Bishop of Limerick, made an appeal for art against the cheapness of much popular entertainment: such appeals are rare indeed from the Irish clergy.

Certainly, Irish censorship has come down heavily on the Irish writers, practically every one of whom suffered from the effects of the ban. Speaking of the relations between those writers and officialdom during the decades following the establishment of the Irish Free State, Frank MacManus commented:

Among many writers one could find suspicion of the state, just as one could find in the state, as expressed through civil servants, a suspicion of them as queer fellows. In fact, the most persistent and permanent contact between the state and the writers was through a state organ, the Censorship Board, which could ban with a savagery which seemed pathological.[1]

[1] In a *Davis Lecture* on *Radio Eireann*, December 13, 1964.

True, there are some startling exceptions to the use of the ban, especially in the case of James Joyce, whose *Ulysses* and *Finnegan's Wake* remain unbanned. These are mainly due to the belief that such work is not likely to be read because of its difficult nature. Irish Censorship Law states that the imposition of a ban on a book must be considered in the light of

(a) the language in which it is written.

(b) the nature and extent of the circulation which . . . it is likely to have.

(c) the class of reader which may reasonably be expected to buy it.

Public protests at the narrowness of Irish censorship led to the establishment of an Appeal Board by the Censorship of Publications Act of 1946. The Appeal Board, having regard for some real literary ethic, repairs some of the worst damage done by the Censorship Board; and the banning and unbanning of books has become something of a farce. This is evident from the following selection of banned books by Irish writers. An asterisk marks those books on which the ban has now been lifted:

Brendan Behan	*Borstal Boy*
O. St John Gogarty	*Going Native, Mr Petunia*
James Joyce	*Stephen Hero**
Benedict Kiely	*In a Green Harbour*, Honey Seems Bitter*
Maura Laverty	*Lift Up your Gates, Alone We Embark*
Walter Macken	*I Am Alone, Quench the Moon, The Bogman**
Edna O'Brien	*The Country Girls, The Lonely Girl, Girls in Their Married Bliss, August Is a Wicked Month, Casualties of Peace*
Kate O'Brien	*The Land of Spices*, Mary Lavelle*
Sean O'Casey	*Windfalls, Pictures in the Hallway, I Knock at the Door**
Frank O'Connor	*The Common Chord, Dutch Interior, Traveller's Samples**
Sean O'Faolain	*Midsummer Night Madness, Bird Alone**
Liam O'Flaherty	*Land, The Martyr, Shame the Devil, The House of Gold, The Puritan, Hollywood Cemetery*
Bernard Shaw	*The Black Girl in her Search for God*

Needless to say, the works of humanist writers have had little welcome in Eire. Some of the works of Nobel Prize winners have not escaped the ban. These include Faulkner, Sartre, Steinbeck, Hemingway, Thomas Mann, Par Lagervist and Sinclair Lewis. Other distinguished writers, some of whose writings have been declared 'indecent and obscene' include Samuel Beckett, Theodore Dreiser, Maxim Gorki, F. Scott Fitzgerald, Aldous Huxley, Arthur Koestler, Wyndham Lewis, André Malraux, Somerset Maugham, George Orwell, John Dos Passos, Marcel Proust, Budd Schulberg, Stephen Spender, Dylan Thomas, H. G. Wells, Tennessee Williams . . .

Irish literary censorship has other lines of defence than the ban itself. An unofficial censorship also exists, as in the public libraries through Advisory Committees on Book Selection, as well as in Catholic and ultra-nationalist book shops. This type of censorship has an important influence in restricting the availability of books. On November 9, 1960, the Longford County Council unanimously decided to exclude from the branches of the county library copies of Edgar Holt's *Protest at Arms* on the grounds that it was a 'clever vindication of England's action in Ireland'. On September 8, 1962, some members of the Cork Co. Library Committee objected to the spending of public money on the works of O'Casey, Joyce, Behan and Tagore. No objection was made to the misuse of public money for the purchase of large stocks of worthless literature, such as cowboy fiction, without which, as a member noted, a 'lot of people would not come near the library'. The work of the librarians – usually intelligent and responsible – is hamstrung by restrictions imposed on them by Committees whose qualifications for literary censorship are by no means obvious.

As a result of the ban – official and unofficial – the Irish writers are poorly represented in the libraries of the Republic, a defect which is aggravated by the indifference of the public to writers whom they have been taught to ignore or distrust. Any available copies of books by Irish writers are being bought by American libraries where alone, apparently, Irish writers are given adequate representation. A continental university looking for the works of Liam O'Flaherty failed to find them in the whole of Ireland. Frank O'Connor stated that present Irish book stocks are 'awful' compared with those in the late twenties when he was a librarian. He referred to the damaging effect of holding up books in the Customs, especially when dealing with the publications of Heinemann, Hutchinson and Cape.[1] Paperback editions are helping somewhat to make up the loss in Irish works, as witnessed in the case of Ernie O'Malley's *On Another Man's Wound*, which was selling for three guineas, if you could find a copy, before it was issued as a paperback.

It is ironic to observe that Catholic Ireland and Marxist Russia have a common fear of individualism. The writers of both countries have been persecuted for the same reason, a distrust of the human mind. In Russia, this is logical, but Catholic Eire professes a moderate individualism. Yet Catholic writers have fared hardly better than others under Irish censorship. In the banned list are to be found A. J. Cronin, Graham Greene, Frances Parkinson Keyes, Compton Mackenzie, Fulton Oursler, Henry Morton Robinson, Harry Sylvester.

The concentration of the Irish Catholic ethic on sex contrasts with the much wider discipline of the original British puritanism which spread itself over almost every form of human expression, being opposed not only to the arts but insisting on frugality, economy, continence in drink, an aversion towards gambling and a personal and sabbatarian reserve. In most of these respects, the Irish are undisciplined by and large, gambling, in the form of the Irish Sweep, being one of our best-known creations. It is noteworthy that the British conscience is far more sensitive than the Irish to the influence of works of crime, horror and violence, which have a relatively free circulation in Eire, even among the young.

Yet the poison from the well of sex was bound in Ireland to spread through the entire human organism, bringing all the human faculties under suspicion, especially when they owed much to sex inspiration. Hence the rigorous Irish clerical attitude to courtship and dancing up to the Second World War. The Irish might and did perpetrate political murder in the ditches, but they were strongly warned against using them for less lethal, if no less exciting, purposes. The Irish still, to quite an extent, spend their lives in a state of semi-intoxicated lethargy; but, being wedded to nothing more than the bottle is seen, apparently, as

[1] *Sunday Independent*, March 25, 1962.

involving a certain kind of innocence; which, indeed, perhaps it does. Likewise there is a reluctance to face up to sex education; and, no doubt, no small number of the numerous Irish girls who go to England to have their illigitimate babies have good reason to regret this omission. Halliday Sutherland's *Laws of Life* was banned by the Irish censors, even though the book had the approval of the Archdiocese of Westminster.

So obsessed is the Irish Catholic Church with sex that ideas lie outside the scope of the Censorship of Publications Act of 1946, even if ultra-nationalist bodies take an independent line. Thus H. G. Wells' bigoted critique of Catholicism, *Crux Ansata*, is allowed to circulate freely in Eire; as is also Paul Blanshard's *Ireland and the Catholic Power*. This is a significant concession from a touchy and heresy-conscious Irish Church, suggesting that ideas are not seen as creative and human reason as of little importance in the shaping of life. Thus, the Irish clergy's view of man pivots on an evil-force – sex – which pollutes the whole mind, making impossible an integrated and wholesome vision.

It is interesting to compare the Irish Catholic view of sex with that adopted by some modern humanists. The line the defence took in *Lady Chatterley's Lover* amounted to the view that passion itself is enough; that sex, as Miss Dilys Powell put it, is a 'kind of holy basis for life'. In Ireland, by contrast, sex is seen as a kind of unholy basis for life. These two positions express the extremes which the puritan Catholic and liberal humanist ethics have reached. Sex is seen as an absolute agent of order or disorder. The optimist view has more of truth in its side. When Lawrence declared 'my sex is to me as my mind is to me, and nobody will make me feel shame about it', he is in a stronger position than those Christians who denigrate sex without qualification.

As in so many other respects, Irish literary censorship has shown the influence of recent liberalism. In a review of this censorship, Ciaran Carty noted that

Undoubtedly, the Board makes mistakes; but my list shows that in the 1960s the mistakes have been few. In addition to not banning the wrong books, the Board has been banning fewer books. Between January 1960 and January 1965, 1,902 books were banned – an average of about 380 a year. Between January 1950 and January 1955, 3,389 books were banned – an average of about 677 a year. In fact, the decisions which earn the Board most criticism belong to the past, to the 1950s and earlier years.[1]

If this relaxation of literary censorship leaves some sense of dissatisfaction, it is because one feels that it is the politic outcome of the new liberalism rather than the result of a clearer appreciation of the nature of art and its therapeutic function, lifting the mind to an impersonal plane from which our human condition can be truly and sympathetically envisaged. In Joyce's *Portrait* . . . Stephen put the point succinctly to Lynch who responded to the beauty of the Venus of Praxiteles by writing his name on the backside of the statue:

> Beauty expressed by the artist cannot awaken in us an emotion which is kinetic or a sensation which is purely physical. It induces . . . an aesthetic stasis, an ideal pity or an ideal terror, a stasis called forth . . . by what I call the rhythm of beauty.

Until the Irish clergy reach an awareness of this, literary censorship cannot serve its true function which is to separate art from non-art. M. Maritain made much the same point when, criticising censorship, he wrote that it is 'less effective . . . than a robust intellectual training, ennabling the mind and heart to resist vitally any morbid principle'.[2] That such a constructive position hardly exists was shown at the trial of *Lady Chatterley's Lover* where, as Gilbert Longden pointed out, 'the prosecution was half-hearted and intelligent Christian support largely lacking'.[3] So it will remain until Christians create a satisfactory literary ethic in which sex finds its due place.

It is the failure to understand art which accounts so often for the cries of obscenity raised by Christian apologists. As Philip Toynbee wrote of the controversy over V. Nabokov's *Lolita*, 'the whole notion of "filthy" seems to me irrelevant in this discussion'. Critics of literature are constantly harassed by this lack of understanding, and are constantly forced on the defensive when they praise a sincere work which distresses because of the work's outspokenness and its preoccupation with sex and violence. Thus Harold Hobson answers those who were shocked by his critique of Bill Naughton's *Alfie*:

[1] *Sunday Independent*, May 23, 1965.
[2] *Art and Scholasticism*, p. 224.
[3] *Observer*, November 13, 1960.

The mistake is to suppose that what makes a play immoral is the behaviour of its characters. This is never so. The essential constituting factor is always the attitude of the author. A play is simply a method of making acquaintance with the mind of its author. If that mind is fine, courageous, strong and sincere, then it matters little what problem it contemplates. Its fineness and sincerity will strengthen the audience . . . Those who do not recognise these facts praise plays in which goodness is identified solely with the absence of sex. They have a negative conception of morality, and, hag-ridden by a perverted puritanism, attempt to guide drama towards a futile superficiality.[1]

Serious writers are not trying to deprave but to comment and interpret. If sex plays a dominant part in their interpretation, that is because rational standards have collapsed, and writers have no choice but to use the values that remain to them. The only real answer to this is to restore rational artistic standards. If this cannot be done, then censorship will not save orthodoxy; and howls of prudish disgust merely advertise the fact that the protagonists of orthodoxy do not really understand what they are trying to save.

A Bill easing Irish censorship law was introduced in the *Dail* on April 28, 1967. It provided that books banned for twenty years – since 1947 – would be subject to re-examination. Banned books of literary merit are likely to be released under the new Bill which also provides no time limit to appeals against the ban, appeals which previously had to be made within one year of the imposition of the ban. The Bill is an implicit acknowledgment of past severity in the moral appraisal of literature, and represents another milestone on the road to Ireland's great need – cultural freedom. For the great barrier to Irish development in the twentieth century was not British imperialism but Irish puritanism.

[1] *Sunday Times*, August 18, 1963.

SELECTED BIBLIOGRAPHY

Barrington (Donal).
  Uniting Ireland, Tuairim Pamphlet, Dublin, 1958
Beckett (Samuel).
  Waiting for Godot, Faber, London, 1956
  Endgame, Faber, London, 1958
  Krapp's Last Tape, Faber, London, 1959
Bedoyere (Michael de la), editor,
  Objections to Roman Catholicism, Constable, London, 1964
Behan (Brendan).
  The Quare Fellow, Methuen, London, 1956
  Borstal Boy, Hutchinson, London, 1958
  The Hostage, Methuen, London, 1958
Blanshard (Paul)
  The Irish and the Catholic Power, Verschoyle, London, 1955
Boyle (Patrick)
  At Night All Cats Are Grey, MacGibbon & Kee, London, 1966
  Like Any Other Man, MacGibbon & Kee, London, 1966
Carroll (Paul Vincent)
  The White Steed: Three Plays, Macmillan, London, 1944
  Shadow and Substance, Macmillan, London, 1948
Casey (Kevin)
  The Sinners' Bell, Faber, London, 1968
Chesterton (G. K.)
  George Bernard Shaw, Bodley Head, London, 1935
Clark (Ruth Elvira)
  Strangers and Sojourners at Port Royal, Cambridge University Press, 1932
Colum (Mary and Padraic)
  Our Friend, James Joyce, Gollancz, London, 1959
Colum (Padraic)
  Arthur Griffith, Browne and Nolan, Dublin, 1959
Coogan (T. P.)
  Ireland Since the Rising, Pall Mall Press, London, 1966

Corkery (Daniel)
   The Fortunes of the Irish Language, Fallon, Dublin, 1954
Cristiani (Leon)
   Heresies and Heretics, Burns and Oates, London, 1959
D'Alton (E. A.)
   History of Ireland, Gresham, London, 1912
Edwards (Hilton)
   The Battle of Harlequin, Progress House, Dublin, 1958
Ellman (Richard)
   James Joyce, Oxford University Press, 1959
   The Identity of Yeats, Faber, London, 1964
Goodspeed (A. J.)
   The Conspirators: A Study of the Coup d'Etat, Macmillan, London, 1962
Gorman (Herbert)
   James Joyce, Bodley Head, London, 1949
Greaves (Desmond)
   The Life and Times of James Connolly, Lawrence and Wishart, London, 1961
Greene (D. H.) and E. N. Stephens
   J. M. Synge, Macmillan, New York, 1959
Gregory (Augusta, Lady,)
   Journals, Ed. Lennox Robinson, Putnam, London, 1946
Guthrie (Tyrone)
   A Life in the Theatre, Hamish Hamilton, London, 1960
Hogan (James)
   Could Ireland Become Communist? Cahill, Dublin, 1935
Hollis (Christopher)
   Along the Road to Frome, Harrap, London, 1958
Hone (Joseph)
   The Life of George Moore, Gollancz, London, 1936
Howarth (Herbert)
   The Irish Writers 1860–1940, Rockliff, London, 1958
Hutchins (Patricia)
   James Joyce's World, Methuen, London, 1957
Inglis (Brian)
   West Briton, Faber, London, 1962
Joyce (James)
   The Day of the Rabblement: Two Essays, Gerrard Brothers, Dublin, 1901
   Stephen Hero, Cape, London, 1944
   A Portrait of the Artist as a Young Man, Cape, London, 1946
   Dubliners, Cape, London, 1947
   Gas from a Burner: The Essential James Joyce, Cape, London, 1948
   Exiles, Cape, London, 1952
   Ulysses, Bodley Head, London, 1960

Joyce (Stanislaus)
My Brother's Keeper, Faber, London, 1958
Kaiser (Robert)
Inside the Council, Burns and Oates, London, 1963
Kavanagh (Patrick)
The Great Hunger: Collected Poems, MacGibbon and Kee, London, 1964
Kenner (Hugh)
Samuel Beckett, Calder, London, 1962
Krause (David)
Sean O'Casey: The Man and his Work, MacGibbon and Kee, London, 1960.
Küng (Hans)
The Council and Reunion, Sheed and Ward, London, 1961
Lewis (Wyndham)
Time and the Western Man, Chatto, London, 1924
Men Without Art, Cassell, London, 1934
McCarthy (G. B.)
The Whip Hand, Duffy, Dublin, 1950
MacDonald (Walter)
Some Ethical Questions of Peace and War, Burns, Oates and Washbourne, London, 1920
The Reminiscences of a Maynooth Professor, Ed. Denis Gwynn, Cape, London, 1925
MacEoin (Garry)
Nothing Is Quite Enough, Hodder and Stoughton, London, 1954
McGahern (John)
The Barracks, Faber, London, 1963
The Dark, Faber, London, 1965
Macken (Walter)
The Bogman, Macmillan, London, 1952
MacLiammoir (Micheal)
All For Hecuba, Methuen, London, 1948
Maritain (Jacques)
Art and Scholasticism, Sheed and Ward, London, 1930
Religion and Culture, Sheed and Ward, London, 1931
True Humanism, Bles, London, 1938
Mercier (Vivian)
The Irish Comic Tradition, Oxford University Press, 1962
Mitchell (Susan)
George Moore, Talbot Press, Dublin, 1919
Moore (George)
The Untilled Field, Fisher Unwin, London, 1903
Heloise and Abelard, Heinemann, London, 1925
The Brook Kerith, Heinemann, London, 1927
The Works of George Moore, Heinemann, London, 1933

O'Brien (Conor Cruise)
   To Katanga and Back, Hutchinson, London, 1962
   Writers and Politics: Essays and Criticism, Chatto and Windus, London, 1965
O'Brien (Edna)
   The Country Girls, Hutchinson, London, 1960
   The Lonely Girl, Cape, London, 1962
O'Brien (Flann)
   At Swim-Two-Birds, MacGibbon and Kee, London, 1960
O'Brien (J. A.), editor
   The Vanishing Irish: The Enigma of the Modern World, W. H. Allen, London, 1954
O'Brien (Kate)
   Mary Lavelle, Heinemann, London, 1947
   The Land of Spices, Heinemann, London, 1949
   The Flower of May, Hamish Hamilton, London, 1960
   That Lady, Penguin Books, Harmondsworth, 1965
O'Casey (Sean)
   Collected Plays, Macmillan, London, 1949
   The Bishop's Bonfire, Macmillan, London, 1955
   The Drums of Father Ned, Macmillan, London, 1960
O'Connor (Frank)
   An Only Child, Macmillan, London, 1961
O'Connor (Ulick)
   Oliver St John Gogarty, Cape, London, 1964
O'Doherty (Rev. E. F.) and Dr E. D. McGrath, editors
   The Priest and Mental Health, Clonmore and Reynolds, Dublin, 1962
O'Donnell (Donat)
   Maria Cross, Burns and Oates, London, 1963
O'Faolain (Sean)
   King of the Beggars, Nelson, London, 1938
   The Irish, Pelican Books, Harmondsworth, 1947
   Summer in Italy, Eyre and Spottiswoode, London, 1949
   Vive Moi, Hart Davis, London, 1965
O'Flaherty (Liam)
   The Informer, Cape, London, 1925
   The Tent, Cape, London, 1926
   Skerret, Gollancz, London, 1932
   The Martyr, Gollancz, London, 1933
   Two Lovely Beasts and Other Stories, Gollancz, London, 1949
O'Hegarty (P. S.)
   The Victory of Sinn Fein, Talbot Press, Dublin, 1924
   A History of Ireland Under the Union, Methuen, London, 1952
O'Neill (Eugene)
   A Moon for the Misbegotten, Cape, London, 1953

O'Sullivan (Donal)
  The Irish Free State and its Senate, Faber, London, 1940
Pakenham (F. A.)
  Peace by Ordeal, Cape, London, 1935
Pearce (D. R.)
  The Senate Speeches of W. B. Yeats, Faber, London, 1961
Pearse (Padraic)
  Collected Works of Padraic H. Pearse, Maunsel, Dublin and London, 1917
Philibin (Bishop)
  Patriotism, Gill, Dublin, 1958
Plunkett (James)
  The Trusting and the Maimed, Devin-Adair, New York, 1955
Price (Alan)
  Synge and Anglo-Irish Drama, Methuen, London, 1961
Robinson (Lennox)
  Ireland's Abbey Theatre, Sidgwick and Jackson, London, 1951
Russell (George), (A. E.)
  Selected Poems by A. E., Macmillan, London, 1935
Ryan (W. P.)
  The Pope's Green Island, Nisbet, London, 1920
Schafer (Boyd C.)
  Nationalism: Myth and Reality, Gollancz, London, 1955
Scott (George)
  The RCs: A Report on Roman Catholics in Britain Today, Hutchinson, London, 1967
Shaw (Bernard)
  The Complete Plays of Bernard Shaw, Hamlyn, London, 1965
Sheehy (Eugene)
  May It Please the Court, Fallon, Dublin, 1951
Stephens (E. N.), see D. H. Greene
Stephens (James)
  A Selection, Macmillan, London, 1962
Sullivan (Kevin)
  Joyce Among the Jesuits, Columbia University Press, 1958
Sutherland (Haliday)
  Irish Journey, Bles, London, 1956
Synge (J. M.)
  The Aran Islands, Maunsel, Dublin and London, 1912
  Plays by John M. Synge, Allen and Unwin, London, 1932
Taylor (John Russell)
  Anger and After: A Guide to the New British Drama, Methuen, London, 1962
Taylor (Rex)
  Michael Collins, Hutchinson, London, 1958

Tracy (Honor)
  Mind You, I've Said Nothing, Methuen, London, 1953
Ussher (Arland)
  The Face and Mind of Ireland, Gollancz, London, 1949
Wilde (Oscar)
  The Works of Oscar Wilde, Spring Books, London, 1963
Wittke (Carl)
  The Irish in America, Louisana State University Press, 1956
Yeats (W. B.)
  Collected Plays by W. B. Yeats, Macmillan, London, 1952
  A Vision, Macmillan, London, 1955
  Mythologies, Macmillan, London, 1959
  Autobiographies, Macmillan, London, 1961
  Collected Poems of W. B. Yeats, Macmillan, London, 1965

Index

Index